Lives of the Australian Chief Justices

SIR JAMES DOWLING

Lives of the Australian Chief Justices

J. M. Bennett

New South Wales

Sir Francis Forbes
Sir James Dowling

Victoria

Sir William a'Beckett

Lives of the Australian Chief Justices

SIR JAMES DOWLING

Second Chief Justice of New South Wales
1837–1844

J. M. BENNETT
M.A., LL.D.

Foreword
Emeritus Professor Bruce Mansfield, F.A.H.A.

THE FEDERATION PRESS
2001

Published in Sydney by

The Federation Press
71 John St, Leichhardt, NSW, 2040
PO Box 45, Annandale, NSW, 2038
Ph: (02) 9552 2200 Fax: (02) 9552 1681
E-mail: info@federationpress.com.au
Website: http://www.federationpress.com.au

National Library of Australia Cataloguing-in-Publication data:
Bennett, J. M. (John Michael)
Sir James Dowling: second Chief Justice of New South Wales

Includes index.
ISBN 1 86287 391 7

1. Dowling, James, Sir, 1787-1844. 2. Judges – New South Wales – Biography. I. Title. (Series: Lives of the Australian Chief Justices).

347.014092

Typeset by The Federation Press, Leichhardt, NSW.
Printed by Ligare Pty Ltd, Riverwood, NSW.

Foreword

(By Emeritus Professor Bruce Mansfield, F.A.H.A.
First Professor of History (1965-1975) and
Deputy Vice-Chancellor (Academic) (1976-1985),
Macquarie University (N.S.W.))

Australia has had a long line of distinguished legal historians, a fact in itself worthy of historical investigation. John Bennett is of their company, and his work readily recalls that of predecessors and mentors, among them the robust C.H. Currey. His range of publications is prodigious. I think of histories of the profession and the courts, studies and biographies of legal personalities and researches in the history of substantive issues in the law, the last including papers he prepared for the Law Reform Commission in New South Wales.

His present project – lives of the Chief Justices – is, merely as a concept, a formidable work of imagination. That he is carrying it through at an initial breathtaking rate of three volumes a year betokens an industry and devotion reminiscent of the great scholarly undertakings of the nineteenth century (when, perhaps, the conditions for such feats were more favourable). I feel a personal stake in this undertaking since it, in a real sense, began with the postgraduate thesis he wrote on Chief Justice Darley in the early days of Macquarie University's History School over thirty years ago. He has himself spoken of "the ultimate flowering of my biographical project that owes much of its genesis to my being inspired at Macquarie University such a long time ago".

The present volume, on the second Chief Justice of New South Wales, Sir James Dowling, demonstrates the qualities that mark Dr Bennett's writing as a legal historian: a sense for historical context that never allows the law to float free of social and cultural circumstances; an interest in personality, which produces here a remarkable cast of idiosyncratic characters; a capacity for the lucid expression of cases that makes the issues accessible to a non-professional reader. All three qualities come together in the depiction of a litigious society, cast down (as it seemed) on the edge of a wilderness at the ends of the earth.

James Dowling did not have the creative powers of his predecessor or his successor, respectively Francis Forbes and Alfred Stephen. But his punctiliousness, his sense of decorum, his regard for the dignity of his court and resistance to those applying to it unreasonable pressures, his very dullness may well have had the stabilizing effect a community in transition from convict colony to liberal settler society required. His uneasiness at doubling his role as Chief Justice with service on the Legislative Council is one of the signs of that transition indicated by Dr Bennett.

At a stricter level of historical analysis, there are important issues here. One is the workings of patronage within the imperial system. All through his career, Dowling was turning to his supporters in London, to members of his family, of course, but also to the Whig chief, Henry Brougham. "Dowling had become adept", Dr Bennett writes, "in striking the right balance between obsequiousness and self-promotion, such as would appeal to Brougham". Another is the applicability of English law to the colony and the beginnings of a local legal tradition. A third – and here I must stop – is Dowling's pioneering work (launched in the earliest days of his career) in legal reporting. Perceptive readers, both professional and non-professional, will find others.

I warmly commend this work to those readers.

SYDNEY **Bruce Mansfield**

6 August 2001

Contents

Acknowledgements

This project, to write of the lives and careers of nineteenth century Australian Chief Justices, originated many years ago. It was inspired by discussions with my mentor in legal history, Dr C.H. Currey, when he was completing his great work *Sir Francis Forbes* (1968). My project took its first shape when I held, briefly, a Senior Research Fellowship in the Law Department (now Program) of the Research School of Social Sciences within the Australian National University. Encouraged, first, by Professors Geoffrey Sawer and S.J. Stoljar, the enterprise has commended itself, in turn, to Professors Paul Finn (now the Honourable Justice Finn of the Federal Court), John Braithwaite and Peter Cane. Much of my research has been conducted in Canberra and the association with the A.N.U. has been sustained by several visiting appointments. The more pressing calls of professional practice conspired, however, to delay excessively the completion of my writing.

For a private author, the cost is daunting of undertaking a project of such a scale as is this series. Much research must be pursued at a distance from home, often inter-State or overseas. I gratefully record my indebtedness to the Law and Justice Foundation of New South Wales for sponsoring my initial research. I acknowledge the personal interest of successive Foundation Directors Terence Purcell and Simon Rice, and of Grants Managers Dawn Wong, Steven Reynolds and Catherine Lloyd.

Later research was assisted by the award of a 2000 Churchill Fellowship, a recognition I am privileged to have received. It enabled me to examine sources in the United Kingdom, Bermuda and the West Indies. I much appreciate the assistance of the Winston Churchill Memorial Trust in facilitating the necessary travel, and I particularly thank Mrs E.L. Munday, O.A.M., Assistant Executive Officer to the Trust, for her help with administrative matters in relation to the grant.

In the case of Sir James Dowling, most research was conducted in Australia where abundant written records of his life survive in libraries and archives. Unlike many of his contemporaries in office as Chief Justice, Dowling was a meticulous keeper of his own records, and his family preserved them.

I have been able to put aside most matters of Dowling genealogy and family history, and to concentrate on issues of legal concern, thanks to the carefully documented publications of Anthony R. Dowling of Mornington, Victoria. They are *Fortis et Egregius or Dowling of Ballyroan* (1996) and an edition of Judge J.S. Dowling's memoirs, *Reminiscences of a Colonial Judge* (The Federation Press 1996). Mr Dowling, who is a great-great grandson of Sir James, gave me the benefit of his vast knowledge of the family's history and assisted me in many matters of detail.

It is a special pleasure and distinction for me that Emeritus Professor Mansfield has enhanced this book with a Foreword. If I manage, at times, to adventure beyond the perceptions of a lawyer to those of a historian, it is due, in large part, to Bruce Mansfield's guidance, many years ago, for which I remain most grateful.

The Federation Press has given me every encouragement to see "The Lives" emerge in print. I appreciate the special assistance of Mr Chris Holt of the Press, and particularly his patience in settling this, as a model volume, for the remainder of the proposed series.

MITTAGONG N.S.W. **J. M. Bennett**

August 2001

List of Illustrations

(facing pages 116 and 117)

"Dramatis Personae"

[A brief introduction to the principal actors]

BAXTER, Alexander Macduff, Attorney-General of New South Wales, 1827-1830.

BOURKE, Major-General Richard, from 1835 Sir Richard, Governor of New South Wales, 1831-1838.

BROUGHAM, Henry Peter, Baron Brougham and Vaux, English barrister, politician and law reformer; Lord Chancellor, 1830-1834; Dowling's principal patron.

BURTON, (Sir) William Westbrooke, Judge of the Supreme Court, 1832-1844.

DARLING, Lt-General Ralph, later Sir Ralph, Governor of New South Wales, 1825-1831.

DOWLING, Sir James, Judge of the Supreme Court, 1827-1837; Chief Justice, 1837-1844; the subject of this book.

DOWLING, James Sheen, son of Sir James; District Court Judge, 1858-1889.

FORBES, Sir Francis, first Chief Justice of New South Wales, 1823-1837.

GIPPS, Sir George, Governor of New South Wales, 1838-1846.

GLENELG, (Lord) Charles Grant, created Baron 1835, Secretary of State for the Colonies, 1835-1839.

GODERICH, Viscount (first Earl of Ripon), Secretary of State for the Colonies, 1827.

GREY, Sir (Henry) George, later third Earl Grey, Under-Secretary (Political) for the Colonies, 1834-1835, 1835-1839.

HALL, Edward Smith, proprietor of the *(Sydney) Monitor*, libeller and vexatious litigant.

HAY, Robert William, Under-Secretary for the Colonies, 1825-1836.

HOWICK, Viscount (title assumed from 1807-1845), *see* Grey, (Henry) George.

HUSKISSON, William, Secretary of State for the Colonies, 1827-1828.

KINCHELA, John, Attorney-General of New South Wales, 1831-1836; Judge of the Supreme Court, 1836-1837.

McLEAY, Alexander, Colonial Secretary (New South Wales), 1826-1837.

MURRAY, Sir George, Secretary of State for the Colonies, 1828-1830.

PLUNKETT, John Hubert, Solicitor-General of New South Wales, 1832-1836; Attorney-General, 1836-1856; Australia's first Q.C.

RUSSELL, Lord John, Secretary of State for the Colonies, 1839-1841.

SCOTT, Thomas Hobbes, Archdeacon of New South Wales, 1824-1829.

SPRING-RICE, Thomas, Secretary of State for the Colonies, 1834.

STANLEY, Edward George, Under-Secretary (Political) for the Colonies, October 1827-January 1828; Secretary of State for the Colonies, 1833-1834, 1841-1845 (from 1844 as Lord Stanley).

STEPHEN, (Sir) Alfred, Judge of the Supreme Court, 1839-1844; Chief Justice, 1844-1873 (successor to Dowling).

STEPHEN, (Sir) James, Counsel (part-time) to Colonial Office, 1813-1825; permanent Counsel, 1825-1834; Assistant Under-Secretary, 1834-1836; Under-Secretary, 1836-1847.

STEPHEN, John, Judge of the Supreme Court, 1825-1833.

THERRY, (Sir) Roger, Commissioner Court of Requests, 1829-1844; Resident Judge, Port Phillip, 1844-1846; Judge of the Supreme Court, 1846-1859.

TWISS, Horace, Under-Secretary (Political) for the Colonies, 1828-1830.

WENTWORTH, William Charles, leader of the colonial Bar.

WILLIS, John Walpole, Judge of the Supreme Court, 1837-1841; Resident Judge, Port Phillip, 1841-1843.

(WILMOT)-HORTON, (Sir) Robert, Under-Secretary (Political) for the Colonies, 1822-1828; took the name Wilmot-Horton in 1827.

PART I
AS PUISNE JUDGE

Introduction

James Dowling was born in London.[1] He spent much of his life thereabouts before removing to New South Wales, where he eventually became the Colony's second Chief Justice. His paternal family's early ancestry is lost in Irish mists of time. The romantic notion, Dowling himself entertained, that his line was founded in Ireland in the 17th century by an immigrant Spanish surgeon, is apocryphal.[2] Dowling genealogy has been, and continues to be, a pursuit of the family, so it need not detain this study of a judicial career.

The only confirmed forebear so far traced is Vincent Dowling[3] of Ballyroan, Ireland. He married Mary Whelan, by whom he had an only son also named Vincent, born in Ireland in about 1756. The grandson of that Vincent faintly remembered him as "not only an Irishman by birth, but possessed of all those attributes that distinguish the Irish Gentleman".[4] Except, he might have added, the attribute of making adequate provision for his own large family.

Vincent, the younger, was a perfect dilettante. He was supposed to have been educated for the Irish Bar, but he was never called, and never practised law. He took a great interest in matters political and literary, without ever being a politician or a writer of consequence. He moved to London in 1780 and, in 1783,[5] there married Elizabeth, the eldest daughter of Joseph Andrews, of Burton-on-Trent, County Lincoln, "a Russian Merchant and Shipowner of an old Saxon family".[6] They had six sons, two of whom died in infancy, and four daughters, three of whom never married. James was the third son (allowing for the early death of Joseph, twin brother of the eldest son Vincent George).[7]

James Dowling was born at Exeter Court, Strand, London, on 25 November 1787, only two months before the English settlement of Australia at Sydney Cove. His father was employed as a journalist and editor by the newspaper proprietor John Bell, but Bell's spectacular enterprises failed, and Vincent Dowling returned to Ireland for a time from 1789. He eked out a subsistence as a Dublin bookseller and retailer of incidental products,[8] and as editor and publisher of an unsuccessful journal. Thus, from the age of two, James Dowling could claim affinity with the land of his forefathers. But only briefly.

Resolving to try his luck once more in London, Vincent Dowling returned there with his growing, and ill-provided for, family in 1801. He ran a bookselling business at Lincoln's Inn Fields for a few years. He then became a parliamentary reporter for the London *Times*, utilizing a skill he had acquired in shorthand writing. He failed ever to make a competence sufficient to support his family, or even adequately to educate his sons. He died in March 1825.[9]

The professional education of James was entirely English and all his maturing years were spent in England. When he was called to the English Bar at the Middle Temple, his allegiances were wholly to Westminster Hall, not to the Four Courts at Dublin. It did not fall to him to be the true pioneer of many lawyers appointed from the Irish Bar to serve as judges in Australia. Yet he was sometimes given a Celtic character, particularly by members of his own family. His son, James Sheen Dowling, for instance, recalled that his father was of Irish extraction, and "no-one could be in his company long without being made aware of it".[10] Furthermore, "He had all the attributes of an Irishman, he was full of fun, of a very happy disposition, fond of his joke, and in his rambles would converse with almost everybody he met". Those recollections do not exactly fit the character of the man as revealed by independent sources.[11]

Moreover, James Dowling's Irishness was decidedly veiled when he was on the Bench. His judicial demeanour and perceptions were thoroughly English.[12]

In that respect he differed from the two men with whom he would eventually begin his judicial career in New South Wales. Chief Justice Sir Francis Forbes and Mr Justice John Stephen both went to Sydney after experience in British colonies elsewhere, not in England itself. Dowling had none of that colonial background. His inclination to be a colonial judge was a pure speculation in advancing himself. It followed that Forbes and Dowling were not cast in the same judicial mould. As Dr C.H. Currey described the contrast:

> The successor of Sir Francis Forbes differed from him in character and capacity. . . We do not detect in the urbane and genial Sir James [Dowling] that touch of austerity and aloofness which distinguish the first Chief Justice. Nor do his letters, opinions, and decisions reveal the discriminating judgment, the grasp of basic principles, and the strength and clarity of mind which characterise those of Sir Francis. One leaves the latter with the impression that he was not only a first-rate lawyer, but also an educated thinker who brought to the consideration of his diverse public problems a definite philosophy. The former knew his law, and did good service in the Legislature, but on the Bench and in the Council he was a less commanding, a more mediocre figure.[13]

1

"Success Under Every Possible Disadvantage"

In the late 1830s, as his career approached its pinnacle and close, Sir James Dowling reflected often on his struggles in life. He dwelt on them in letters to his son, James, then in England reading for the Bar. The letters' homiletic flavour makes them unreliable guides to the truth; for the father clearly exaggerated his own suggested triumphs to encourage the son to greater things. Qualified accordingly, they reveal Sir James Dowling's estimation of himself.[1]

The nub of his assessment was that he had been less than well provided for by his father Vincent, who had done little more than point the way to the family interest in the law. Sir James often marvelled at the success he had attained "under every possible disadvantage". As he told his son:

> I persuade myself that you are making the most of the opportunities for improvement, which through adverse circumstances were denied to me. After 15 I had no direct instruction, and my knowledge subsequently acquired was the result of personal exertion, often called into action in a scrambling and snatching manner. I have had to struggle through life under the disadvantages of a neglected education, and I attribute my good fortune, through Providence, to laborious industry and unconquerable perseverance.[2]

The last phrase, at least, was scrupulously accurate. Industry and perseverance were the hallmarks of Dowling's accomplishments. Again, in remarking to his son on the receipt of the Queen's warrant appointing him Chief Justice, Sir James made the like point, expressing gratitude to God:

> that after a youth chequered by the adverse discouragement of scanty means – a narrow education, and the hopeless opposition of a crowded profession – that after struggling against the vested interests and connexions of the more favoured sons of wealth and family weight – and abiding with patient industry the cares of life with a large family, I have at last attained the most sanguine aspirations of ambition, in youth, I could never have anticipated.[3]

One gift Sir James Dowling, along with his brothers, acquired from their father was a proficiency in shorthand writing. Joseph Dowling, one of the brothers, made his living from it.[4] All were adept also in longhand writing of artistic quality. James had as well from his father the benefit of a year or two at St Paul's School, Hammersmith, where he was an enthusiastic pupil.[5] But, on the father's becoming practically insolvent, James had to fend for himself from the age of 16.

He turned first to his shorthand for an income. He progressed – perhaps with a helping hand from his father – to writing, for London newspapers, reports of parliamentary debates. The work liberally educated him in the functions of government, the personalities of British politics, and the operation of parliamentary procedure. All the while his qualities of industry and perseverance shone through. He managed, aged 27, to secure his call to the Bar at the Middle Temple on 5 May 1815.[6] He practised in the courts at Westminster, on the Home Circuit, and at Middlesex and Essex Sessions.[7] There he came under favourable judicial notice, but languished under the "closed shop" system that kept the Bar the wealthy domain of the anointed few. His small share of practice, much augmented by law reporting fees, returned him £1000 a year by 1827.

Reporting, rather than law practice, made his name. He published, in conjunction with Archer Rylands, *Dowling and Rylands' Reports* covering decisions of the Court of Kings Bench and at Nisi Prius from 1832. The Nisi Prius reports did not prosper, but those at Kings Bench[8] continued over some years and brought Dowling into contact with judges and leading practitioners in that court. In a pretentious "Address" in the first volume, the compilers begged for "a fair and impartial examination of the Work" and fairly observed that:

> The duty of a Reporter, even under the highest encouragement and patronage, is an anxious, a laborious, and with reference to his

> reputation, a momentous one. By none, perhaps, except those who have been actually engaged in a similar pursuit can the assiduity, anxiety, and research necessary to the completion of his task, be duly estimated.[9]

Not long after his 39th birthday, Dowling took stock of his circumstances and concluded that, having to provide for himself, his wife[10] and six children, he could not support them all as he would wish on his existing income. As his son later summed up the position, "success marched with very slow steps".[11] So Dowling boldly decided to seek advancement in the British Colonies. He first approached the Vice-Chancellor, Lord Lyndhurst, soliciting that he might "condescend to write a favourable line, or speak a single favourable word on my behalf". Dowling never forgot that his request was "not honoured with any notice on the part of his Lordship".[12]

But Mr Justice Bayley, of the Court of Kings Bench, and the Solicitor-General (Sir Nicholas Tindal) were more forthcoming, each agreeing to be a referee. On 7 June 1827, Dowling wrote to Lord Goderich, Secretary of State for the Colonies, a letter[13] that would transform his career. He was disarmingly direct, given the niceties then observed in correspondence with great men – not least the convention that a supplicator have the prior intervention of a patron. Dowling, without even a formal introduction to Goderich, was moved to write, so he asserted, by desires to be of public usefulness, to advance the welfare of his family, and "to tender . . . his services as a candidate for some judicial, or other professional appointment, in any of the British Colonies".[14] He relied on the assured support of Bayley and Tindal, and mentioned the names of Mr Justice Holroyd, of Serjeant Onslow, and of some leaders of the Kings Bench Bar, including that of "Mr Brougham".[15]

"A Very Excellent Person for Any Such Station"

Henry Brougham was then in his ascendancy. A "new chapter" opened for him in 1827 and, next year, when the Whigs resumed power, he "became once more indispensable", soon going on to greatness with his parliamentary championship of law reform, accomplished by exalted oratory, and then to the occupancy of the woolsack.[16] Although Goderich caused Dowling's supplication to be acknowledged[17] no hope was offered to him. His referees were not consulted. But that was not the end. Writing to Goderich, in July 1827, in another connexion, Brougham emerged as Dowling's champion. "There is an idea", he wrote:

> in the Ct of K.B. [Court of Kings Bench] (to which I belong) that a Mr James Dowling wishes to go abroad in a professional situation. Him I have known for some years and he is certainly very well qualified in all respects – both professionally and personally. . . He would be a very excellent person for any such station and his name is well known in Westminster Hall.[18]

After discussion between Goderich's office and Brougham, the latter soon wrote that Dowling was "anxious for" a judicial or "other legal situation" at Gibraltar, but would accept an unpopular judicial seat at the slave colony of Dominica if he had no chance of any other. Having inquired "widely in the profession", Brougham found the opinion in Dowling's favour "very strong",[19] and he submitted written testimonials from Mr Justice Bayley and from Solicitor-General Tindal. Brougham wrote, "I have rarely known Mr Justice Bayley go so far" in a reference.[20] The judge made it clear that his judicial oath precluded any active patronage. But he assured Dowling, "with every wish for your success either here or abroad", that it would give him great satisfaction to be instrumental "in forwarding your wishes", and vouching for "your fitness for any judicial or professional appointment in the Colonies".[21] The Solicitor-General also undertook to answer inquiries made of him in such fashion "as will be serviceable to the views and objects of Mr Dowling".[22]

Dowling, even more decisively, enlisted the aid of his contemporary and "excellent friend" Serjeant Henry Stephen.[23] Henry was the elder brother of James Stephen, then permanent counsel to (later Under Secretary in) the Colonial Office, and already a man of influence and power. Dowling knew Henry well enough to write seeking his help. The response, charmingly ceremonious, was all that could have been wished. Serjeant Stephen wrote:

> On receiving your letter I immediately called on Mr James Stephen, apprised him of your object and requested permission to introduce you. He will receive us with pleasure on any morning that you may find it convenient to accompany me from 11 to 12. Tomorrow would suit me as well as any other time. . . My brother will best explain for himself whether he can in any degree be useful to you. I can only say that if this should turn out to be the case, it would give me very sincere pleasure.[24]

That meeting markedly turned the tide. James Stephen was "friendly" and equally well impressed by his brother's testimonial as by his own summation of Dowling. It followed that Dowling was invited to wait upon Goderich himself, which he did on 5 July 1827, being received in "the most kind and condescending manner".[25] In the light of Brougham's representations, Goderich thought that Dowling would disembarrass him of the problem at Dominica. The post of Chief Justice there was offered at £1200 a year: alternatively, there was a vacancy at Sierra Leone. Dowling was torn by the prospects. The opportunity for advancement was tempting. Yet the two locations offered, with their unwholesome climates and unattractive conditions, must promise great hardship for his family. His wife obviously insisted that he have second thoughts before committing them all to such a move. Was there no prospect, he asked Goderich, of any other appointment? The Secretary of State replied:

> there was another situation, . . . the office of the puisne judge at New South Wales, more eligible in many points of view, though not of equal rank with the others he had offered, but for that situation there were too many candidates, who were so powerfully supported in their claims, by persons of rank, and political influence, that he could hold out no hopes to [Dowling] of a preference.[26]

Dowling, sent away to think about the matter, wrote to Goderich on the very same day, thanking him for the audience and formally staking a claim upon the opening in New South Wales.[27] He was not to know it, but his claim was timed most opportunely. The Colonial Office had earlier resolved to send to New South Wales a Scottish practitioner, William Menzies,[28] who had no special qualifications for judicial office in Australia. Indeed, his mastery of Scots law, with its foundations in Roman law, was incompatible with the position. Perhaps it was thought that his Gaelic character would appeal to the Colony's Chief Justice Forbes. At the eleventh hour, Goderich's advisers realized that a foolish mistake was being made. Menzies' legal background better suited him for the Bench at the Cape Province, where Roman-Dutch law prevailed, and an extra judge was needed to administer a recently reorganized court system. Menzies must go there.

The decision to transfer Menzies to South Africa inflicted a great disappointment on another aspiring judge, William Westbrooke Burton.[29] By chance, he and Dowling would be placed later in contest for judicial promotion. For the moment, though, neither could foretell that their paths would cross. Burton, an English barrister, thought, in 1827, that he had a firm appointment as Senior Puisne Judge at the Cape.[30] He went to Holland, not, as is sometimes said, to master Roman-Dutch law, but "for the purpose of . . . acquiring the Dutch language".[31] In his absence, Menzies was appointed over his head as the Cape's Senior Puisne Judge.

James Stephen seized upon the fortuitous opportunity and recommended Dowling so strongly for New South Wales that Goderich caused a formal offer to be made to Dowling on 6 July, the day after their interview.[32] Convinced that Stephen had engineered these changes in fortune, Dowling wrote to thank him and to present him with one of the law books he had written. With his typically demure, lofty and detached air, that would have become a headmaster, Stephen replied enigmatically:

> I have placed the book on my shelves where it will remain as a memorial of you. I fear that I am but very little likely to be called again to the general practice of our profession so that I cannot pledge myself to become a very religious student of your work. I am very happy to find that you think I have been useful to you, and I should be still more happy if the fact were such as your kindness induces you to represent it.[33]

So the game of "musical chairs" among the contestants ended. After another interview with Goderich, Dowling accepted the Sydney offer on 9 July 1827.[34] Menzies was sent off to the Cape: Burton had to make do with what was offered as a judge junior to Menzies. Furious at being so passed over, and to all intents, demoted, Burton pressed the Secretary of State so relentlessly as to receive a written assurance that "you forfeit no prospect of future advancement".[35] Burton was to invoke that assurance when, years later, his course and that of Dowling not merely converged but ended in serious collision.[36]

Dowling's judicial salary in New South Wales would be £1500:[37] no great advance in money terms, but he reckoned that the Colony would offer him other material advantages, such as land ownership.[38] In his letter of acceptance he tried on his new mantle of public commitment. His literary style on such occasions, florid yet vaporous, no longer has much appeal. But it was then the fashion:

> It shall be the study of my life to deserve the high trust thus reposed in me, and my constant effort, to hold forth, in my personal conduct, an example which shall contribute to the maintenance of his most sacred Majesty's Government and authority in the remote region to which I am destined.[39]

Yet there were reasonable boundaries to upholding the public weal. Dowling soon turned to more practical considerations. He would need a free passage for his family; an advance of salary; and he would like a grant of land in the Colony.[40] Land grants, he was told, were within the gift of the Colony's Governor. The new judge would be conveyed with his family by the first available convict ship (Dowling demurred to any ship picking up convicts from Irish ports – "a deviation often attended with great inconvenience and delay"); and he might have a small advance, say £200 (which dismayed Dowling who claimed that making arrangements to move had already cost him some £1000).[41]

Suddenly the members of the "closed shop" at the Bar were among Dowling's most devoted friends.[42] The "largest assembly of members that [one of them had] ever met at the Home Circuit" rallied to congratulate their colleague and lament his departure.[43] The size of the assembly may have owed something to the haunch of venison Dowling presented to the Bar mess as a farewell gift. Meanwhile, Dowling set about studying Commissioner Bigge's *Reports*, and settling the details of the contract for passage of his family and himself by the convict ship *Hooghly*.[44] Dowling also made time to acknowledge Brougham's support. A set of *Dowling and Rylands' Reports* "handsomely bound in Russia Leather" was despatched to him with a fulsome letter of gratitude, and assurances that his patronage would be vindicated. "You have made me a very happy man! Let me be judged by my conduct how much I deserve this auspicious turn in the wheel of fortune".[45]

Dowling then called on James Stephen, with whom he had a "long conversation", much of it confidential, which led to yet another interview, this time with R.W. Hay, Permanent Under Secretary at the Colonial Office.[46] Those confidential exchanges reflected that office's concern about deteriorating relations between Governor Darling and the judges in New South Wales. Hay and Stephen, hoping to recruit Dowling as a source of intelligence on their behalf, disclosed to him their views, which were unfavourable to the judges, but in sympathy with the Governor, who was supposed not to have received from the judges the support due to him. That the Colonial Office was committed to those opinions demonstrates the success of lobbying by the Macarthurs of Parramatta and others of the "exclusive" class. Moreover, the Colonial Office was, at that time, quite unconcerned where the legal merits lay: "the official tone and formal manner which the difference of opinion had assumed, was not to be commended, on account of its necessary tendency to produce disunion".[47] Dowling would have remembered those words when, shortly after his arrival in New South Wales, the intransigence of Governor Darling evoked a typical contest between his office and the judges concerning Dowling's seniority on the Bench.[48]

Meanwhile, Dowling was gratified to be asked to call on the new Secretary of State, William Huskisson, who had replaced Goderich (raised to the Prime Ministership on Canning's death). Huskisson had at first rebuffed Dowling's suggestion that there be a discussion between them. But Hay and Stephen obviously wished to impress upon Huskisson and Dowling alike their concern at the unsettled state of government in New South Wales. Dowling was accordingly summoned to the feet of the Minister who rehearsed his impression that, in the Colony, the judges had:

> kept too much aloof of the Governor, and had left him to act upon his own responsibility, in a manner not quite consistent with what he had a right to expect from gentlemen who must reasonably be supposed to be more conversant with professional matters.[49]

It was conceded that Chief Justice Forbes had distinguished himself by his careful accounts of the constitutional disagreements that had plagued the Colony. Huskisson admired the "great ingenuity" of Forbes' arguments and was convinced that he was "certainly a man of considerable talent". Nevertheless, he felt persuaded (wrongly, because he was not in command of the facts) that the judges had been delinquent in their duty to advise the Governor and to do so "in the spirit of conciliation and cordiality".[50]

Dowling was then sent on his way, Huskisson outwardly being keen not to "dictate any rule of conduct for [Dowling's] own guidance, or to impose any shackles upon the free exercise of [his] own judgment".[51] Inwardly, Dowling was meant to understand that he had best take care not to precipitate any further fuss at Sydney, and that he should be astute to promote what he understood the real wishes of the Colonial Office to be.

It is not easy to fathom why the Colonial Office, having such fixed views about the circumstances of New South Wales, should have placed its trust in a man who had neither knowledge of colonial administration, nor judicial experience, nor a professional reputation beyond the solidly unremarkable. Yet the man had abilities that were instantly recognized by Brougham and James Stephen and testified to by significant referees. On the faith of those commendations, the Colonial Office was, as it were, sending into choppy and unchartered waters a seafarer with, as yet, no knowledge of the open seas.

"I Devoutly Wished Myself Back Again"

On Saturday, 3 November 1827, the Dowling family and some servants were in the *Hooghly* as it was towed down the Nore by one of those remarkable inventions – a steam boat.[52] Dowling was captivated by the *Hooghly*. It was a sailing vessel of 465 tons, under the command of a part-owner P.J. Reeves. The ship was then eight years old, and Dowling thought it "remarkably fine tight fast . . . and admirably adapted for the purposes for which she was chartered".[53] That was fortunate, too, for the preponderance of the passengers (about 100 of them) who were convicts under sentence of transportation. Their severance from home was completed in a speedy journey of four months.

James Sheen Dowling, aged eight at the time of the voyage, vividly remembered their departure and its consequences for him:

> We left London in a large coach of a style not now in existence and crossed "Old London Bridge" to embark at Woolwich. Most of the incidents of that day made a lasting impression on my mind . . . and well do I remember many of them; for instance I had but just set foot on the deck of the ship when, partly through my own carelessness, and that of others, I was knocked into the main hold . . . by a cable, and the fall well nigh terminated my voyage before it could fairly be said to have commenced.[54]

News of the intended augmentation of the Bench was already public knowledge in Sydney by late November. Although little was known of Dowling, it was assumed that "his legal information cannot be trifling", as it was hoped that his appointment would be "fortunate".[55] Meanwhile the journey passed quickly enough for the Dowling family who thought the time "agreeably spent making the usual abatement for seasickness and other trifling disagreeables incident to marine travelling".[56] The parents applied themselves to their children's education; and Dowling himself started writing a "narrative" of the circumstances that had brought him to his then station in life. On Sunday afternoon, 24 February 1828, they arrived in Port Jackson, sparkling, but steaming, under a hot summer sun. The *Sydney Gazette* hailed the occasion remarking that, "with our three Judges, we think the Colonists may indeed say – 'ADVANCE AUSTRALIA'".[57]

Dowling wrote at once to Governor Darling to report his arrival.[58] The next day, Monday, was busy. The arrival of any ship was a matter of moment in such a remote settlement. And the arrival of a dignitary further elevated the occasion. Runners brought letters of welcome from the Governor, appointing that very afternoon for Dowling's swearing in, and from Chief Justice Forbes. The latter wrote more personally, extending congratulations on arrival "after a voyage which always teaches the traveller that he did not know the pleasure of being on *terra firma* before": and Dowling and his wife were invited to a "family dinner" at Forbes' house. Mr Justice Stephen and several officers of the colonial administration waited upon Dowling in the *Hooghly*: the new judge found these attentions almost overwhelming.[59]

In a companion study of Forbes, the diverting mental picture is presented of Dowling's descent, in full judicial attire, from the *Hooghly,* on the afternoon of 25 February, to an artillery salute and the greetings of the unwigged Forbes.[60] The formalities gone through, of meeting colonial magnates at the quayside, Dowling was marched off by the official retinue to be received by the incumbent of Government House. Governor Darling was as chilling as the day was hot. Dowling's impression of him, much quoted since, needs to be allowed to flow again in his own words. The Governor, he wrote, "appeared to me to be a cold, stiff, sickly military person. He had none of the frankness and ease of a soldier and I absolutely froze in his presence".[61] In that icy atmosphere, Dowling was sworn into office as a Judge of the Supreme Court.

The new judge found nothing to please him in his company or environment on that day, though he conceded that "the ceremony was as imposing and formal as I had expected".[62] He dismissed the "very unwell" Chief Justice with his contemptuous (but enduring) "round head, republican look" epithet; thought Mr Justice John Stephen "marked down for another world"; and found Colonial Secretary McLeay betrayed by "his carriage and look (which were) altogether ungentlemanly and discouraging".[63] He contemplated in dismay the prospect of his new circumstances.

> My first day in the Colony was anything but pleasant . . . I got melancholy, anticipating that I should have a very difficult card to play, and ten to one get myself into a scrape from my utter inexperience in intriguing and "trimming" . . . The whole proceedings . . . gave me a sensation which I had never experienced before. My heart sank within me at the prospect in view, and I devoutly wished myself back again in London, to go on with the quiet slavish drudgery of my bygone existence.[64]

Brighter greetings from Bench and Bar celebrated his taking of his seat on 1 March, when his judicial commission was read by the Registrar.[65] There were soon other consolations. He and his family moved into a good residence, though the judge called it a "very small cottage",[66] in Kent Street, Sydney (still standing and still sometimes called "the Judge's House"), which, with its then delightful outlook over a yet undeveloped inner harbour, afforded agreeable accommodation. Its annual rent was £200, and the lease ran for three years.[67]

The judge was eligible for a town grant and a country grant of land.[68] For one who never had, and probably never would have, been a landowner in England, that was a source of great satisfaction. He picked out about 9 acres of what is now Darlinghurst as his town grant. It was not very prepossessing country to English eyes in those days, being "covered with scrub, much water-worn by flood rains, and infested by snakes and other reptiles".[69] For his rural grant, Dowling eventually selected somewhat more than 2500 acres on the banks of the Williams River near Dungog, later adding to the property, which he called "Canningalla". Never particularly comfortable, as a town man, with his country estate, Dowling did not visit it much, and left it substantially to the care of others. When he did visit, the countryside tended to overawe him. As his son, James, recalled:

> he [Sir James] was no horseman, and would prefer . . . to lead his horse rather than ride it. Once when at the farm he went for a stroll

> on foot, lost his way, wandered about all night, and at last turned up in the morning near his own cottage, having been all the time but a short distance away.[70]

Back in Sydney, Dowling's concern about land was to tame the "wasteland" at Darlinghurst. The property having been fenced, the architect Ambrose Hallen - soon Colonial Architect[71] - was engaged by Dowling to design a handsome Georgian residence. When completed, it was for a time in splendid isolation but, with its imposing circular drive, was a very distinguished gentleman's residence. Dignified further, while at the same time perpetuating indebtedness to a patron, the house was called "Brougham Place". Its construction was much more costly than the judge had expected and, to see it through, "he was compelled to borrow money at a high rate of interest".[72]

Money often dominated Mr Justice Dowling's thoughts. His new fixed income, in a settlement notorious for its inflated cost of living, was quickly eroded and could not be supplemented unless by working his rural land. He owed money to his sister Ann who had lent him funds to cover the unexpectedly heavy cost of removing from London.[73] The claims of his dependants upon him became greater: the amount of liquid cash at his disposal, smaller. But, all things considered, he was well placed. His standing as a landed gentleman far exceeded any expectations he could ever have attained had he stayed in England.

"His Majesty is Highly Satisfied"

Although so well forewarned about the state of public business in the Colony, Dowling could hardly have expected that the mere taking of his seat in court would create a colonial storm. As it was to turn out, even had the incident been a deliberate test of his diplomatic skill, he could not have acquitted himself better. But the *contretemps* that awaited him was not deliberate and probably originated in a mere clerical slip.[74]

In a despatch of 4 August 1827, Goderich advised Governor Darling that "the King has been pleased to appoint an additional Judge [Dowling] for the Service of [the] Colony, who will take rank in the Supreme Court next to the Chief Justice".[75] Had that been so, it must have represented a calculated slight to Mr Justice John Stephen, the coadjutor judge then in office. Any sensitivity on the

Governor's part would have compelled him to seek the Chief Justice's opinion, or to question the accuracy of the despatch. Darling took none of the steps that common sense dictated, but treated the despatch as if an order to be translated unquestioningly into action. He had Colonial Secretary McLeay pass the order to Chief Justice Forbes[76] who would, he supposed,[77] resolve the matter, as junior officers should, in implicit obedience to the will of the high command. The Chief Justice, quite properly, regarded the letter as merely informative, if vexatious, and as requiring no action by him. In any event, McLeay's letter identified Dowling as "John", not as "James", so grounds for special pleading existed if needed. Nothing having been said by any of the judges on the subject, Stephen took his accustomed place as senior puisne judge at Dowling's inaugural sitting on Saturday, 1 March 1828.[78] Darling, hearing of this, at once sensed insubordination on the part of the provocative Chief Justice. He wrote directly to Dowling, pointing out that, under the Secretary of State's "Instructions", Dowling must take precedence over Stephen and "it was not in my power to consent, so far as the Government was concerned, to his waiving his right in this respect".[79]

There then began an exchange of blunt views, tempered only by the highly formal language that matters of honour then required. Mr Justice Stephen, in quite unsporting mood at the prospects of being demoted, wrote a confidential letter to Dowling as a trap. "Permit me", he beguiled, "to solicit your private sentiments on the subject, in what manner I may most conveniently conduct myself on the emergency – on the one hand to avert the effects which may ensue to my character – on the other hand not to compromise my rights".[80] Stephen added that it seemed extraordinary that the Colonial Office should write "to a *Military Governor* to degrade a *Judge on the Bench*".[81]

Dowling was "painfully embarrassed" at being caught in the trap. He could not see how, with propriety, he could express any independent views on a matter "of so much delicacy, and so peculiarly of a personal nature".[82] The best amends he could tender lay in his assurance that, were the matter left to his private inclinations, he would not accept the higher judicial station. "But", he insisted, "as the pleasure of His Majesty's Government has been so distinctly notified upon the subject, I do not feel that I should be justified in frustrating its arrangement".[83]

The two correspondents came face to face in the judges' room at the court house on the following morning. Stephen, in a truculent humour, told Dowling that he intended, in a statement from the Bench, to ventilate the injustice proposed to be done to him, especially as:

> he was not conscious of having deserved the mark of degradation thus attempted to be put upon him, . . . as he had received no intimation from Home upon the subject, and . . . as his own Commission in express terms designated him as the *second* Judge.[84]

Dowling was shocked and still more embarrassed. He tried to dissuade Stephen from a course of publicity that must provide grist to the newspaper mills, and unsettle public confidence in the court. Stephen being unmoved, Dowling agreed, for the time being, to occupy the junior judicial seat, provided that Stephen would see to it that the instructions from the Secretary of State were clarified. Dowling reported these events to the Governor, indicating that he was not to be understood as "giving up any substantial right conferred on me by His Majesty's instructions".[85] He wrote, in somewhat similar terms, to Stephen, subscribing himself as "with great respect, my dear Sir, yours faithfully and truly", placing their conversation on record and repeating that, "If by this regard for personal feelings I have been understood as waiving the right conferred upon me by His Majesty, I may beg to state that I by no means intended to have my concession carried to that extent".[86]

For his part, Governor Darling could not allow the matter to rest there, and countenance the possibility that the parties might compromise. Orders had been given. The same orders had been disobeyed. He thundered at Dowling that any discomfiture suffered by Stephen was irrelevant in the light of those orders: "I do not conceive . . . that Your Honour could consistently, with what you owe to His Majesty, waive a Right, which His Majesty has been pleased to confer upon you".[87] The Governor, convinced that Stephen "will not on reflection agitate the question any further", made a tactical error in inviting Dowling to send a copy of the vice-regal letter to Stephen and to Forbes. Dowling did write to Forbes, but added observations of his own that completely controverted the Governor's real intentions.

From Forbes, Dowling sought particular and general advice. Would it be proper, he asked, to send a copy of the Governor's pronouncement as an enclosure to a further letter he intended addressing to Stephen.[88] Forbes replied that so conveying the Governor's views would "render the matter less easy of adjustment": this he gave as "a mere opinion", not as considered advice. The only means of settling the matter without "some unpleasant difference" would be its reference to the Secretary of State.[89] As usual, Forbes was right. But Dowling, hoping for a more immediate resolution, begged the Chief Justice not to withhold his advice on the substantive questions, lest Dowling be denied the "opportunity . . . thus afforded of relieving me with honour from the dilemma in which I am now placed". "I should really have been grateful to you", he added, "for a candid avowal of your opinion whether there is any legal or formal objection to the arrangement [of yielding place to Stephen out of courtesy without concession of any rights]".[90] Forbes replied the same evening. He had been approached also by Stephen, and was at that moment studying "the means of giving the best advice in my power upon the several points submitted to me".[91] His earlier opinion, he insisted, was limited to curtailing a possible misunderstanding between the judges: he had not intended to avoid the nub of the controversy.[92]

In his ensuing formal advice, the Chief Justice found an abundance of objections.[93] In his view, judicial precedence was to be determined by seniority of commission, in accordance with "the usage of England . . . part of the Law of the Land". As the "*New South Wales Act*" made no contrary provision, colonial precedence was governed by English law and practice.[94] It was open to doubt whether the royal prerogative alone could give a junior judge precedence above a senior and, even if it did, could the prerogative be enlivened in the Colony merely by a despatch from the Secretary of State? The proper course was to refer those questions back to that department.

Forbes meanwhile enmeshed the Governor in another tangle, because the misnaming of Dowling, in McLeay's original letter on the subject, suggested that the despatch had been misquoted. Forbes sought to inspect the despatch itself, a request Darling grudgingly conceded, while denying any ordinary obligation to divulge to the judges the contents of official despatches addressed to him.[95] Irritated by the unexpected turn of events, the Governor sent a copy of Forbes' letter, (to Dowling), to the Secretary of State, soliciting "your Orders for my guidance".[96] He was certain that those orders would vindicate him. So much so that he was even more forthright in a private letter to Under Secretary Hay which he wrote a few days later:

> I cannot consider Mr Dowling's yielding the precedence to Mr Justice Stephen, after the communications I made to him . . . as at all consistent. But Mr Forbes from the first professed to doubt the Authority of a Secretary of State's Despatch in such a case. He said the precedence should have been given in Mr Dowling's warrant under the Sign manual.[97] I had occasion not long since to point out that it appeared, by my Commission under the Great Seal, that any Instructions conveyed in the King's name by the Secretary of State, were to be considered the same as Orders under the Sign manual.[98]

Darling was, once more, completely astray in his comprehension of the relevant sources of power. As the law then stood, the royal prerogative to appoint judges in New South Wales did not contemplate any delegation of that power to the Governor. Executive instructions could not usurp a purely prerogative power. Because of his demonstrated inability to understand such things, and because of his misplaced preoccupation with "orders", Darling was dumbfounded by the response from Downing Street. The new incumbent as Secretary of State, Sir George Murray, signed a despatch in November 1828 assuring the Governor that "His Majesty's Government can have no wish, but that [Mr Justice Stephen] shall retain the Station to which his seniority entitles him. This you will signify to Mr Stephen without delay".[99] The Colonial Office's explanation was brief and disingenuous.[100] The arrangement first made had been intended to accommodate the supposed wishes of Stephen himself, who had been understood (though how is unclear, as Stephen denied any knowledge of the matter)[101] to prefer, because of his uncertain health, not to be liable to be called upon at any time to act as Chief Justice.[102]

Darling did not disguise his frustration as he responded to Murray in terms suggesting that he had been betrayed and demeaned in the faithful discharge of his duties – "it then appeared to me, as it still does, that I was doing no more than I was bound to do in endeavouring to give effect to the orders I had received".[103] He regretted that his motives might have been misunderstood or misconstrued. But, of course, they could not have been had he acted with sounder judgment or with the benefit of the very advice he declined to take.

All of the judges emerged from the incident with credit. Stephen had to be admired for his unexpected resoluteness in insisting on his rights. Forbes was typically circumspect, conciliatory and legally right. For Dowling, it had been a *tour de force* that helped him to establish his credentials at the outset. He had deferred to Stephen's position and feelings, he had properly submitted the problem to the adjudication of the Chief Justice, and he had declined merely to subserve the Governor's will. Crowning all of these, his moderation had won rare acclaim at the Colonial Office. As the hapless Governor was eventually instructed:

> you will inform Mr Dowling that His Majesty [*scil.* for this purpose, James Stephen] is highly satisfied with the courtesy and forbearance, which he has shown on this occasion, and by which Mr [Justice] Stephen has been spared much of the mortification which he would have experienced, had Mr Dowling persisted in assuming the superior station on the Bench.[104]

Dowling had demonstrated, for all to see, that he would readily place the public interest, and the interests of the judicial Bench as an institution, ahead of his private aspirations.

"I Stand Well in All Quarters"

The brooding melancholy, and reaction to the unaccustomed climate, that had so overwhelmed the new judge on his arrival, soon had to be cast aside. Such were the burdens of judicial business, and of settling in, that there was not even time enough to continue his autobiographical "narrative". For this early period of Dowling's judicial career, one must look elsewhere to reconstruct his doings, his impressions, and the impressions others had of him.[105]

A little over a month after his arrival, he felt that he would serve his function of observer for the Colonial Office by writing privately to James Stephen. He wrote also to Brougham. In this way he kept alive connexions that would continue to benefit him.

The judicial duties, he reported to Brougham, had been incessant as they had been much more burdensome than he had expected. There had been a heavy gaol delivery simultaneously with *nisi prius* sittings – "the gaol calendar, as may be expected in a community containing so many transports from the parent state, contained a catalogue of many enormous crimes".[106] The civil cases were frequently significant as to the property or money in dispute, notwithstanding that "nice or difficult points" were rare. Dowling had not found the abruptness and isolation of his elevation to the Bench easy to manage. The Chief Justice, who, at Dowling's landing, looked so unwell and appeared to be ten years older than his true age, soon succumbed to his indisposition. For several days, Mr Justice Stephen being also unwell, Dowling was the only judge fit to preside in court.[107] At least Governor Darling's anxiety, on just such grounds, as to the need for a third judge, proved to have been justified. Dowling, more self-servingly, told Brougham that "the numerical addition to the Bench has been hailed with unqualified approbation, not only by the judges themselves but all persons interested in the character of the Supreme Court"; and that "I have reason to believe that I have not yet disappointed the favourable anticipations indulged respecting me".[108]

In matters of procedure, Dowling noticed "a good deal of laxity" in applying the rules of evidence, and many other "irregularities" in practice – all of which were attributable to Forbes' attempts to adapt adjectival law to suit colonial circumstances.[109] At odds with the Chief Justice in that respect, he also, surprisingly, took a view contrary to that then entertained by Forbes about trial by jury, a subject to be examined further.[110] Given his own recent experience with the Governor, Dowling had little to say about relations between the Viceroy and the Bench, beyond reporting the regrettable nature of the "disunion that cannot, I fear, be easily corrected" and offering his views, which he would later translate into attempted mediation, as to the need for better understanding on both sides. His conclusion, colourful yet realistic, pointed out that "very trifling scratches have been fretted and rubbed into gangrene wounds, which if not speedily healed, may seriously affect the body politic".[111]

Dowling did not fail, in his letter to Brougham, to suggest that better provision should be made for his judicial salary. His first impression, that his stipend would serve him better than had his faltering income at the Bar, turned out, in the Colony, to be a mirage. "I fear", he wrote, "that my salary will be wholly inadequate to meet the enormous expense of living here, many of the essential articles of life being exceedingly high in price".[112] Soon afterwards, he complained privately to James Stephen, in similar terms. "My salary", he remonstrated:

> is so inadequate even to the purpose of decent living in so expensive a colony that I could not spare a shilling for the improvement of [my] land if I had it in my possession. . . The salaries of the puisne judges here are inadequate to enable them to maintain that appearance of decent respectability which their station requires should be observed. . . Without the most parsimonious economy I cannot keep out of debt.[113]

In that department, he was to receive no support from Brougham, Stephen, or anyone else. Until his elevation as Chief Justice in 1837, Dowling had to do as best he could on a fixed income that was hindered, rather than advanced, by his persisting with rural landholdings that were less than proficiently managed.

Only two days after Dowling signed his report to Brougham, Governor Darling was writing to Under Secretary Hay, as if to rub up another gangrene wound.[114] Chief Justice Forbes, complained the Governor, in obtruding upon assignments of government staff to court duties (the Governor could never grasp the fact that the appointment of subordinate court ministerial staff was reposed by the Charter of Justice in the Chief Justice and in no-one else),[115] had been prompted by ulterior motives. Dowling brought out with him his nephew Willoughby Dowling[116] (eventually admitted as a solicitor), and proposed that he serve as his associate and clerk. Forbes readily agreed, authorized the appointment and sought the Governor's approval to fund it at £200 per year. Forbes felt that the result was economical, especially if his proposal to abolish the office of Master, at £600 annually, were adopted. Darling, however, had his own, very improper, ideas about foisting upon the court a Master of his own choosing.[117] Typically, he perceived the arrangements, to accommodate Dowling's wishes for an essential assistant, as being conspiratorial and sinister.

That such a harmless and normal engagement should have been of any consequence to the Governor is remarkable enough in itself. But, so exercised did Darling become over the matter, that he allowed his imaginings and words to run unbridled:

> The appointment . . . had, I have no doubt, also another object, that of securing the support of Mr Dowling. . . You are aware . . . how desirable it must be for Mr Forbes to receive Mr Dowling's support;

> and he is too crafty not to use any means in his power to obtain it . . . Mr Forbes's constant aim has been to set the Government aside, and to show that the Chief Justice and the Supreme Court alone are competent to decide here . . . I hope that Mr Dowling will prove that he possesses sufficient firmness to resist him, until matters shall be put on a proper footing, and that he will not allow himself to be made such a tool as his associate.[118]

Suffice it to say that, if the Governor looked to win Dowling's respect, he would better have done so by yielding graciously to the appointment of Dowling's preferred nominee as his clerk, and not have elevated the matter to one of contest between the Court House and Government House.[119]

Resolving to rise above these differences, Dowling decided to try to be peacemaker between the Governor and the Chief Justice. If he succeeded, it would gratify his self-importance and win further praise from the Colonial Office. As he confided to James Stephen in August 1828, "At present *I* stand *well* in all quarters, keeping myself to myself and quietly going through the labours of my vocation".[120] The attempted mediation on which he embarked was probably thought presumptuous by the other parties, especially as it came from a newcomer of relatively junior status. Nevertheless Forbes did not countermand the proposal when Dowling put it to him in February 1829.

On 7 February, Dowling drew up a "paper" which he presented to the Governor and the Chief Justice "in order to cement the breach which had arisen between them".[121] The paper viewed with deep concern the prejudice caused to the King's service "from the apparent want of personal cordiality" between the Colony's two senior officials. The paper flowed on, in Dowling's grandiloquent style, but, in essence, urged a private composition of all differences.

> Impressed with these conjectures Mr Dowling hopes that his station in the settlement may excuse an attempt on his part to restore that state of right feeling, which in the present condition of affairs is so essential to the public welfare. He would therefore venture to propose that without inquiring too minutely into past transactions, or compromising any differences of opinion which a sense of rectitude on the one side and on the other may hitherto have . . . induced, – the *whole* shall be cast at once into the shade of oblivion and that the parties do henceforth reunite on terms of amenity [*sic*] and kindness.[122]

The next day, Dowling sent a copy of the paper to Forbes. To avoid "circuity and too much negotiation", Dowling had resolved to bypass the usual communication through the Colonial Secretary, and to seek an audience with the Governor personally. "I purpose talking the matter over with him", Dowling wrote, "and if terms of pacification are not accepted or the *pont d'or* be not immediately crossed I shall leave with him the memorandum of which the enclosed is a copy, in justification of my interposition".[123] Alas, the golden bridge remained uncrossed, the "paper" commended itself to neither of the disputants, and Dowling's naive hopes, of becoming the source of reconciliation, were dashed.[124] Eventually the Colonial Office would enforce peace on terms that neither party could resist – unless at the peril of recall to England.[125]

Forbes must have been more grateful, for practical support which Dowling gave soon afterwards, when the mentally decayed John Macarthur sought to have the Chief Justice "impeached".[126] The circumstances in which Macarthur's quarrel with his neighbour John Raine, about the diversion of dam water, degenerated into a riot and Supreme Court proceedings for a criminal information against Macarthur, have been sufficiently canvassed by other writers.[127] The Supreme Court (Forbes, Stephen and Dowling) granted a rule *nisi*, but, on hearing argument, declined to make it absolute, chiefly because "the party applying does not appear to us to be quite free from blame" and because "the Court sees much to discommend in both parties".[128] But costs were awarded against Macarthur.

The response of the latter was explosive. He set out to petition the King for leave to be heard before the Privy Council (there was then no provision for any other form of appeal from the Supreme Court) or to deal with the Chief Justice "by impeachment in Parliament". The second course, Macarthur made plain to Stephen and to Dowling, would be visited upon the Chief Justice alone, not upon them.[129] Macarthur tried to recruit the Governor's assistance, but Darling was, on this occasion, relieved to report to the Secretary of State that "I have not moved in [the matter] either directly or indirectly".[130] James Stephen, at the Colonial Office, headed off a crisis by declining to intervene apart from reproving Macarthur for proposing actions that were intemperate and vexatious. Meanwhile Forbes had been obliged to protect himself against Macarthur's attack, by official representations and private explanations to Wilmot-Horton.[131]

Central to the case was Macarthur's allegation that the unusual penalty in costs was a gloss on the court order and that it had been added by the Chief Justice alone without the concurrence of his brother judges. With that sense of whimsicality Forbes could bring to the relief of testy circumstances, he invited the other judges, as "competent witnesses in my behalf", to confirm where the truth lay.[132] They corroborated him. Dowling, in forthright terms, thought it unnecessary that the Chief Justice should have had to appeal to his colleagues for vindication of his honour and integrity. The court order had been unanimous, he said, and followed "the most anxious, dispassionate and mature deliberation of all the Judges".[133] For more abundant caution, he continued:

> I with like solemnity declare that throughout the whole proceeding I observed but one feeling manifested by you [Forbes] in the case, namely, a great anxiety to do justice in a case in which there appeared to me to be much of error on both sides.[134]

Things had travelled far since Dowling's nervous and unhappy arrival in Sydney. He had come to enjoy cordial relations with his judicial colleagues. As he remarked to James Stephen, "We agree admirably in temper and disposition and go on with great smoothness".[135] He had tried to attain equal cordiality with Darling, but had given up the attempt as being hopeless. The greatest change he experienced was not in personalities but in physical wellbeing. It was a change for the worse. His robust health, on arriving in the Colony, had collapsed under the pressures of court business and the stressful circumstances of his life. By March 1831, the tables were so turned that only Chief Justice Forbes was fit enough to preside in court, Stephen being ill, and Dowling "so indisposed as to be unable to attend to his customary routine of the day in the Supreme Court".[136] Diminished health would come increasingly to impose a heavy burden on the effective discharge of his judicial duties.[137]

2

"The Intention of the Legislature"

On 31 July 1828, Sir George Murray transmitted to Governor Darling a copy of the *Australian Courts Act* 1828 (9 *Geo.* IV *c.* 83).[1] In a covering despatch he explained "the motives by which His Majesty's Government have been guided in proposing those Enactments to Parliament", but added, in words later to assume greater import, that "in the execution and interpretation of the law, the intention of the Legislature must be collected exclusively from the language they have employed".[2]

As concerned two sections of the Act presently relevant – sections 9 and 24, relating respectively to revocation of convict assignments, and the reception of English law in the Colony – these utterances from Downing Street would, in practice, prove to be duplicitous. English draftsmen of the Bill for the Act (even with advice from Chief Justice Forbes)[3] had too little understanding of colonial conditions to be able always to prepare appropriate legislation. Conversely, even though in those days reference to extrinsic matter to ascertain parliamentary intention was frowned upon, the colonial judges could rarely have had public or private knowledge of any legislative intentions of the Parliament at Westminster beyond the statutory words used.

In numbered paragraphs of his despatch of 31 July 1828, Murray added a gloss to particular sections of the Act. Paragraph 21, relating to s. 9, observed:

> The power of the Governor of New South Wales to issue Tickets of leave or to withdraw assigned Convicts from their Masters is so obviously essential to the good government of the Colony, that Parliament has in the present Act been induced to place it beyond dispute. I perceived, however, that in the printed copy of the Act,

this Clause is inserted by accident in a place where it should not have been introduced.[4]

By May 1829 Darling reported to Murray[6] that the mischievous Judges of the Supreme Court had again been apprehended *flagrante delicto* in their disobedience of superior orders. They had handed down a judicial decision "at variance with the intimation conveyed in Paragraph Numbered 21 of your Despatch, dated the 31st of July last". The innocent precipitant of the difficulties flowing from this, was a woman convict, Jane New.[7] Transported from England to Tasmania for shoplifting, she eventually received the Lt Governor's permission to transfer, with her freeman husband (to whom she was an assigned convict), to New South Wales. There she again practised her shoplifting arts until, being taken into custody and brought to trial, she was convicted, sentence of death being recorded by Mr Justice Dowling. On review of the sentence by the Executive Council, Chief Justice Forbes considered that the legality of the conviction was doubtful because the Act (12 *Ann c.* 7) on which it was based was repealed and inoperative in New South Wales at the time.[8]

The Governor sought a report from the judges. Forbes replied on behalf of all, that they adhered to a view they had previously taken, in the case of Joseph Lee and others,[9] tried and sentenced under English statutes which had since been repealed, that no colonial conviction could be supported by a statute that was not in force locally.[10] Meanwhile, Darling revoked Jane New's assignment to her husband and caused her to be removed from the gaol to the "Female Factory" (where convict women not assigned as servants were kept), "in order to prevent her continuing her depredations on the Public".[11] The husband, in the Supreme Court, sought and was granted *habeas corpus* for her appearance before the court.

The court then heard argument as to the wider consequences of the application: in particular, whether Jane New was illegally detained.[12] There was also an extraordinary submission by Attorney-General Baxter and Solicitor-General Sampson, to the effect that "to guide the discretion of the Executive Government in other cases now under consideration" the judges should give virtually an advisory opinion on the proper construction of s. 9 of the *Australian Courts Act*.[13] The judges *viva voce* resisted that proposal, as they thought that the limited factual boundaries of

New's case did not require a determination of the Governor's powers to renew or revoke assignments granted by the Lt Governor of Tasmania.

On reflection, and ill-advisedly as it was to turn out, the judges yielded to Baxter's importunings and agreed to make a pronouncement about s. 9. On 21 May 1829 they assembled in banc to hand down their reserved judgments. That of Stephen was perfunctory, merely acceding to the views of Forbes.[14] The Chief Justice and Dowling gave very lengthy reasons for their decisions. The unanimous result was that a Governor of New South Wales had no power to renew or revoke an assignment of a convict granted by the Lt Governor of Tasmania (and *vice versa*), with the consequence that Jane New was unlawfully at large within New South Wales and must be remanded to the custody of the government for transportation back to Tasmania.

On that point, the Chief Justice rested his opinion on the binding application upon the court of the imperial Acts for the transportation of convicts. It was his opinion that:

> When a prisoner, who is transported to one Colony, is permitted to remove to another Colony, such prisoner is no longer within the provisions of the Acts of Parliament; he is not transported to such other Colony, and consequently not subject to the summary jurisdiction of the Magistrates. . . The fact of his being a convicted felon does not in itself subject him to the legal consequences of the transportation Acts; those Acts are very particular in their details; they must be strictly followed; and, where they are silent, there is no law.[15]

Dowling, as to the specific point affecting Jane New, was adamant that the court had no power to discharge her and was bound to remand her, as a prisoner unlawfully at large, by virtue of the court's "paramount ministerial jurisdiction".[16] Her going to New South Wales amounted to an "escape" from Tasmania and the permission of the Lt Governor of that island "would be no defence in law to an indictment for such escape". There would be great inconvenience in allowing prisoners of the Crown to go from one colony to another, because the jurisdiction of magistrates (to which jurisdiction such prisoners were amenable) was exclusive to the colony of their location and commission.

Had the matter rested there, the result might have been embarrassing to Darling and inconvenient to his administration, but have done little serious damage. It did not rest there and the judges soon proved to be authors of their own injuries in having agreed to step beyond the limits of the case and to offer their judicial opinion on s. 9 of the Act.

"The Question has been Pressed upon Our Attention"

Chief Justice Forbes considered the section to be "certainly expressed in an ambiguous manner".[17] The power of revocation of convicts' assignments was confined to prisoners going to New South Wales from some other part of the King's dominions:

> Van Diemen's Land is now, to all intents and purposes, a distinct Colony from New South Wales, and the Governor of the latter can no more revoke any act of the former than of the Governor of any other Colony under His Majesty's Crown. The mere circumstance of the prisoner being under sentence of transportation from England, and being found within the limits of His Excellency's Government [in New South Wales], cannot confer the power contended for; it must derive its force from some positive enactment, or it cannot exist.[18]

No such positive enactment, said Forbes, could be found. There was the stronger reason for needing the reassurance of such an enactment. Baxter, in his submissions in favour of a broad power, in the colonial Governors, to revoke or renew assignments, admitted that such a power could be used at pleasure to revoke any assignments, thus leaving free colonists, who depended for their livelihoods on the assured labour of assigned convict servants, at risk of having the value of their estates depreciated were the servants withdrawn. That estimation would, in time, prove to have been well founded.[19] For the moment, Forbes politely speculated to the contrary:

> That His Excellency will not exert such a power may be assumed; but it is upon the existence of such power, not the exercise of it, that we are called upon to express our opinions; and, before the bare abstract claim of such a power can be sustained by the adjudication of this Court, it must be established to its entire conviction upon the clearest manifestation of the intention of Parliament.[20]

Forbes proceeded to do so by a study of legislative history and a review of the alterations to the previously existing law. It followed, in Forbes' view, that the conjunction "and" in s. 9 did not confer two grants of power, but required reading down so that the latter part of the section formed an entire clause investing in the Governor of New South Wales the single power of revoking the assignment of a convict servant for the purpose of remitting his sentence.[21] Forbes stressed that the point was incidentally raised, and was not essential to the final disposal of the case, and that his remarks on s. 9 were *obiter dicta*.

Mr Justice Dowling equally stressed that the s. 9 point, although "of great importance", arose only incidentally to the arguments in the *habeas corpus* proceedings. So he was guarded in developing the point:

> I should have been strongly disinclined to give any opinion upon the construction generally of [s. 9], because it does not properly arise; but inasmuch as the question has been pressed upon our attention on both sides, and the opinion of the Court urgently sought for by the Law Officers of the Crown, I feel no hesitation in giving my present views upon it, although it is a matter which may possibly require hereafter more advised consideration.[22]

In a study of the antecedents of the legislation and of a number of precedent cases (including one from *Dowling and Rylands' Reports*), Dowling agreed with Forbes that the conclusion was imperative that "and" in s. 9 did not confer additional powers. The matter following "and" was, he considered, to be construed "by reason of its punctuation, as one substantive enactment . . . to give a power of revoking assignments for the merciful purpose of granting . . . temporary remissions of sentence".[23]

Like Forbes, Dowling was concerned at the risks, inherent in Baxter's arguments, that the section be read as enabling a Governor to withdraw arbitrarily a free settler's assigned labour:

> Parliament having given this Authority to the Governor, it appears to me that, from its very nature, it ought to be exercised *sub modo;* that is, in such a way as is consentaneous with the rights of the subject. It implies solemn enquiry and adjudication by means known to the Law of the Land. The Authority is created, but must be exercised in a manner agreeably with the scope and principal [*sic*] of municipal Law. . . The Governor's high office, I apprehend to be purely executive and not judicial.[24]

Were it otherwise, said Dowling, the Governor must be exposed, not merely to difficulty, but also to "unseemly odium" in personally exercising a power of revocation capable of producing controversial and prejudicial results.[25] Moreover, Dowling was satisfied that Parliament had shown a clear intention that the person to whom a convict's services were assigned, under the prevailing Acts, had an absolute right of property in the services of the prisoner, which right could not be divested without compensation.

After dwelling for some days on these pronouncements, Governor Darling addressed the judges curtly. The view they had taken was "contrary to the intentions of Parliament, as signified to me".[26] He demanded an explanation. The judges did not allow their "laborious avocations in Court" to be interrupted by the demand. Three weeks passed before Darling had a reply that must greatly have displeased him.[27] The judges jointly signed a letter to the Governor in which they referred to "the intentions of the Legislature" as being "of doubtful import";[28] they enclosed copies of their respective judgments; and they added only one comment. It elaborated upon a point made by Dowling in his formal decision. If the matter required legislative attention, the proper course would be to refer it to the colonial legislature so that remedial steps could be taken in Sydney with local circumstances well in mind.[29]

Such a broad hint passed for nothing with Governor Darling. There had been orders issued; again they had been disobeyed; duty demanded that a full report be made to superior officers. A despatch accordingly went to Sir George Murray,[30] pointing out that Darling had persistently claimed an absolute power to revoke assignments, and that any curtailment of it, particularly as regards prisoners transferred from Tasmania, would be productive of great inconvenience.

"A Censure on the Judges"

Other tangles in the skein meanwhile gathered in the Colony, but it is convenient to put them aside[31] and examine instead the "separate" despatch returned on 30 January 1830 by Murray to Darling in response to his report.[32] That despatch must have represented, in Darling's mind, the sweetest personal triumph and vindication of his vice-regal authority. If so, the sweetness would soon sour. The despatch was, however, damning of the judges' views and critical of the judges themselves. Accordingly, the despatch was "separate" and Darling was instructed by Under Secretary Twiss:

> that the portion of it which contains a censure on the Judges may not be communicated except to themselves, because, though [Sir George Murray] much disapproves their conduct in this affair, . . . anything which would tend to detract from their responsibility in the eyes of the public, would be a disparagement to the Government itself and a check to the general well-being of the Colony.[33]

The case, while demonstrating hypocrisy at the Colonial Office, would make plain to James Dowling that, under the Darling administration, no judge, however aloof and independent; could avoid being drawn into a whirlpool of contest and disagreement Darling excited among those of his "subordinates" who cavilled at his commands. Dowling, as will be seen, later shifted his ground to try to be seen as a supporter of the Governor: and later still recanted and shifted back again.[34]

Meanwhile, on the one hand, the Colonial Office criticized the Chief Justice at large for failing to assist the Governor.[35] On the other hand, in the present case, the same office castigated the Chief Justice and the whole Bench for giving their judicial opinion beyond the boundaries of *Ex parte Jane New*.[36] That censure stood, notwithstanding the universal understanding that the colonial Crown Law Officers, speaking for the Executive Government, had besought the court to give a ruling. Equally abhorrent was resort to the Colonial Office's entrenched custom, when convenient to that office, of sitting in effect as an appellate tribunal from the decisions of commissioned colonial judges. The Secretary of State first sought a confirmatory opinion from the English Crown Law Officers, who, in an *ex cathedra* pronouncement, observed:

> We are clearly of opinion that, under the 9th section of the 9th *Geo.* 4, *c.* 83, a Governor can revoke the assignment of a convict, of whose sentence it is not intended to grant any remission; and we think that there is nothing, either in the context or the apparent policy of the Act, which militates against this construction.[37]

The matter went also to Under Secretary Horace Twiss. He added his *ipse dixit* at length,[38] with neither detachment nor any pretence of understanding colonial circumstances. He accused the judges of participating in some political intrigue. They had gratuitously "travelled out of their straight path" to give an opinion not squarely raised in *Ex parte Jane New*, and had done so provocatively: "It was an opinion which, with the party opposing the Government, was but too sure to be popular; and every one will readily perceive how prejudicially it must work against the authority of the Government, in a Colony where the great majority of the population are . . . convicts".[39] Then Twiss conceded precisely what his paper controverted – that it was not for the Colonial Office "to determine whether the decision, thus *obiter dictum*, be or be not the true construction" of the Act.[40] But, being the man who had seen the Bill through its latter stages in the Commons, he was able to say "that the real intention of the Enactment was the very opposite of that which the Sydney Judges have construed its words to import".[41]

Whatever Twiss might have thought and whatever might have been in Parliament's inner mind, a form of words had been cast into a statute. It was then for judges, not for lawmakers or public servants, to decide what those words meant.[42] The suggestion that the Sydney judges had contrived a warped interpretation to suit colonial political purposes was as preposterous as it was without foundation or substantive evidence. It is superfluous here to canvass the lengthy criticisms Twiss applied to the decision of Chief Justice Forbes. Dr Currey, in particular, has disposed of them.[43] It reflected the parlous state of Forbes' reputation at Downing Street under the Colonial Office regime *post* Wilmot-Horton, that, for a joint curial pronouncement, Forbes was made to bear almost sole responsibility – "the weight of his judicial authority is . . . impaired",[44] so Twiss was pleased to say.

The views of Mr Justice Dowling were much more rapidly dismissed, especially as they accorded so much with those of the Chief Justice. Dowling's judgment, Twiss asserted, had proceeded, "upon the fallacy that the settler has the same right of property in the labour of the convicts at this day, as he had under the old system, when he paid for their transportation and gave security against their return".[45] While Dowling was entitled to some leniency for having insisted that the s. 9 point did not directly arise for decision, his excuse that "the Court was urged to it by the Counsel" (albeit the Attorney-General and the Solicitor-General) afforded merely "an indifferent reason" for his participation in a joint expression of judicial opinion "destitute . . . of the authority which belongs to legal judgment duly and directly obtained".[46]

A condensed version of the pronouncements of Twiss formed the basis of Murray's "separate" despatch. The Secretary of State declared that the Government had framed s. 9 of 9 *Geo*. IV *c*. 83, and recommended it to Parliament, "with the distinct intention of conferring on the Governors of the Australian Colonies an unlimited discretion to revoke the assignment of convicts".[47] The decision of the Sydney judges to the contrary was as surprising to the Colonial Office as it was unacceptable. The opinions of the English Crown Law Officers and of Twiss were to be regarded as "conclusive", especially as the *obiter* remarks of the judges were so "destitute of authority".[48] The Secretary of State hoped that other proceedings might arise to enable the judges to alter their opinion.[49] If they did not so repair the matter, the Governor (whose boundless gratification can but be imagined) was to disregard any related pronouncement from the Bench "until either the judgment shall have been reviewed by His Majesty in Council, or the law placed beyond doubt by the authority of Parliament".[50] Murray would not shrink from the "painful duty" of introducing a declaratory Act "on the ground of the difficulties imposed on the Colonial Government by an *error* of the judges, when that error is declared by the highest legal authorities here to be destitute of even a plausible foundation".[51] In such a fashion the colonial judges, who held office during pleasure and, as Dowling observed, could be dismissed "by the scratch of a pen",[52] were bludgeoned into submission.

Dr Currey has sufficiently exposed the absurdity behind the suggestion that the judges' views were not plausible.[53] It may be added that the description of their careful observations as an "error" debased the separation of executive and judicial powers. It was not for the English Crown Law Officers to sit in final judgment on any colonial judge's public pronouncements in legal proceedings. Dr Currey recites Forbes' "cogent, respectful reply" to Murray[54] – a reply that was not even acknowledged.

Dowling wrote, independently to the Secretary of State,[55] a fawning and exculpatory letter. He penned it in contrition, not wishing to shrink from his "just proportion" of any blame attributable to the Bench. The judges had been so hard pressed by the colonial Crown Law Officers that they were "prevailed upon (I confess much against my own inclination)" to go into the question; they then received virtually no assistance by way of argument from the Bar table; and they persevered with the matter "very reluctantly".[56] The judges had conferred to seek a "sound and safe" construction, but Dowling now disclaimed close involvement. He was the junior judge: his experience in the Colony had lasted only a little over 12 months: and Forbes had drafted the *New South Wales Act* on which 9 *Geo.* IV *c.* 83 was based. Forbes was, so Dowling apprehended, "more conversant with the intentions of the Legislature than I could be supposed to be".[57] Dowling had yielded assent to the majority view and had been "induced" to participate in it because of the seniority and greater experience of his colleagues. "Most assuredly", he pleaded:

> I should studiously have forborne giving any opinion whatever upon the point, did I not conscientiously and honestly believe, from the declaration of the Attorney and Solicitor General, that the local Government, from doubts entertained by itself, was desirous of having an intimation of the opinion of the Court for more abundant caution.[58]

These protestations expanded into an entreaty for self-preservation. Dowling could never, he said, be a party to any "unworthy purpose" such as gratifying political interests. He had striven to be independent and do his duty, notwithstanding that: "The Supreme Court has constantly been the scene of most difficult, painful and disagreeable discussion, independently of the immense mass of general business constantly arising in a territory of such wide extent, and amongst a population remarkably prone to litigation".[59] He felt that, if the propriety of his conduct were doubted, reference should be made to Governor Darling, and Dowling would "fearlessly abide by the judgment of his upright, honourable and discerning mind".

The respective letters of Forbes and Dowling stand in marked contrast. The one, polite but unyielding in its intellectual and legal persuasiveness of the soundness of the judges' position:[60] the other, timidly defensive, abandoning the Chief Justice to his fate, and hoping to be excused. It would be easier to admire the more a coadjutor judge who, having the breadth of experience at Westminster Hall, claimed by Dowling, (in distinction from his colleagues), had stood by the previously published point of view – acquiesced in by all the judges – and left the Colonial Office to procure an alteration to the statute or to submit the matter to the Privy Council.[61]

"You Will Never Revoke an Assignment Except After Previous Consultation"

It might also have been recalled to the memory of the Colonial Office that absolute power to revoke the assignment of convicts had been exercised by Darling already, and in precisely the manner the judges had criticized, to put assignees of convict labour out of business. The most telling example was that involving "a troubled spirit in this Colony", as Dowling called him,[62] the newspaper editor and publisher Edward Smith Hall.[63] Applying the columns of the *Monitor*[64] against Darling and his administration, Hall attacked with such ferocity that he was eventually imprisoned after conviction for criminal libel, as noticed in detail later.[65]

Darling, before and after the operation of s. 9 of the *Australian Courts Act* 1828, had shown himself more than willing to use the power he regarded as reposed absolutely in himself to withdraw convict assistance from enemies of his administration. The presently relevant events cannot be more succinctly summarized than was done by Professor R.B. Walker, when he wrote:

> In 1827 a convict printer "lent" but not formally assigned to Hall was suddenly withdrawn and when Hall tried to retain him he was fined by the Police Court. Then early in March 1829 by authority of [s. 9] of the *Constitution Act* [*sic*] the assignments were revoked of Peter Tyler, Hall's foreman printer, Joseph Monks, another printer, and Edward Ledsham, his reporter. Tyler, having been persuaded to return to work was gazetted as a prisoner illegally at large, arrested, and sent to Wellington Valley. Hall failed to obtain his release by a *habeas corpus* and was himself fined for harbouring a runaway convict. All this was done by lower courts in disregard of a recent Supreme Court judgment [*scil. Ex parte Jane New*] which ruled that the Governor might revoke an assignment only for the purpose of remitting the sentence.[66]

Hall, while imprisoned, and only two months after Darling had sent to Murray his report on the alleged misconduct of the judges in *Jane New's Case*, himself addressed the Secretary of State,[67] through the Governor – the latter dismissing the representations as "rhapsodies".[68] But Hall disclosed the very excesses to which Darling's claim to absolute power of revocation was exposed and which Darling had exploited so much to his own advantage. As Hall wrote:

> according to Governor Darling's interpretation of the new Act, His Excellency can send constables to the farm of a settler, just when the convict labourers of the latter are entering the ripened wheatfield; and, though the settler's clothing be on their backs and his shoes on their feet, His Excellency can take them into custody, and place them in the charge and keeping of . . . our Superintendent of Convicts.[69]

Thence, Hall added mischievously, it would be unsurprising to find the same convicts drafted to work on the wheatfields of the Governor and his relatives.

The Colonial Office, already sensitive to Hall's overblown complaints,[70] had to take notice when Darling, driven by a sense of vengeance, overreached himself. In his jubilation at the receipt of Murray's "separate" despatch of January 1830, effectively reversing the judges' views on s. 9 of the *Australian Courts Act*, Darling demonstrated who was in regional command. Hall, having retrieved his own freedom, and recovered the services of Tyler,[71] found his foreman suddenly spirited away again as the Governor once more peremptorily revoked the assignment.[72] Darling visited the like favour upon A.E. Hayes, editor of the *Australian*.[73] Sir George Murray, on this occasion, was appalled. "It is not suggested", he admonished Darling:

> that any necessity existed for the removal of [the newspaper editors'] assigned servants, nor is it even shewn that any reasonable cause required your interference. The single object of Parliament in enabling the Governors of New South Wales and Van Diemen's Land to remove assigned convicts was the advantage of the convicts themselves, or the protection of the public against an improper use of his master's authority.[74]

Having read thus far with mounting indignation, Darling must have been shocked at the unsparing censure upon him that followed:

> whatever your motives for removing [the editors'] assigned servants may have been . . . it would be vain to expect from the public at large any other construction than that you were endeavouring by this use of your power to harass a political opponent and to cripple his operations. I deeply regret that any ground whatever should have been given for such an imputation.[75]

The Governor was then commanded that his power to revoke assignments was never to be used unless on the clearest proof or most evident probability that the master of the convict was acting harshly or contrary to the requirements of justice. Adding to Darling's humiliation was advice that the Colonial Office had reflected again on the opinions of the Sydney judges and, in the circumstances which had happened, was very likely to propose that the statute law be amended.

Darling, in one sense, was unlucky. He had, at the material times, no knowledge of a despatch already on the high seas from Sir George Murray.[76] It would express concern at the *Monitor's* observations on the Governor's power of revoking assignments. It noted that Darling was reported to have acted only in the case of the newspaper editors, and trusted that the statements were untrue. Nothing could be more opposite to Parliament's intentions "than that the right of revoking assignments should be made subservient to any political purpose". The imputation necessarily arose "that the indulgence of your own personal feelings rather than the Public welfare had been consulted".[77] If the power of revocation were used as a resource for patronage or an instrument of punishment for offences allegedly committed against the Governor personally, the result would be "a total abuse of ... trust". The despatch ended in terms that a soldier could well understand: "So invidious indeed is the duty, which this devolves upon you, and so great the danger of misrepresentation to which you will be exposed, that you will never revoke an assignment except after previous consultation with the Executive Council".[78]

Had Darling known of those instructions he would scarcely have embarked upon his foolish despatch of April 1830 in which he reported, as if with pride, the revocation of the assignments of the servants of Hall and Hayes.[79] Yet, even when he did know of Murray's views, Darling was consumed with incredulity and intransigent self justification. He had previously assumed that the Secretary of State's despatches had been intended purely "to correct the view taken of this subject by the Chief Justice".[80] The Governor:

> entertained no doubt that I was as fully warranted in revoking the assignments of the men in question, as I should have been in the case of an individual ill treating his servant, the offence of the editors being in fact much the more serious of the two, their proceedings being likely to prove injurious to the public at large.[81]

Such protestations were ill calculated to persuade the Colonial Office that their Governor was right. Once again, the soundness of

Chief Justice Forbes' law and practicality was vindicated. James Dowling might have pondered on the wisdom of his course in distancing himself from Forbes, and clinging to the recognition of Darling. Forbes, as was so often the case, had been right: Darling had been wrong to so flagrant a degree that even the Colonial Office needed no further witnesses but the Governor's own admissions. The matter was resolved as Forbes had proposed – "And so", as Dr Currey summed it up, "the wheel turned full circle".[82]

"Keeping Aloof of All Parties"

Dowling, in these proceedings, had shown himself to be but a fairweather friend to the Chief Justice. His equivocation was due to judicial inexperience and to a realisation that the standards of pure judicial objectivity he had set himself could not be met in the then circumstances of New South Wales. It seemed superficially attractive to adopt the moral high ground as he vowed he would in a letter to his patron:

> On my arrival I soon saw the difficulties of the position in which I should be placed, and accordingly I laid down a plan of acting for myself, which I have since religiously pursued, namely – keeping aloof of all parties, squabbles and societies of men in this small community – living in the utmost state of seclusion in private with my family – but faithfully and fearlessly discharging my public duty when called upon, to the utmost of my ability.[83]

There is no doubt that Dowling attempted to manage his judicial career independently. Commendable though it may have been in some other circumstances, it was not a practical curriculum for New South Wales. Dowling could have strengthened the standing of the Bench at that time by giving undivided loyalty to the Chief Justice. But even his private comments on his judicial colleagues were much less than generous. Forbes, he wrote, was "a very superior man" who had been "*dragged* into politics, and placed in positions incompatible with the station of a judge".[84] From this, said Dowling, had arisen "much of the frigid, uncompromising, heartless state of public feeling" in the Colony.[85] Poor old Stephen, "a worthy and excellent man", was not up to contributing much because of his infirmities of health and age, so that most judicial business had to be carried by Forbes and Dowling to the detriment of both. All three were badly done by, in that:

> Our conduct is (I fear) unfairly represented to the "powers that be" at home no allowance made for the difficulties and anxieties of men called upon, by Act of Parliament, to administer the law of England to the people of this settlement, when that law is too frequently opposed to the conduct which requires its administration.[86]

Finally, Dowling altered his position once more as to Governor Darling. No longer concerning himself with that officer's approbation of Dowling's services, the judge reverted to the impressions he had formed on the day of his landing in Sydney, "By nature he [Darling] is a cold unapproachable soldier of the old school – (blind to the signs of the times) and by *manner* alone, he keeps aloof those who from honest and upright intention would cheerfully tender him advice and assistance".[87] Darling, he thought, was a well meaning man, but "as unpopular as can possibly be imagined" – one who had been "betrayed into many injudicious acts" by the generally incompetent advisers upon whom he relied. "Things went wrong at the commencement – they have continued worse" and they would not recover so long as the government continued to be administered as it was. In that, at least, Mr Justice Dowling was right.

3

"The Life of Man is Above All Price"

While Lord Brougham was Dowling's patron, it cannot be said that he was Dowling's tutor in the arts of speaking and doing in furtherance of great public issues. Brougham's commitment to law reform in England, and his powerful articulation of it, earned praise as "perhaps the most striking indictment of our legal system which has ever been delivered by an English lawyer".[1] Few such statesmanlike perceptions came from James Dowling during his judicial career. He played a part in reshaping the Colony's laws and institutions: but as a skilled legal technician rather than as an inspired jurist.

The greater part of his service on the Bench was in the criminal sittings, where he was efficient and fair – fair, that is, when seen through the eyes of the Victorian age. When it came to civilizing the savagery of inherited criminal laws which still bore the "barbarism of the fourteenth . . . century",[2] his was a blinkered view. Most criminal cases did not evoke great principles of public law in the Supreme Court of New South Wales in the 1830s. But the circumstances of *R. v. Farrell, Dingle and Woodward*,[3] disposed of by the Full Bench of Forbes, John Stephen and Dowling, in 1831, were different.

That case tested the application to the Colony of an old English rule of evidence whereby an attainted felon could not be sworn as a witness.[4] Chief Justice Forbes summarized the conventional principles:

> The law of England provides in two ways for the elicitation of truth; it excludes infamous persons as witnesses; and it binds such as it

> admits by the solemn sanction of an oath, fortified by the penal consequences of false swearing. . . These are the two bulwarks which the law has raised up for the protection of the subject. . . The law of England presumes an infamous person to be regardless of an oath; – and what penalties can reach a man under sentence of death?[5]

As Dowling described the facts of the case, the Bank of Australia had been robbed in September 1823, the vaults being entered by underground excavation. The then huge sum of over £12,000 was stolen. The planned operation was, said Dowling, "executed with a degree of cunning, contrivance, and perseverance, scarcely paralleled in the history of human villainy".[6] The participants managed for years to escape detection until all was revealed by a self-confessed participant named William Blaxstone. He claimed that Farrell and Dingle were fellow principals in the theft and that Woodward was a receiver of part of the proceeds. The three accused persons were put on trial before Dowling and, on the evidence of Blaxstone as Crown witness, the jury found them guilty.[7]

Blaxstone, a transported convict who had re-offended within the Colony, had been convicted, and had judgment recorded against him, for a capital felony, which had been commuted to 14 years' "transportation" to Norfolk Island. He had not been pardoned. A defence objection being pressed to the admission of his evidence, Dowling rejected it, but agreed to reserve the point for the Full Court's consideration. Such an appeal, as it might loosely be described today,[8] showed the inconvenience of the reserving judge's being one of the bench of review. Dowling had already, at the trial, expressed his view. He could hardly bring a completely detached mind to the Full Court. In this case, the review was unsettling. The Chief Justice applied the English rules of evidence to the Colony, thus excluding Blaxstone's evidence. Dowling decided to the contrary. Stephen concurred with Dowling, giving *ex tempore* reasons that were not reported. As to the major questions, Forbes and Dowling were poles apart.

The first question concerned the status of the Colony. Forbes conceded that it was still a penal colony, but its character was changing for the better.[9] Accordingly, a necessary exception had to be made to the laws of evidence to permit acceptance of transported persons as witnesses. Unlike convicted persons in

England, who were confined or exiled so as not to form part of the community at large:

> in New South Wales they are liberated on arrival, and are admitted to certain qualified rights – they are no longer *in vinculis* but the actors or witnesses in nine cases out of ten that come before a Court of Justice. To exclude such persons, therefore would be to shut out of court nine-tenths of the witnesses to every ordinary transaction which might become the subject of judicial investigation.[10]

So, said Forbes, they should be admitted as witnesses out of a necessity which formed the exceptional case, not the rule.

For Dowling, on the other hand, New South Wales was and remained a place dedicated by the English Government for the punishment and reformation of criminals:

> In no sense of the word has it been, nor can it have been considered, as a free settlement and colony of Englishmen. In this respect it has been in the lowest grade in which a society of English subjects could be placed to form a community, and differed from every other colony under the dominion of the British Crown.[11]

It followed, he thought, that Mr Justice Blackstone's celebrated principle, about reception of English law in settled colonies,[12] was not able to be applied to New South Wales, *a fortiori* because "the general municipal laws of England" could not be administered there. Moreover, "almost every" provision of the *Australian Courts Act* 1828 (9 *Geo*. IV *c*. 83) suggested to him Parliament's continuing acknowledgement of the "peculiarity of the Colony since the foundation".[13]

The latter Act was the one which, by s. 24, provided, with great equivocation, that all laws and statutes in force in England at the time of its passing, were to be applied in the administration of justice in New South Wales "so far as the same can be applied". Forbes, in the present case, expressed his view that s. 24 was "merely declaratory": it placed the Supreme Court on the same footing as before, of declaring what laws did or did not apply. He could not construe the section to mean that there was a "positive recognition of the power of this Court to apply the law only so far as circumstances will admit" and therefore a correlative power to dispense with so much of the law of England as seemed inconvenient to apply.[14] To take such a dispensing step would place the court, so Forbes contended, in the position of legislators. "If", he said, "the law require amendment or adaptation, it must be done by the makers of the laws, and not by the expounders of the laws".[15]

Dowling, while "utterly disclaiming and repudiating" the idea that the judges should take the lead of the legislature,[16] considered s. 24 to impose on the court the positive "duty of determining the applicability of any of the laws of England" to the Colony. Performance of that duty, in his opinion, had been rendered unpractical because the judges were constantly "obstructed by local difficulties and peculiarities",[17] compelling them "to lay down principles, and adopt resolutions, which would perhaps startle a lawyer in Westminster Hall". This was such a case and, as it dealt merely with laws of evidence, and not with the substantive law, he felt the judges constrained, by a statutory duty, to resolve the problem sympathetically to the needs and circumstances of the Colony.[18]

Applying those premises, Dowling declared that the traditional exclusion of the evidence of a convict attaint was, for colonial purposes, no more than "a dry canon" of the law and was wholly technical in spirit.[19] Local circumstances differed so much from those in the mother country, that the court was justified in dispensing with a traditional rule where the ends of justice commended it. He contended that a line of earlier authority in the Supreme Court,[20] and a consistent course of practice, not only warranted, but compelled, the court's accepting the evidence of "retransported" felons.

The gulf between the judges was on the question of "necessity". In Dowling's view, the evidence of the overwhelming majority of the ex-convict community of New South Wales was necessarily received because it was not practical to send to England for documentary and legal proof of their status as convicts attaint. If, in consequence, they were beyond the strict application of the laws of evidence, he could see no distinction in principle in accepting also, as witnesses, persons who had been retransported within the Colony itself.[21] As he put it, rhetorically:

> Are the lives and personal safety of the unhappy men who may be transported to these penal settlements less the objects of care and solicitude than the lives and personal safety of the rest of God's creatures placed under the dominion of British laws? *The life of man is above all price.*[22]

Forbes had some rhetorical questions of his own, in rebuttal. For him, the evidence of the ex-convict community was received out of necessity, not because of nice questions of proof of conviction or of great seal pardon, but because those persons represented the bulk of the colonial community – "set at liberty, depending upon their good conduct, to earn a future character and station in society". For him, the case turned on the exceptional class of re-offenders drawn from that group. The very fact of re-offending, and being sentenced to domestic "transportation" or worse, was sufficient, on traditional rules of evidence, to destroy the credit of that person's oath. And, to come to his rhetorical tests of the logic of the matter:

> What was the situation of a witness in this case? Originally a transported felon from the Mother Country, he is not only convicted of a capital offence in this Colony, and receives sentence of death, but also comes into the box a self-convicted accomplice. . . Is there not a broad and tangible difference between such a case, and that of a transported population from the Mother Country? His accumulated crimes render his testimony valueless – the sanction of an oath of no force – and the punishment of perjury cannot reach him: all the safeguards of the law consequently fail. Is cumulative crime nothing? is attaint upon attaint nothing? is there no point where the law of the civilised world can come into operation – where must the Court stop.[23]

Forbes continued that, taken to their inevitable conclusion, these propositions would seem to place the Colony's free inhabitants at risk, if ever put upon trial, of having evidence given against them by condemned criminals brought up from the cells or from the foot of the gibbet itself.[24]

Dowling conceded that such a conclusion would be intolerable.[25] But he considered the example to be extreme. In ordinary circumstances, the Colony's long usage and previous court decisions should be binding. His exhortation was:

> Let the doors of justice be thrown open to all men short of a person in the extreme case . . . whom it may be practicable to admit, in order that those who are to execute the laws may have the benefit, as much as it is worth, of any human testimony which may develop truth, and give vigour to the arm of justice.[26]

Rarely again would Dowling reveal the foresight he brought to this particular problem. He had reached his conclusions, he admitted, with "anxiety" and somewhat against the disposition of his mind, imbued as it was "with the inclinations of an education acquired in Westminster Hall". The judges must all have known of changes in England to the laws of evidence as recently as 1828,[27] that went some way to admitting the testimony of convicts. Those changes vindicated Forbes' conclusions rather than those of Dowling. The latter's boldness, in embracing changes that would within a decade acquire the force of law in England and derivatively in the Colony, was remarkable.

The majority decision accordingly was that the Blaxstone evidence was admissible and that the jury's verdict of guilty would stand. There was assuredly some feeling of community satisfaction, at a time when interests in property were among the most cherished in colonial society, that the enormity of the crime perpetrated upon the Bank of Australia had at length been set to rights. Dowling's view in this case was not universally shared. By the time he succeeded to the Chief Justiceship, there was a concerted opinion that the principles he had enunciated would be overturned should a test case arise. It did not arise, and those principles were, in due course, embodied in the colonial statute law.[28] His construction of s. 24 of the *Australian Courts Act* 1828 was less compelling, Forbes' interpretation being consistently rehearsed with approval until well into the 20th century.[29]

The two principal prisoners must scarcely have believed their luck when Dowling and Stephen declared that, out of deference to the Chief Justice's dissent, sentence of death would not be passed, but judgment of death would be recorded only.[30] The prisoners' application, in advance of judgment, for leave to appeal to the Privy Council, was rejected as being a novelty, unsupported by authority, and doomed to futility:

> All that could be transmitted would be the record of the proceedings. . . There would be nothing, therefore, upon which the King in Council could adjudicate as an appellate tribunal. It is a long settled rule, that no writ of error lies upon a judgment in cases of felony, but even if it did, a writ of error, at common law, would not operate as a stay of execution.[31]

Overshadowing which was the reality that no avenue of appeal then lay from the Supreme Court to the Privy Council.[32]

Dr C.H. Currey, in *Sir Francis Forbes*, states that "in August 1833 Farrell and Dingle appealed for a reconsideration of their case, since the Judges who tried them had been divided in opinion" and Stephen had been superseded by Mr Justice W.W. Burton.[33] With great respect to Dr Currey, that seems a highly improbable course, and the present writer has found no contemporary material to support it. The proceedings, by way of Crown case reserved, were not amenable to any "appeal" in the modern sense of the word: though there was the outside possibility of seeking a review of the Full Court's decision by the Governor. The time for moving for arrest of judgment had long since gone: and it would have been futile to seek a prerogative writ going to the Supreme Court itself. The question of appeal to the Privy Council had been raised and rejected. Even had there been any machinery for review of the decision of the Full Bench, and it is submitted that there was not, its use would have involved unattractive risks. The offenders had long since escaped with their lives. Had any review been available, it might have resulted in the ultimate severity of the law being reimposed.

It seems likely that Dr Currey has confused the conclusion of *R. v. Farrell* with its sequel, the case of *R. v. Ryan*, which had many similarities to the former case and produced the outcome – of suggested legislative reform – that Dr Currey describes. On 15 December 1832, Samuel Ryan, William Steele, Thomas McGrath and Patrick Daley, on their trial before Chief Justice Forbes, were convicted of murder and sentenced to death. As the Chief Justice reported to the Executive Council, the trial was beset with problems.[34] No body had ever been discovered, and the evidence, which was at best "speculative", was flawed, and showed what Forbes claimed to be the weaknesses of the *R. v. Farrell* principle in practice: "the whole case rested upon the evidence of one witness, who besides being by his own statement an accomplice in the crime itself, had been called up from a penal settlement where he had been transported under commutation for a capital sentence".[35] The case thus had direct affinity with the procedural circumstances of *Farrell's Case*. There was also new evidence that pointed to an almost certain acquittal had that evidence been forthcoming at trial – but that is by the way for present purposes.

As Governor Bourke wrote to Viscount Goderich, concerning the admission at trials of the evidence of convicts attaint: "The opinions of the Judges Stephen and Dowling were given on a former occasion in favour of receiving this description of evidence. The Chief Justice took a view of the matter different from theirs, though not entirely opposed to the admission in some cases".[36] Given that John Stephen had been superseded by Burton, who had the Governor's ear, Bourke was able to add that he "had reason to believe" that, were the matter re-argued before the Bench as reconstituted, Dowling's would be the minority view. Bourke thought that the other two judges would "probably either recommend the introduction of a legislative enactment suited to the particular circumstances of the Colony, or return to the practise [*sic*] of the Law of England".[37]

Although the reply by the then Secretary of State, E.G. Stanley, authorized a pardon of the prisoners under sentence, the question of the admissibility of the testimony of convicts attaint was ignored.[38] In the result, Dowling's view of the law remained authoritative during the whole of his continuing term on the Bench.

The matter came to be resolved by statute in a way that owed nothing to the difficulties that had arisen in court cases in New South Wales. The *Civil Rights of Convicts Act* 1828[39] had already taken effect to render convicts attaint competent to be tendered as witnesses, provided that they had served their sentences and had not been convicted of perjury. That, in effect, was the position Forbes recognized as operating *de facto* on convicts transported to New South Wales. Not until 26 June 1844 (just three months before Dowling's death) was an even more liberal provision adopted in New South Wales, in conformity with the English *Evidence Act* 1843.[40]

The 8 *Vic. No.* 1, "An Act for Improving the Law of Evidence", provided that: "no person offered as a witness shall hereafter be excluded by reason of incapacity from crime or interest from giving evidence either in person or by deposition . . . on the trial of any issue".[41] Dowling's view had thus, at length, come to prevail, and the fact of a conviction became "a matter which concerns the cogency and not the competency" of the convict's testimony.[42] At least, for a brief moment, and exceptionally (generally his decisions were much more prosaic), Dowling had been something of a Brougham come to judgment.

"Justice Has At Length Overtaken You"

When, however, it came to putting the fine rhetoric of *Farrell's Case* into practice in the routine administration of the criminal law, Dowling showed a very different perception about the price of "the life of man". He was content to take the criminal justice system as he found it. In a penal settlement, harshness and deterrence in criminal punishment were matters of course. Many of the transported community had come involuntarily to Australia, their transportation being in mitigation of the death penalty then called for in crimes that now shock the conscience for having been so characterized, because they seem to have been so trifling. But they were not trifling in the early 19th century. In particular, in the Colony in those days, cattle stealing was a serious felony. Theft of a beast could be equated with heinous crimes like murder and rape because the ownership of cattle was then, for many people, their principal possession and investment. The law lent much more of its protection to property than it did to human life. Since feudal times, interference with such possessions had been visited with condign punishment.

In June 1828, before Dowling and a military jury in the Supreme Court, John Curtis was found guilty of stealing one cow at Bringelly. Profound silence being ordered by the court, the judge proclaimed the inevitable, by his assuming the black cap, and addressing the prisoner "with becoming solemnity". Dowling had no words of concern about the barbaric state of the law. On the contrary, he declared that the law "for wise reasons" made cattle stealing a capital offence. It made an example to the community that those who took advantage of others, by stealing their cattle, could expect nothing but the due severity of the law.

> I am sorry to observe that in your case, prisoner, there is no circumstance to justify me [*sic*] holding out a hope that this dreadful penalty can be in any way averted. There is against you every circumstance of aggravation. You had not the plea of distress – no large family and wife perishing for food. You . . . were actuated by a lawless disposition to plunder your neighbour, without any possible inducement but from indulgence in a course of predatory habits . . . Justice has at length overtaken you, and considering the nature of your offence, justice requires such an example in you as may tend to operate as a warning upon others disposed to pursue so mischievous a course. It is therefore my duty to warn you of the precipice on

> which you stand, and to tell you that in this instance the law must certainly take its course. Ere long you will be ushered into the awful presence of your Maker.[43]

Then followed admonitions to submit patiently to the requirements of justice, to undertake "the work of repentance" while there was yet time, and to be preoccupied with prayer until the dreadful day when the prisoner would be "led to the usual place of execution, and there be hanged by the neck until your body be dead". A man's life for a cow!

There was not the slightest indication that such severity in administering the criminal law worked as any deterrent or that cattle stealing stopped. It was as good an example as could be wanted of a monstrous penal system in which no attempt was made to fit the punishment to the crime. These were not cases in which "the life of man is above all price", and Mr Justice Dowling showed none of the characteristics required of a reformer of oppressive and antiquated criminal laws. He did not see the law as Brougham had seen it.

It would not be profitable, in a work of this kind, to attempt further to trace the course of individual criminal cases over which Dowling presided.[44] But it is appropriate to examine a collateral aspect of the system for administering justice, in order to appreciate some of the difficulties under which contemporary judges laboured.

"There Existed Great Neglect in the Attorney General's Office"

In many cases of great public importance at that time, Dowling, along with the other judges, found the court poorly served by the Crown Law Officers. The early Attorneys-General were inferior lawyers, ill-equipped to conduct forensic contests with private counsel like Wentworth and Wardell. Crown counsel often could not prepare prosecutions effectively, make charges for aggravated crimes stand up in the face of evidence given by the Crown's own witnesses, or even have mental agility enough to move for a conviction on a lesser count if a greater could not be sustained.

A striking example of the incompetence of Attorney-General Baxter occurred in 1829 on the hearing before Dowling of *R. v. Hackett*.[45] In that prosecution, five men were charged with piracy of the brig *Phoebe*, and its cargo of cedar, "on the high seas". The case had but opened, when Baxter submitted that it would waste time to go through all the evidence as he found he had nothing to prove the commission of an offence on "the high seas".[46] He asked that the indictment be quashed, with a view to substituting another for the non-capital offence of stealing. It would emerge that the *Phoebe*, at the time of the alleged stealing, was not in open waters but within "Shoal Haven Port"; though it was later taken out of the port. Dowling responded:

> I told the Attorney General that of course he was the best judge of his own case, having, I presumed, duly considered the force and effect of the depositions before him, and to which I had not access. If, upon due consideration, he was of opinion that the charge of piracy could not be substantiated, certainly there would be no use in going on with this case. I was entirely in his hands and must be governed by his intimation as the Public Prosecutor.[47]

Clearly the effect of the depositions had not been assessed by Baxter until the eleventh hour. And then, as it happened, his assessment was wrong.[48] He proceeded with an indictment for feloniously stealing, and secured convictions, for which the prisoners were sentenced, not to death as they would have been if pirates, but to transportation to a colonial penal settlement for seven years.[49]

Governor Darling was exercised that the opportunity, of making an example of men he prejudged to be pirates, had been missed because of administrative ineptitude. He demanded a report from Baxter, who responded, falsely, that the five prisoners were found to be, not principals, but the unwilling assistants of "ringleaders" yet to be apprehended. Baxter claimed, equally falsely, that "an objection was taken by the learned Judge to the higher Charge contained in the information".[50] Baxter compounded his incompetence with dishonesty.

In summing up, Dowling had told the jury that "most undoubtedly there was abundant evidence, as it turned out, to have supported the case in point of law".[51] Dowling had even tried to shield the ungrateful Baxter, remarking that the Attorney might not have been aware, when he presented the indictment, of the full extent of the evidence that would be disclosed. Dowling said:

> Had I been apprised of the fact that the vessel had been actually carried off, I should in the discharge of my duty, [have] directed the

> case to proceed; for, although the first taking was in a *Harbour*, yet the subsequent carrying out upon the *high* seas made the offence Piracy in all persons concerned in the taking of the vessel.[52]

On reading the judge's report, Darling urgently complained to the Secretary of State about Baxter's want of professional soundness in his conduct of the entire proceedings:

> Feeling how important it was in a Colony of this description that the convicts should be made aware that no pains would be spared to bring them to punishment, should they attempt to escape . . . I confess that my disappointment at the course adopted for [this] trial has been proportionate.[53]

In 1830 Dowling was again greatly embarrassed at the consequences of the conduct of criminal proceedings by Baxter in the case of Dennis McHugh (sometimes rendered Maccue or McHue). The latter, a transported convict who had already re-offended within the Colony, was charged with stealing a note of the Bank of Australia – one of the items allegedly stolen from the bank in September 1828, which enterprise had its conclusion in *R. v. Farrell, Dingle and Woodward*.[54] For his pains in offering two irreconcilable explanations of how he came to have the note, the Sydney Bench of Magistrates, in September 1828, found McHugh guilty of "wilful and corrupt perjury in a matter under investigation" and sentenced him to serve three years' imprisonment in a colonial penal settlement.[55]

On 3 January 1829, when Dowling had sat all day hearing Crown cases, an application was made by Sydney Stephen of the Bar just before the rising of the court. Stephen moved, on affidavit evidence, for the Principal Superintendent of Convicts (A.F. Hely) to bring to the court, by the authority of *habeas corpus*, the incarcerated McHugh, so that the court might entertain submissions that his conviction had been illegal. Stephen argued that the Bench of Magistrates had acted of its own motion, without objective proof of perjury, and simply on an impression it had formed of McHugh's demeanour. He also submitted that the Bench was illegally constituted for the purposes of the case, one of the magistrates (A.B. Sparke) being personally interested in his capacity as a director of the Bank of Australia.[56]

Dowling's minute of the proceedings recorded that Attorney-General Baxter at once conceded the accuracy of Stephen's submissions, acknowledged that it was impossible to sustain any conviction, and undertook for the Crown that McHugh would be discharged without need for formal prerogative relief.[57] Stephen thereupon withdrew the motion, and the supporting affidavit was not filed. Baxter gave a written order to the sheriff to cause McHugh to be discharged from the *Phoenix* (an abandoned vessel which had risen from its ashes to become a prison hulk) where he had been held.[58]

The Colonial Secretary, Alexander McLeay, somehow came to the conclusion - probably promoted by the "exclusives" - that McHugh had been released by Dowling on a technicality "because his actual offence did not come within the legal definition of that crime [perjury]".[59] In the meantime, McHugh was shipped off to Moreton Bay by order of the Principal Superintendent of Convicts who was convinced that "McHugh was strongly suspected of being privy to the Bank Robbery, and that it was desirable to keep him from any communication with his fellows".[60]

Thereafter, who should stumble upon what had happened but Edward Smith Hall, editor of the *Sydney Monitor,* then engaged, as noticed elsewhere,[61] in prolonged litigation - some voluntary and some not - in the Supreme Court, much of it before Mr Justice Dowling. Hall, whose tactics were to unnerve Dowling by making trouble implicating him, and who also had accounts to settle with Hely, soon published in the *Monitor* "a certain false, malicious and defamatory libel" of Hely.[62] The innuendo was (and no doubt it was true) that Hely had continued to hold McHugh "in the hot putrid air of the Barrack dungeon" by his own authority long after the order had been given for the prisoner's release - and then caused the man to "disappear" very suddenly to some remoter penal settlement.[63]

So much publicity was directed to these disclosures, with friends of the "exclusives" putting it about in Downing Street that the Supreme Court, and Dowling in particular, had "gone soft" on convicts, that the matter came under notice in the House of Commons. There, however, the debate was critical rather of Governor Darling.[64] It was resolved by the House that addresses to it, calling for the tabling of all documents relating to McHugh's release by the Supreme Court, be acceded to. The Secretary of State accordingly commanded Darling to furnish them.[65] Colonial Secretary McLeay did so with enthusiasm, adding to the documents bespoken unsolicited testimonials as to McHugh's bad character. Through Baxter's deviousness, it was made to appear that Dowling had discharged his judicial duties negligently. On 6 January 1829, Baxter, presumably to protect himself, (for he could, if energetic, have caused McHugh to be held in custody to await prosecution on alternative criminal charges), wrote to McLeay. Baxter described the brief Supreme Court proceedings as resulting in a "peremptory order" being made by Dowling for McHugh's discharge on the ground that the sentence passed against him by the magistrates was illegal "there being no case of *legal perjury* committed by the prisoner to warrant the record of the conviction by the magistrates".[66]

If that were true, it amounted to accusing the judge of deliberately lying in giving his certificate, on 21 December 1830, that his own judicial minute of the proceedings on 3 January 1829 was correct when it recorded that Sydney Stephen had withdrawn his motion on the concessions made in court by Baxter, and that no formal order of court was made. In corroboration of the judge's minute, J.E. Manning, Registrar of the court, confirmed that no order was enrolled, and that there was no affidavit on file concerning the proceedings.[67] The only document contemporaneous with the court proceedings was the "order", not by the court, but by Baxter himself, directing the sheriff to release McHugh from the *Phoenix*.[68]

McLeay, who disliked Dowling, and may have wished to gratify the Governor, was convinced that the judge had made a peremptory order. McLeay, on the basis of no other evidence than his feeling convinced, reported to Darling that the judge's certificate, dated 21 December 1830, had been composed entirely from Dowling's memory.[69] McLeay embroidered upon that fiction some trumpery remarks about Dowling, intending to disparage his judicial probity.

Well had Dowling formed the impression, on his first arrival in Sydney, that McLeay was "ungentlemanly".[70] The Colonial Secretary had, however, underestimated Dowling's greatest judicial strength – he was a meticulous taker of notes and keeper of records, a practice inherited from his law reporting days. Dowling's record of the proceedings could not have been fabricated after the event: it appeared, exactly as he quoted it, in his judicial notebook for 3 January 1829 in circumstances where it was physically impossible for it to have been added to or altered after the event.[71] In the margin, Dowling later wrote: "N.B. A copy of the above was given by me on the 21st Dec. 1830 for the information of the Govr. to be sent home".[72] McLeay's attempt to denigrate the judge's character was preposterous.

Dowling was the only principal participant to emerge from this episode with his character not merely unscathed but enhanced.[73] Baxter had been incompetent and devious; the "exclusives" had again tried improperly to politicize the court; and the Colonial Secretary had demeaned the stature of his office by his unworthy treatment of the judge. Baxter's reputation was such that Dowling had nothing more to fear from him. In a strikingly inappropriate appointment, the Colonial Office got Baxter out of the way by elevating him as puisne judge in Tasmania. Lieutenant-Governor Arthur correctly summed up Baxter when he called him a "sot", a man of straw, and a wife-beater – to which he might have added that Baxter must have suffered an acute mental illness. Arthur would not permit him to take his seat on the Tasmanian Bench lest there be "a violation of all public decency".[74] Baxter had to resign and, in effect, submit his insolvent estate to be sequestrated in bankruptcy. Dowling and New South Wales were well rid of him.

One further illustration will suffice of the effect on Dowling of the shortcomings of early Crown Law Officers in New South Wales. In May 1832, a case in court drew to his notice serious defects in the discharge of the duties of the Coroners Court. In coronial proceedings, with a jury in attendance, Ann M'Court was alleged, during a bout of drunkenness, to have murdered her daughter, aged four, by battery. Questioned about the death, she claimed that the child had been poisoned by some other person. No post mortem examination was conducted. According to the *Sydney Gazette*,[75] the Coroner wished to order a medical examination of the body, but the coronial jury had overruled him and acquitted the accused. The Crown attempted to present new evidence in proceedings on indictment before Dowling in the Supreme Court. The proceedings failed because the evidence broke down. Rival newspapers gave different accounts of the result.

The *Gazette* reported that, when the Attorney-General disclosed why the Coroner had not obtained a medical examination:

> The learned judge, with very great warmth, said, "A Coroner is a Judge of Record, and is the sole master of his own court. He has a right to have such witnesses called and examined as he thinks proper, and no man has a right to control him in his office as a judge. If he does wrong, he is alone responsible for his acts, and is not to suffer a jury to presume to dictate to him the course he shall pursue in the administration of justice".[76]

The *Sydney Monitor* found those comments to be inaccurate and claimed that, though quarrels between the Coroner and his juries were not uncommon, the jury on this occasion had not attempted to obstruct the taking of medical evidence.[77] According to those columns, when the matter was before Dowling in the Supreme Court, "The Court expressed itself in severe terms upon the neglect of the Coroner in omitting to call in a surgeon to view the body, and in the absence of any proof as to the real cause of death of the infant, the jury were directed to acquit the prisoner".[78] Given that the very same issue of the *Monitor* contained a grossly distorted report of another criminal case, the object of the distortion being to discredit Dowling, its version of the aftermath of these coronial proceedings is not to be preferred to that of the *Gazette*.

Early in 1834, the judges were prompted by difficulties in the conduct of criminal business to propose radical changes. All were weary of the problems that have been illustrated here – the depressing effect of lengthy calendars of major and brutal crimes, the want of ability in the early Crown Law Officers in applying themselves to those calendars and otherwise, and the inconvenience of trying to administer justice beyond the boundaries of metropolitan Sydney.

To Dowling, much of the initiative was due. On 8 August 1833 he was on the Bench to hear a criminal trial. Two Crown witnesses were temporarily incarcerated in the hulk *Phoenix*.[79] After Plunkett, an efficient lawyer still new to the office of Solicitor-General, had proceeded with the prosecution for two hours, he called the incarcerated witnesses, but they were not in court. Nothing had been done to bring them up from the *Phoenix*. Dowling, in short temper before taking an enforced journey to Norfolk Island,[80] made his displeasure known when it became necessary to adjourn the court for two hours. As the judges reported to the Governor, "The Solicitor General . . . disclaimed all blame . . ., as he had nothing to do with the arrangements in the

Attorney General's office".[81] The *Sydney Monitor* tried to accelerate the complaint by publishing a commentary on the proceedings, which the judges conceded was a fair account: "Mr Justice Dowling, who sat on the Bench, remarked that there existed great neglect in the Attorney General's office, and that he should be compelled to make a formal complaint to His Excellency the Governor, if the evil were not remedied".[82] The matter, being thus publicly brought to his attention, Governor Bourke, through the Colonial Secretary, sought a report from the judges, who responded at length. Most of their recommendations travelled beyond what is relevant here.[83] But it was a seminal document that stimulated a review of the administration of justice out of urban Sydney, encouraged the establishment of Supreme Court circuits, the appointment of stipendiary magistrates "in each district",[84] and proposed important changes in criminal procedure.[85]

As to the postponement of criminal trials – the grievance over which Dowling had expostulated – a number of reforms were put forward.[86] As matters then stood, those committed often languished in gaol "for indefinite periods" awaiting trial; witnesses, at great public expense, were frequently brought from and returned to country districts without their evidence being tendered in court; and:

> a vast number of prisoners who ought to be tried, and who might be tried if due diligence were exercised by those entrusted with the preparation of their cases, remain untried at the end of each criminal Sessions of the Supreme Court, notwithstanding that the Sessions of the Court are fixed, and as certainly known as its terms for the conduct of civil business, and notwithstanding that each criminal Sessions of the Supreme Court is by its rules a Sessions of Gaol Delivery.[87]

Such reforms as were attained were granted by reluctant governments in meagre instalments. Necessary improvement and expansion of the system usually foundered on the rock of expense. But Dowling, when he became Chief Justice, would return to many of these areas of complaint and preside over some significantly beneficial measures, as will be noticed later.[88]

It would take upwards of two more years before the then Attorney-General, the deaf and doddering Dr Kinchela, could be displaced.[89] In the meantime, he could not pretend to enjoy the confidence of the judges. In their report of 1834 they acknowledged the "extreme anxiety and laborious attention" applied by Kinchela to his official duties, but only to offset their condemnation of the:

> entire want of proper system and management in the Criminal Department . . ., a want of due investigation of cases, of discrimination in prosecuting them, and of diligence in preparing them for trial; [and] a want of co-operation between him [Kinchela] and the Crown Solicitor [Moore] . . . and unfortunately there exists a misunderstanding between them both personally, and as to their relative public duties, which greatly impedes and frequently prevents the performance of the duties of either.[90]

In his contribution as a puisne judge Dowling showed characteristics that would, in due time, typify his Chief Justiceship. They included an attentive regard for court administration, but a generally conservative approach to the law, that placed heavy reliance on precedent and showed little sympathy for innovation.

4

Edward Smith Hall – "The Cobbett of New South Wales"

James Dowling's brave ideal, of standing aloof from party feeling, politics and personality in New South Wales, proved to be illusory.[1] He found, as had Chief Justice Forbes, that there was little room for official detachment in the Colony. The pronouncement of a court order to the prejudice of some powerful individual's claims or interests, condemned the judge to be that individual's enemy. Dowling had many such painful lessons, few more striking than in a series of proceedings brought by or against Edward Smith Hall[2] and Atwell Edwin Hayes,[3] editors and publishers of the *Monitor* and the *Australian*, respectively.[4]

Improbably, the litigious chronicle began in church. Hall, already in contest with Governor Darling who had withdrawn Hall's assigned convict servants in retaliation for the *Monitor's* criticisms of the government,[5] now came into dispute with Archdeacon Scott.[6] Hall, on the surface a very religious man, rented a family pew at St James' Church of England in King Street, Sydney.[7] In June 1828, church officials required him to move to another pew. The reason, so the public thought, was that the Archdeacon entertained "animosity" towards Hall,[8] and that Hall's pew was inconveniently close to the vice-regal seating.[9] Hall, disliking the new arrangement, remonstrated unavailingly. Attending at evensong soon afterwards, he and his six daughters, finding their old pew locked, climbed into it from above. Next time they found the pew "roofed in" and guarded during the service by constables bearing staves: they were "rudely thrust from the door [of the pew] and compelled to sit on the Communion steps".[10] The controversy went on for months.

The mental pictures, thus evoked, and the testimony they bear to days of great religious diligence, are a diversion. The relevant issue is that Hall, far from being "in love and charity with [his] neighbours" over these pew incidents, felt slighted. His feelings erupted in a *Monitor* editorial on 5 July 1828.[11] Depicting Scott as "a greater enemy to the liberties of New South Wales than Mr M'Arthur[12] himself", Hall declared that, "the Archdeacon has descended from his high station, to take upon him the office of Church-warden or director of the pew-openers . . . he will presently, we suppose, turn chief grave-digger and manager of the Churchyard". Hall concluded that Scott was "not a MAN of peace".[13]

Thus, on 29 September 1828, Mr Justice Dowling started along the serpentine road of Hall litigation that would burden all the judges for years. On this first occasion, Hall, as editor, printer and publisher of the *Monitor*, was proceeded against by *ex officio* information charging that his publication had criminally libelled Scott. Dowling presided. The "jury" comprised seven officers of the armed forces – a relic of the early convict days. Attorney-General Baxter, prosecuting, urged upon the jury's notice, not so much the "violence of the language" of the offending article, as:

> its mischievous tendency, in upsetting the whole moral and religious fabric of society; upsetting it too, in a country, and in a society where the character of its clergy is of the most vital importance to its well-being. . . Libels on individuals engaged in other walks of life, may frequently, without much injury to the Public or the individual, be passed over with silent contempt, but when a Clergyman is attacked, the case is widely different.[14]

Hall, in his own defence,[15] said that he had published fair comment on a matter of public interest, and that a man receiving an official salary, as the Archdeacon did, became a legitimate subject of public criticism should he "transgress the line of duty . . . marked out for him".[16] Dowling summed up "at some length", as the *Sydney Gazette* remarked, without itself reporting his observations. The military jury pronounced Hall "guilty".[17] For his part in this, Dowling was not forgiven by Hall. In a petition to the Parliament at Westminster, submitted in January 1831, Hall perceived judicial bias:

> in summing up . . . the learned Judge made allusions which tended to aggravate the alleged libel . . . [in telling the jury] that it was no part of the Liberty of the Press to libel the constituted Authorities of Government, to blacken the reputation and wound the spirits of private individuals, and pour forth columns of matter as offensive to good taste and good feeling, as it was opposed to the real welfare of the promising settlement of New South Wales; of thus insinuating to the said Jury, that the [alleged libel and columns of printed matter in fact had the character attributed to them by the prosecutor].[18]

The matter came up for judgment on 6 January 1829 when Dowling, so Hall further protested, "reproved your Petitioner in a very severe manner"[19] while "passing eulogiums on the Venerable Archdeacon" (who made a charitable gesture of "begging" the court to inflict only nominal punishment),[20] and complimenting the Attorney-General "on the attention and zeal he had displayed throughout so long and arduous a term".[21] Attorney-General Baxter must have savoured the moment: compliments rarely went his way.

"At the trial of this case", said Dowling, "I rigidly abstained from delivering to the Jury my opinion upon the character of the publication in question, being willing that they should be in no degree influenced by any direction from the Bench".[22] But, the jury having reached its independent conclusion, Dowling thereafter freely disclosed his own. It was against Hall; the publication being, in the judge's estimation, "a most indecent and scandalous libel" upon Scott.[23] The alleged grievance, as to the occupancy of pews, raised issues for which the law already provided redress.[24] Hall had no right, said Dowling, to air the matter in his newspaper in the "tone and spirit" he affected – least of all, against the character of a clergyman. In the judge's opinion, the publication tended not only to degrade the Archdeacon, but also to bring religion into contempt. Had Hall acted in good faith, as a public writer, on public grounds, and for the community's general welfare, there might have been justification; but the court could not "shut its eyes to the fact, that this libel emanated from personal motives".[25]

That was a reasonable assessment, and Dowling might well have left his remarks there. But he warmed to the theme with a general criticism of the Colony's newspapers. The *Sydney Gazette* published it. The press, he asserted, had too often "exceeded those bounds which fairly and justly belong to its province".[26] Sydney's citizens were entitled, he thought, to expect their loyalty, patriotism and integrity to be recognized "at home" from a reading of the colonial newspapers. If the press were indiscreet, great risks accrued of losing public sympathy in England and even of ceasing to "enjoy the radiant advantage of His Majesty's paternal protection".[27] Those remarks, calculated to appeal to Governor Darling and the Colonial Office, equally decided colonial newspaper editors to ignore judicial homilies, inevitably drawing Dowling further into the warfare of local politics. He would not henceforth find the press – least of all the *Monitor* – disposed to see things his way.

The Archdeacon's request, for moderation in the sentencing of Hall, saved the court, so it said, from subjecting the offender to "considerable inconvenience". He was fined 20 shillings. Inconvenience came instead by a side-wind. The court order required him, on his own recognisance, in £500, to be of good behaviour for 12 months, "and that you be imprisoned in His Majesty's gaol at Sydney, until such fine be paid and such security entered into".[28] Hall, with eight children to provide for and a newspaper to run, had few ready assets: and £500 was then a huge sum.[29] He tried unsuccessfully to sell the *Monitor*.[30] Unable to raise sufficient money, to gaol he went, thinking dark thoughts about those who had wronged him, particularly the Governor and Mr Justice Dowling.

The latter showed clemency when, in December 1829, the Attorney-General moved the court to estreat the unsatisfied recognisance – in other words, to have Hall's goods levied upon to pay the sum due. The judges discouraged the motion. When the Attorney-General pressed it as being formal, Dowling rejoined, "Certainly it is not quite a motion of course to estreat a recognizance of £500 Mr Attorney-General".[31] The matter was then allowed to drop: but was reopened a few days later, when the Chief Justice made the order.[32]

Hall persistently sought to justify himself, and, while in gaol, complained earnestly but unprofitably to the Secretary of State about defects in the Colony's court system, where "the Judges are distinctly and notoriously dependent on the Crown"[33] and trial by jury was but a farce: "The Jury, Sir, that tried me, were many of them my political antagonists. They were military men. They were under the dread control of military law and military discipline.

Their commander [the Governor] was their constituent, and virtually he was my prosecutor".[34]

"The Learned Judge Behaved in a Rude, Arbitrary and Dictatorial Manner"

On 12 March 1829, the next round began when Dowling presided, (this time with two assessors, there being still no trial by civil jury), at the hearing of *R. v. Hall*.[35] The proceedings attracted a "numerous auditory".[36] Despite its citation, this was not another criminal prosecution but an action in trespass brought in the name of the Crown for the alleged "breaking and entering" (the pleading formula apt for trespass) of a nominated pew "of His Majesty" at St James' Church, causing damage claimed at £100. Hall, represented this time by the able solicitor-advocate Edward Keith,[37] pleaded not guilty and set up a defence of entitlement to the pew by payment of rent. Keith challenged the right of the Crown to proceed as plaintiff in an action of trespass, a point Dowling agreed to reserve, though inclined to the view that there was such a right "by virtue of . . . high prerogative".[38]

Argument followed about the powers of the Archdeacon to let pews. After some time, Dowling refused to hear counsel further on that point, no evidence having been adduced that St James' Church ever was constituted a Parish Church. The judge felt "bound to discard all knowledge of the Archdeacon as a party in the cause, and to treat the case as a mere temporal matter, confined to the question of trespass, without reference to any ecclesiastical authority whatever".[39] He delivered a long *ex tempore* "charge" to the assessors. It was reported in the *Sydney Gazette*[40] and a modified version was transmitted to the Colonial Office.[41] Despite praising the "simple and compendious mode of technical pleading" allowed by court rules devised by Chief Justice Forbes,[42] Dowling managed to offset their benefits by his complex remarks and, in the teeth of his own ruling that only temporal matters would be considered, he adventured far into realms of ecclesiastical law.

The real question, he said, was whether Hall's claimed title to the pew would excuse his taking possession of it forcefully:[43] a question that was unprecedented. Much English authority could not apply in the absence of proof that New South Wales had been divided into parishes, or that St James' Church had been dedicated to the use of the inhabitants of any particular district.[44] None of the incidents of English parochial government applied in Australia.

So far as the evidence went, it emerged only that St James' Church had been built by the Crown and maintained by the "Home Treasurer", such that the soil and freehold were in the Crown.[45] Nothing showed that the building had ever been dedicated to the general uses of a parish church, or vested in persons with authority akin to that of churchwardens. Likewise, although, the matter might be determined in England by a Bishop as Ordinary, the Archdeacon, as senior cleric and equivalent to an Ordinary in New South Wales, had no such powers over a church not dedicated as a parish church.[46] Nevertheless, the assessors had to consider that premises used for religious services needed to be under the control of some authority with discretionary powers to preserve decorum and decency. The demanding of pew rents in advance further removed the case from usual legal principles as to landlord and tenant.[47] Applying that consideration, "those, who have the letting of pews in this Church, had a right to exercise a discretion, whether they would or would not continue the letting to a particular individual after a previous tenancy had expired".[48] The assessors found that Hall had not proved an unequivocal title,[49] and accordingly the Crown was entitled to nominal judgment. Hall regarded that as a moral victory, damages of only one shilling being awarded.

On 30 March, Keith appeared before the Full Supreme Court seeking a new trial, because the verdict was against the weight of the evidence. The court decided that "the verdict had better rest where it was" as Hall had "sustained no injury in consequence of the decision".[50] The matter did not rest there, the conclusion of it being noticed later. Hall deplored Dowling's conduct of those civil proceedings alleging that:

> the learned judge behaved to the counsel of your petitioner in a rude, arbitrary, and dictatorial manner, so as to cause the said counsel to complain thereafter in open Court to the other learned judges, of his having been unable to do justice to your petitioner, his client, in the said trial. Moreover, the learned judge, instead of finding the facts only, as had been agreed by the parties, at the suggestion of the Court, influenced the two magisterial assessors, appointed by the Governor, to join him in finding a *general* verdict.[51]

Keith, a reliable counsel, would have known that claimed denial of procedural fairness should have been agitated at once in court. No independent record suggests that it was. Hall's criticism of Dowling, for taking positions judges have to take to resolve difficult contests, may be dismissed as the outburst of a disappointed litigant. His reflection on the system of assessors was more substantial,[52] for the Governor's power to appoint assessors was open to potential abuse. Here, however, the result ran quite the other way: the Governor must assuredly have regarded the assessors' treatment of Hall as excessively lenient.

On 10 April 1829 Hall was again before the Supreme Court to be tried on a charge of seditious libel, relating to some of his fulminations in the *Monitor* about the Governor. The matter was heard before the Chief Justice,[53] Dowling being preoccupied with a libel case involving Hayes as editor of the *Australian*. Hall was found guilty – "as he anticipated", so the *Australian* remarked.[54]

Back at the bar, before Mr Justice Dowling, only five days later, Hall was proceeded against by yet another *ex officio* information for criminal libel. The allegation was that Captain Francis Crotty, when Commandant of the settlement at Port Macquarie, had been defamed by the *Monitor's* assertion that he had appropriated government grain without paying for it. Hall complained that Dowling's summing up was "distinctly in favour of the Crown" such that a verdict of guilty was inevitable,[55] leading to his further imprisonment.

As 1829 closed, Hall's cup of gall was brimful. His editorial aspersions on the Governor, on the Colonial Secretary, and on other worthies, were visited with a spate of rules absolute, verdicts of guilty and severe punishments.[56] In these Dowling played no part except, sometimes, that of a silent constituent of the Full Bench. But, on Christmas Eve, Dowling presided with a jury at the hearing of two further informations against Hall. One was for libelling Deputy Commissary-General Laidley by representing in the *Monitor* that Laidley had dishonestly managed the calling of tenders for salt pork.[57] No point of legal substance emerged.[58] Dowling reminded the jury that, although the information was filed with the court's leave, it did not follow that it had the court's support. Allowing for that, the jury needed only a short consultation before declaring Hall to be guilty.

The other case alleged a libel on Alexander McLeay, as Colonial Secretary, by imputing to him, through the *Monitor*,[59] an attempt to pervert the course of justice by placing a false document on the Supreme Court files. Edward Keith again had the awkward task of defending Hall. Having failed in a challenge to the attendance of the same jurymen, he attempted to urge upon them forgetfulness of what had passed in the Laidley case and in the notorious earlier proceedings. "I say this", he declared:

> because it is not in the nature of men wholly to forget that he has been already convicted on several cases of libel, and that with such a weight of prejudice against him it is not too much to apprehend that you might be led to suppose him a systematic libeller – one whose delight it is to assail the character of every member of society – and that, without looking at the merits of this case, you would at once pronounce him guilty.[60]

Keith's substantive defence was that Hall had merely adopted observations from an affidavit, read in court but not accepted for the court file. The question then became one of press licence to report matters ventilated publicly in court. "If you gentlemen", he argued, "should come to a conclusion that Editors of newspapers are not authorized to publish reports of what takes place in a Court of Justice, the name of the liberty of the press is a mere farce".[61] Keith called Wentworth[62] of the Bar to testify that the affidavit had been read, that Hall's account of it was accurate, but that the court had declined to accept it on file because it was thought to contain defamatory matter. Dowling rejected Wentworth's evidence as being irrelevant.[63]

Dowling advised the jury that a newspaper editor might publish all that occurs in a court of justice "provided the report contains nothing of a defamatory, scandalous, or immoral nature which would be calculated to raise a prejudice against a person out of doors". He relied on four decisions, but they were not in direct point, except for one case relating to republication of a blasphemy.[64] The *Sydney Gazette* was unimpressed by the judge's reasoning and thought his remarks a threat to press freedom.[65]

> Having much confidence in the learning, experience, and diligence of Mr Justice DOWLING, it is fair to infer that this solitary case was the only one he could find; and even this (*The King v. Carlile*) was so *extreme* a case, that it can barely be said to establish the general principle against which we are pleading. It was a case of

> BLASPHEMY – of blasphemy in its blackest, foulest, most infernal forms; and yet this appears to be the *only* case, within the vast compass of law precedents, that at all bears upon the point![66]

The *Gazette* fairly concluded that it was in the nature of trials, particularly criminal trials, that imputations injurious to individuals would be made. If Dowling's view of the law were correct, nice questions would arise constantly as to what the press might or might not report of court cases. Hall, who was again found guilty, was harshly treated this time, and justice did not appear to have been done. The Laidley jury should have been discharged and a new jury empanelled. Dowling's *ipse dixit* on what might be published about contentious court proceedings was unconvincing.

It is convenient to break the thread of Hall's many appearances in court, so that similar proceedings instituted against Hayes, as editor of the *Australian,* may be noticed. Those proceedings had preoccupied Dowling when Hall was before Chief Justice Forbes earlier in 1829. Hayes was presented on an *ex officio* indictment charging him with seditious libel in having published in his newspaper matter defamatory of Governor Darling. The details are not relevant here,[67] but some of Dowling's remarks on the law of libel are. He began with a fulsome compliment to Wentworth, who had conducted the defence case "with great temper and moderation" such that he had, "done himself infinite credit by the good and discreet part he has taken in the proceedings. I confess that I expected this, from his natural good sense, his great experience, and the station he holds at the Australian Bar".[68] Wentworth, who needed no judicial testimonials, doubtless found these condescending.

The judge dilated on the liberty of the press in New South Wales. It had been observed in Parliament, he said, that the Colony was to enjoy press freedom to the full. Only to accommodate cogent reasons of state would restraint be imposed:

> the distance from home, and the political circumstances of the Colony, may well excuse a manly, free, and unshackled discussion upon the measures of Government, so long as the discussion is conducted with temper, candour, good feeling, and without the imputation of bad motives. If a public writer goes beyond these bounds, if he says or insinuates that the Governor acts from any partial or corrupt view, or with an intention to oppress any individual or class of men, I apprehend the writer would subject himself to the penalties of the law.[69]

The jury applied that test adversely to Hayes. The *Australian,* while commending the judge's "luminous and impartial charge" as doing him "unfading credit", expressed editorial "surprise – chagrin – astonishment" at the verdict, and feared that it would encourage extinction of a free press.[70]

Hayes and Hall in effect appealed together from their respective sentences to the Full Court. Strictly, the applications were not appeals in the modern sense, but motions in arrest of judgment. Practically, the result was the same: neither applicant was successful, both were sentenced to imprisonment,[71] and Hayes additionally was fined £100 (promptly defrayed by public subscription).[72] The proceedings were unusual as the judges sat *in banco* but dealt with the matters severally. Mr Justice Stephen briefly dissented from the majority, saying that he would have arrested judgment.[73] The Chief Justice delivered his judgment as to Hall, and then Dowling his as to Hayes, each virtually concurring in the decision of the other. Finally each pronounced sentence in the relative case.

Dowling's observations about jury trial are noticed below.[74] As to the libel, he was not satisfied that the proved defamation of the Governor was *seditious.*[75] But it mattered not, as the averment of sedition was surplusage, allowing the matter to be disposed of as an ordinary libel. The *Australian,* shortly before those remarks were made, had published a letter suggesting that it was absurd to associate sedition with a mere reference (however hubristic) to a public officer:

> To publish the fact, that his Excellency, his Venerability, his Honour, or his Worship, is unpopular, or that a violation of the Law, or of the Constitution, is arbitrary or illegal, subjects an unfortunate public writer to an *ex officio* prosecution for "SEDITIOUS (!) LIBEL".[76]

The Jury – "An Institution – the Proudest, the Most Useful, the Most Venerated of All"

Next month, Hall was back before the Full Bench seeking a rule for a criminal information to issue against magistrates Rossi, Bunn, Browne and Wollstonecraft for conspiring with the Superintendent of Convicts to deprive Hall of the services of his assigned convict printer Peter Tyler,[77] and in having held that Hall had harboured Tyler when a Crown prisoner. Wentworth read Hall's supporting affidavit which suggested that the magistrates had acted under the "schooling" of Colonial Secretary McLeay. That suggestion was not denied. According to Wentworth's argument, the magistrates had disqualified themselves by compromising their sworn duty of independence.

The Full Bench dismissed the rule, but awarded costs against the magistrates. Dowling's was the principal judgment, in which his colleagues concurred. The court, he said, though conscious of its corrective jurisdiction over magistrates, would have preferred not to entertain this controversy. Faced with contradictory affidavits, the court was unpersuaded that a rule should issue, as the magistrates had plainly acted "under malicious motives. . . That they had acted wrong, however, was most certain; and, therefore had the Court determined that the rule should only be discharged by the Magistrates paying costs".[78] The case further showed that the Crown Law Officers as well as the magistrates had been delinquent:

> The decision of the Court in the case of Jane New had been pressed upon the Magistrates,[79] they ought to have attended to it. The Crown Law Officers heard the mature opinion of the Court in that case. It was their duty to have set the Magistrates right, as it was of the latter not to have meddled with Mr Hall in the face of that decision, rather to have deferred it to the consideration of the judges.[80]

Moreover, these magistrates had consciously "set their opinions" against those of the judges, arid cast contempt upon the dignity of the court. "It would be an extraordinary novelty, indeed", said Dowling, "if subordinate tribunals were to be allowed to call in question the justice of a SUPREME COURT".[81] Why, then, was the rule not granted? The court, he declared, would pardon the contempt on this occasion, but all magistrates were on notice that such provocative conduct would not be tolerated again. The court, as Dowling revealed its mind, would similarly forgive the suggestion that McLeay had tutored the magistrates in their proceedings. The judges would not assume in the Colonial Secretary any disposition to act in a manner "so subversive of all honour and rectitude". While Dowling was astonished that the affidavits of the magistrates failed to controvert the allegation, the court would look the other way: "In the absence of positive proof, it would be best to dismiss such an idea, however unopposed and astonishing".[82]

The irrepressible Hall, well advised by Wentworth, reckoned that, on flimsy grounds, he had been denied his chance to proceed criminally against the magistrates. His new moral victory inspired him to greater efforts. If he could not succeed by way of the criminal law, surely he could proceed against the same magistrates civilly. Thus, on 15 March 1830, Dowling found himself again presiding over a matter involving Hall, when the latter sued Rossi, Browne, Bunn and Wollstonecraft in the Supreme Court[83] for allegedly convicting him unlawfully on the charge of harbouring the supposed runaway prisoner. It may be recalled that the honorary magistrates in those days wielded vast powers, often arbitrarily, to which a brake had been applied only since the opening of the Supreme Court in 1824. Magistrates became answerable to the court's supervisory powers.[84] Another sanction, used by Hall in this case, was that the magistrates might themselves be sued for improperly using or exceeding their powers. These proceedings were also remarkable because a special jury – one composed of men of a specified station in society – was empanelled, in pursuance of changes just made towards reform of the jury laws.[85] Dowling offered some lofty words. "I cannot refrain, as a man", he exhorted the jurors:

> from congratulating you gentlemen upon the inoculation of this great Southern continent with an institution – the proudest, the most useful, the most venerated of all that the freest nation on earth can boast; but even as a Judge – (the frigid expositor of the law), I cannot abstain from hailing with gratulation the introduction of a system which places the Judges of this Court upon a proper constitutional footing with their fellow subjects in the sacred Temple of Justice.[86]

Wentworth this time appeared for Hall and, while voicing his own approbation of extended trial by jury, took some gloss from Dowling's remarks when he pointed out:

> Gentlemen, . . . you are . . . not the first jury which I have had the honour of addressing in this Colony. Under the old Act of Parliament, it was competent to this Court to grant a jury for the trial of civil issues, if both parties agreed in the application; but as the latter provision evidently rendered the enactment a nullity, it was in only one or two instances, through the liberality of the government, in the administration of Sir Thomas Brisbane, that this right was exercised.[87]

Wentworth's address to the jury made as much as Dowling would permit of Governor Darling's efforts to silence the *Monitor* and isolate Hall. Wentworth told the jurors that they would weaken public confidence in the new civil jury if they failed to act decisively.

> Let it not be said that the first effort of Trial by Jury here, was to sow deep the seeds of discord and of mischief in the bosom of society, but rather that when the noble institution of which you are this day the representatives stretched forth its prerogative, conciliation came, and the ascendancy of the laws was established in the sovereign mercy of their nature, and the wisdom of their dispensation.[88]

The defendants, silent in the face of this sententiosity, offered no evidence. Dowling summed up: the jury found for Hall, awarding him £10 damages and costs. The taste of victory gave Hall a new impetus as he returned, again as plaintiff, before Dowling on the civil side of the Supreme Court on 6 April 1830.[89] This time Hall would settle a score with Archdeacon Scott, whom he caused to be served with process on board ship just before Scott left the Colony, having resigned his position – thus carrying with him a "lasting memorial of colonial vindictiveness".[90]

Ever since the start of the pew controversy, Hall had sniped relentlessly, through the *Monitor*, at the Archdeacon: "Not an issue passed without some derogatory reference, largely by suggestion or innuendo".[91] Hall now sought, in his action in trespass against Scott, damages for having been dispossessed of the pew to which payment of rent had, he insisted, entitled him.[92] Again a special jury was empanelled. Hall urged Dowling to disqualify himself from hearing proceedings that duplicated much of the St James' matters he had already determined.[93] Dowling declined the request, though he told to the jury that his "private inclinations" were to grant it.[94] Mr Justice Stephen was out of town, and the Chief Justice was "unhappily confined to a sick chamber", so indisposed that his life might be at risk were he to attempt court duties. Dowling was not prepared, of his own motion, to cause the trial to be postponed.

Hall could not reasonably have complained about Dowling's participation at this trial. With detachment, the judge instructed the jury not to be influenced by anything they knew of the earlier proceedings concerning the same pew. He explained that, in England, an action for trespass to the occupation of a church pew, could not be brought. There, possession of the whole of the church "is in the parson". In the Colony the circumstances of the Church and of the law stood on a different footing. There were, as yet, in New South Wales, none of the typically English incidents of parochial church government. Hall had proved the letting to him of a pew at St James' Church. It was not established for the defendant that Hall had been given any reasonable notice to vacate it. "I am bound to hold", said Dowling, "that the plaintiff was entitled to some notice before his tenancy could be determined".[95] In its absence, the law would recognize in Hall a right of possession entitling him to maintain trespass against anyone threatening his enjoyment of the use of his pew. The defendant, *qua* Archdeacon, exercised only spiritual functions. He had no power to determine a temporal contract with Hall. No law authorized the forcible removal of Hall from his pew, no matter how indecorous his behaviour, provided that the minister and congregation were not disturbed during services. The summing up made it plain to the jury that Hall's action had substance, and that the law tended his way if the facts were as Hall represented them to be. The jury so found and awarded Hall £25 damages with costs, which the government quite improperly defrayed.[96]

It was a tribute to Wentworth's skill as an advocate that this jury achieved the Gilbertian result of finding the facts to be precisely the opposite of those found by the assessors in *R. v. Hall* in the previous year concerning the right of occupancy of the very same pew. To judge from the affidavit evidence in *Hall v. Scott*, the assessors' conclusions had been quite wrong. Hall did not hesitate to press upon the Secretary of State the paradoxical consequences:

> For my comments [on the original conduct of Scott], which I respectfully contend, in opposition to the opinion of the learned Judge [Dowling], were neither "indecent" or "scandalous", nor yet did they (immorally) "emanate from personal motives", but were fair remarks, decorous reflections, and true statements; for these comments, I say, I was punished by the very same Court and the very same Judge, which within the last month have rewarded me with pecuniary compensation for the indignities and wrongs which were the occasion of those comments.[97]

Yet another link in this complex chain of litigation occurred in March 1830[98] when Hall and Hayes severally and successfully sued Hely, the Principal Superintendent of Convicts, for wrongly abducting and detaining their assigned convict servants. For the detention of his printer, Peter Tyler,[99] Hall recovered £25 and costs[100] – and an infinitely greater moral triumph, given that Hely was acting on Governor Darling's explicit orders. As those proceedings took place before Chief Justice Forbes, they will not be pursued here.

"Judges are Not at Liberty to Mould the Law as it Ought to Be"

A new participant entered upon this saga of litigation. In 1828 a Methodist missionary, the Revd Ralph Mansfield,[101] resigned that calling in protest at attempted interference with his ministry by the Wesleyan Committee in London. To supplement his income, he became joint editor, with Robert Howe, of the *Sydney Gazette* – still regarded as the official organ of government, and supportive of Governor Darling. Early in 1829, only a few months after beginning the joint venture, Howe was drowned. Mansfield became sole editor and was soon drawn into Hall's magnetic field of litigation.

Wentworth was then seeking to "impeach" Governor Darling.[102] Mansfield, at Darling's suggestion, published addresses to the Governor, by various landed proprietors and merchants, declaring their support for him.[103] Editorially, Mansfield lauded the subscribers to the addresses, and attacked newspapers hostile to Darling, including (very imprudently) the *Monitor*. Darling's effusive acknowledgements of the addresses were also published. In them he animadverted against the "opposition journals", deprecating their claims to represent the public when they well knew "that they are not countenanced by any man of character or common respectability".[104] He denounced the "infatuated incendiaries who have attempted to assail my character".[105] All this Mansfield dutifully published, while Darling was reporting to Under Secretary Twiss that "Wentworth and his Party are not countenanced by one respectable Individual".[106]

Wentworth sued Mansfield for libel in having published words that adopted the Governor's defamatory remarks. The matter was so sensitive that Chief Justice Forbes required it to be tried before the Full Bench which, he said, would, if need be, discharge the committal functions of a grand jury. The court made absolute a rule for an information to go against Mansfield, and the case was heard, on 3 June 1830, before Forbes and a military jury. Mansfield was found guilty. The Full Bench refused a motion for a new trial.[107] The details cannot detain us here except to notice some observations by Dowling (who gave the leading judgment) on the defamation laws, particularly as to there being no need to prove malice, and as to the need for the colonial court to adhere to English law and practice:

> The circumstances of our being in New South Wales, cannot, ought not, I hope, to have any influence in swaying the judgment of any man in the high office which I have the honour of holding, when called upon judicially to administer the law. The trust reposed in us, is not for the occasion – the fleeting influence of ephemeral circumstances, but for the perpetuation of those principles of justice which the matured experience and ripened judgment of the most enlightened men have rendered sacred, as the inheritance of civilized beings. . . In administering justice in cases of this particular class, judges are not at liberty to mould the law as it ought to be, or as some persons wish it to be, but as they find it sanctioned by the wisdom of the legislature and approved by its practical application in preceding cases of like nature.[108]

Applying those principles, Dowling was convinced that Forbes, at first instance, had correctly directed the jury to the effect that the Colony's Governor, when replying to a citizens' address concerning his administration, had the right and privilege to express himself in whatever terms he thought appropriate. Dowling concluded that, "unless it could be successfully contended, that the voluntary address to, and reply from, the Governor of a Colony, upon an occasion like the one alluded to, stand on the same footing with the solemn proceedings of the High Court of Parliament, [precedent authority] could not avail the defendant to justify him in printing and publishing the matter now charged to be libellous".[109]

Hall, meanwhile, taking his cue and professional advice from Wentworth, instituted proceedings against Mansfield. There were three actions for libel: Hall succeeded in two. The first went to the publication of the Governor's replies to the signatories to the addresses, and claimed as the innuendo the suggestion that the *Monitor* was not read by anyone of common respectability.[110]

The second action concerned publications in the *Sydney Gazette* alleging that John D. Shelley[111] had been influenced by the

Monitor's editorial criticisms of Governor Darling[112] to attempt to assassinate the Governor. Darling claimed that Shelley had "associated himself with Mr Hall, the editor of the *Monitor*, when in jail",[113] and considered that, "the circumstances which led to his [Shelley's] coming to this Colony, whether of a domestic nature or otherwise, had made so strong an impression on him as to disturb his mind. Naturally of an irascible and impetuous temperament, he has been worked upon by the *Monitor* newspaper".[114] Mansfield, who had reproduced the drift of Darling's remarks with much embellishment, was tried before Dowling and a special jury for "two alleged false and scandalous libels". They included the depiction of the *Monitor* as a "prostituted press", the editor of which was "branded from head to foot with convictions before the tribunals of the land".[115] It was poetic justice that the reverend gentleman went to trial, not in the new court house, then undergoing extensive repairs, or in the old court house which was completely occupied with criminal sittings, but in the Wesleyan Chapel in Macquarie Street, turned for the nonce into a temporary court room.[116]

Wentworth and Keith appeared for Hall: Dr Wardell for Mansfield. Mr Justice Dowling told the jury that the publication could be seen as libellous as to Hall's moral character, and that it had been proved that the publication related to Hall. The jury returned a verdict for Hall with £50 damages and costs. Hall, fairly but unavailingly, remonstrated from his prison cell about his incongruous position:

> For a libel on his Excellency, I am now incarcerated. Surely when the Governor had procured a verdict and a sentence against me, and had inflicted the sentence, he should not have added to my troubles by almost immediately afterwards causing the Government Editor [Mansfield] to publish a libel on the man whom his Excellency had just incarcerated for libel on himself?[117]

The third action, in which Hall was unsuccessful, was against Mansfield for the *Gazette's* assertion that Hall's attempted private prosecution of Captain T.E. Wright[118] for murdering a convict at Norfolk Island was "a malignant prosecution".[119] Wardell was so confident in his defence of Mansfield that he called no evidence and merely addressed the jury briefly.[120] They found for Mansfield, without retiring, or waiting for any charge from Mr Justice Dowling.[121]

In July 1830 Mansfield moved the Full Court to grant a new trial in Shelley's case. The motion was unanimously refused. Dowling's lengthy judgment concluded that Mansfield had travelled far beyond the bounds of fair and free discussion by dealing quite specifically with the reputation of Hall and the *Monitor* in a manner that no-one in the Colony could misunderstand. Because Hall was a public writer, it did not follow that "every thing and any thing may be said or written of him or of his works, without any regard to the fair province of discussion and argument".[122] It followed that no grounds existed to disturb the jury's verdict.

"A Judge Cannot Pick and Chuse the Cases He Will Try"

Having thus seen Scott, Mansfield and some others, on their way, Hall directed his spleen to Dowling. Early in 1831 he preferred his petition to Parliament, praying an inquiry into Dowling's judicial conduct, and a review of the judge's fitness to remain in office. Dowling was so concerned at being pilloried by the "troubled spirit in the Colony" that he again implored the protection of Lord Brougham.[123]

Hall's petition recited, with exaggerated complaints, his appearances before Dowling, usually as the defendant to *ex officio* informations.[124] The petition was swollen with many other representations which, at first sight, did not reflect well on the judge.[125] In particular, Dowling, at criminal trials, was alleged to have treated matters of substance superficially, to have asserted an improper influence over jurors, and to have shown bias in favour of accused members of the armed forces.[126] One such instance was said to be the trial, which Hall himself had instigated, of Captain Wright for the alleged murder of a prisoner (Clynch) at Norfolk Island.[127] Hall claimed that the witnesses for Wright – all fellow military men – conspired to give such contradictory evidence as to make an acquittal inevitable.[128] Yet, claimed Hall, "they were not reproved by the Judge for their contradictory testimony, but were addressed by him in accents of courtesy, forming a contrast with his manner towards the other witnesses for the prosecution, whose testimony went to criminate the prisoner".[129] Hall insisted that, at a point when the Crown evidence stood unshaken, the prosecutor discontinued the proceedings, whereupon Dowling, "evinced publicly on the Bench the greatest satisfaction at the abandonment thereof by the counsel for the prosecution; complimenting the latter . . . and directing the jury forthwith to acquit".[130]

This, said Hall, revealed "the most indecent party feeling" by the judge.[131] In the *Monitor* of 6 June 1829, Hall represented that Clynch, when in custody awaiting trial, was ordered by Wright to be shot dead.[132] Yet the Colonial Secretary held a report, describing how Clynch came to be shot while attacking a constable and a soldier with a crudely made spear – after earlier attempting to kill Wright and to threaten the principal overseer.[133] Clynch's actions had been part of an intended mutiny.

Wentworth, for the prosecution, obtained leave to call two alleged accomplices in the murder.[134] That did nothing to help the Crown case. Wentworth, immediately their testimony was given, "frankly acknowledged that the case had broken down under him, stating that he would not press Captain Wright to a defence".[135] Dowling told the jury that, "Mr Wentworth had done himself infinite honour by the manner in which he had presented this case to their notice"[136] and directed them to acquit Wright, which they readily did. Governor Darling considered that "a fouler conspiracy against the life and character of an Officer never existed" than that which Wright's trial exposed.[137] The conspirators, he alleged, were two other military officers, and Hall and Wentworth. "The merit of the latter", he added, "seems to be in having prudently abandoned the prosecution. . . The result, however, in my humble judgment, is as little flattering or complimentary to Mr Wentworth's Head as it is to his Heart".[138] Suffice it to say that, like the judges, Wentworth was not one of the Governor's favourites.

Hall attacked the Governor for having "stacked" this military jury with men who would never find against a brother officer.[139] Wright, however, was completely vindicated, and Hall's stature correspondingly diminished.[140] Viscount Goderich considered it due to Wright "and to every principle of justice" that he be informed that the imperial government considered him "entirely free from even the remotest suspicion of" having merited the imputations cast upon him.[141] Wright was appointed Police Magistrate at Emu Plains – "a measure of necessity as well as an act of justice".[142] In due course promoted Major, he was a significant witness, concerning the state of things at Norfolk Island, before the Select Committee on Transportation (the "Molesworth Committee") in England in 1838.[143]

To return to Hall's unworthy petition, other cases were cited. In one, he alleged that, because of a slanted summing up by Dowling, the jury was led to an acquittal, whereby "one of the most wanton murders ever committed in any civilized country, was suffered to pass entirely unpunished".[144] In these cases, Hall's outrage was so vehement that he presumed to sit in final judgment on judge and jury alike. In implicating Dowling, he necessarily implicated the jurors. Hall achieved nothing more than to show that his perception of the court proceedings differed from the perception of those sworn to administer justice. The want of substance to his allegations showed how shallow was the whole petition.

In February 1831 Dowling sent to Lord Brougham a copy of Hall's petition. Hall, said the judge, had been "perpetually in hot water with the local authorities" and the source of many "difficult, anxious and troublesome" cases which Dowling had been obliged to hear.[145] "Now, although I anticipate nothing disagreeable as to the result of this petition", Dowling wrote:

> I am not at all insensible to the annoyance of having my name as a judge even called in question, whatever may be the motive of the petition. I only hope that the petition may fall into some judicious and candid hands, and be well considered before an unnecessary, and certainly unjustifiable wound is inflicted upon the feelings and character of a man in my situation; because, if called upon to explain my conduct officially, I pledge myself to do so in the most satisfactory manner. Many things stated in the petition are grossly untrue – all the statements are garbled, imperfect, and most uncandid.[146]

Wanting no other shield but his own integrity, Dowling assured Brougham that he approached him, not to procure some untoward influence, but to vindicate his own good character. Dowling believed that he had acquired, with everyone in the Colony but Hall, the reputation of being upright and impartial: and had done so in the face of the peculiar difficulties of New South Wales, especially the antipathy between Governor Darling and the Bench.[147] Dowling contended that, if Hall had suffered wrong, it was not in the Supreme Court, and that Hall deserved little sympathy, being "a powerful popular writer . . . the *Cobbett* of New South Wales, [who] has done, I fear, more mischief than good".[148]

Hall pursued his complaints in a letter to Viscount Howick. But Howick had long since resolved that the Secretary of State for the Colonies should receive any charges from Hall "with great caution and suspicion".[149] Accordingly, Hall's letter was marked "no answer" and relegated to the file.[150] There, it seemed, the matter might rest. But, in May 1832, Hall's resentment of Dowling was rekindled.

On 7 May 1832 three prisoners were severally indicted as principals and accessories to the rape of "Catherine Hayes, at the Wheather-boarded [*sic*] Hut" – a stopping place for travellers on the western road to Bathurst.[151] Hayes was examined by Attorney-General Kinchela, and separately by the judge and by some members of the jury (it was not uncommon for jurors to take a spontaneous part in court proceedings in those days), and cross-examined by Roger Therry for the defence. Thereafter Kinchela rose to say that he could carry the case no further as the complainant had not established the essential elements of the crime of rape.

> Mr Justice Dowling said, "Be so good, Mr Attorney-General, as to raise your voice [Kinchela was somewhat deaf], in order that the grounds on which you mean to abandon this prosecution may be audibly proclaimed to and distinctly understood by the world. Do I understand you to say, that there are no grounds for the prosecution?" [152]

Kinchela would not go so far, but insisted that the evidence at his disposal could not sustain a prosecution. Therefore he would not call further witnesses. Therry demanded an acquittal. Dowling was cautious – "the public eye is upon this case" – and he again pressed the Attorney-General to disclose the grounds for abandoning the prosecution. Kinchela repeated that the evidence adduced could not establish rape. Dowling directed the jury to acquit, (as they did), telling them that: "Most undoubtedly the poor woman has been grievously ill used, but the question for our present consideration is whether the prisoners are guilty of a rape, in the legal sense of the charge. It had been insinuated that this prosecution has been got up in some quarter or other, but with that we have nothing to do".[153]

In the *Sydney Monitor* of 12 May 1832 the earliest report of these proceedings was published, and, through Hall's guile, corrupted. It was made to appear that Dowling, convinced that the charge had been concocted for partisan purposes, "wished it to be proclaimed to the wide world, that there were no grounds for the charge".[154] That misrepresented Dowling's efforts to fix the Attorney-General with the consequences of throwing away an ill-prepared and amateurish prosecution. Nothing said by Dowling attached him to any point of view. He was circumspectly neutral.

Sir John Jamison, one of the Bench of Magistrates who committed the prisoners for trial, wrote to the *Monitor*, seeking to justify the committal. His action was inappropriate: the magistrates had completed their duty and, being each *functus officio*, could have no more to say upon it unless asked by the Supreme Court or the Governor. Nevertheless Jamison wrote, as he put it, "in conformity with the desire of . . . the Judge for explanation". He concluded:

> had the learned Judge perused the depositions before he sat on the trial he would have seen the grounds for the complaint. . . The acquittal of these men is calculated to encourage attacks on unprotected women travelling in the interior, and must certainly discourage Magistrates (when soldiers are concerned) from discharging their duty.[155]

That was misconceived. Any grievance Jamison may have entertained could only be brought home to the Attorney-General's door: it was not for the judge to direct how the prosecution should be conducted.

Nevertheless the opportunity was grasped by Hall to compose another letter to the Secretary of State, which he immediately published in the *Monitor*, seeking to influence public opinion, before the recipient of the letter could know that he was even to be addressed on the subject.[156] Hall took up Jamison's point about the application of the law to soldiers and, harking back to his own petition, singled out Dowling as particularly disposed to favour military defendants. Hall claimed that the acquittal of the three prisoners in the case under review was due to perjury which Dowling had disregarded and, crowning all, to judicial misconduct:

> the Judge who sat on the Bench, heard and saw all this; yet so far from discountenancing such proceedings, his Honour did all but express in direct terms, his satisfaction thereat, reflecting in a loud voice [due, it may be recalled, to Kinchela's deafness], and in a manner the most energetic, upon the party or parties who had got

> up the case, and stating, that he wished to proclaim to the wide world, that the prisoners at the bar were innocent of the crime laid to their charge.[157]

All of this was so spurious that Dowling had an objective report of the trial published in the *Sydney Gazette*.[158] As he wrote to Governor Bourke, requesting that the newspapers and his letter be transmitted to Viscount Goderich, "it is very painful for a Judge to be put into the situation of vindicating himself against newspaper slander".[159] Dowling observed that, as the Attorney-General had taken over the traditional functions of the grand jury, he was responsible for the conduct of proceedings on *ex officio* informations. The presiding judge had no control over his exercise of that discretion.[160]

Bourke transmitted the materials without comment.[161] The response was a final triumph for Dowling over the vilification to which Hall had subjected him for years. Goderich was satisfied that Dowling had acted correctly, and could have acted in no other way. Rather, the actions of the Attorney-General, in abandoning the case without attempting to secure a conviction on a lesser charge were to be explained. In the view of the Colonial Office, the imputations on Dowling's character were so extreme that he would have been justified in taking defamation proceedings against Hall.[162] Transcending all of these was a testimonial which Dowling must have read with the greatest and most justifiable satisfaction:

> Mr Dowling may be assured that I have too much respect for the character of the King's Judges in every part of His Majesty's Dominions to permit myself to entertain even a momentary impression to his prejudice, without some better foundation than the censures of an anonymous writer, actuated by such a spirit as [is] exhibited in the paragraphs which he has brought under my notice.[163]

Justice had been done! Perhaps some virtue lay in Hall's editorial pursuit of Darling, Scott, Mansfield and others. But there was none in attempting similarly to tarnish the reputation of Mr Justice Dowling.

PART II
AS CHIEF JUSTICE

5

"This Simple and Natural Course of Proceeding"

After their initial difficulties had been resolved by Dowling's tact, Dowling and Mr Justice John Stephen worked in harmony for several years. Stephen's health during that time was never robust, and judicial business was accomplished only through Dowling's willingness to take more than his ordinary share. When Stephen's constitution had so broken down that he resigned conditionally on the receipt of a pension, there was an awkward interval during which he rejected the pension offered, as being too small, and would not vacate his seat, even though a successor to his office had already arrived in Sydney.[1] The government stood firm, and Stephen was sent on his way in December 1832 with a small gratuity which he lived to enjoy only for 12 months.[2]

Dowling's *modus vivendi* with John Stephen, and his friendship with the latter's son Alfred, of which more will be said later,[3] were not emulated in his relationship with the new judge, William Westbrooke Burton, who was sworn in on 22 December 1832.[4] Burton, as earlier noticed, had served as a judge at the Cape Province where General Bourke, as Acting Governor, formed a favourable opinion of him and relied on him to draft Ordinances for submission to the local legislature.[5] It was no accident that, as Governor of New South Wales, Bourke, perceiving the need to fill a judicial vacancy, privately reminded the Colonial Office of Burton's accomplishments and proposed that it might be possible "to hold out to him the prospect of succeeding the Chief Justice in N. S. Wales".[6] Burton, who had very elevated ideas of his own importance,[7] found it gratifying to arrive in Sydney as if the Governor's nominee.

Bourke's biographer, Dr Hazel King, detected such common cause between the Governor, Chief Justice Forbes and the new judge, as to have aroused resentment on Dowling's part:

> The intimacy between these three – Bourke, Forbes and Burton – caused some heartburning on the part of . . . Mr Justice J. Dowling, who felt himself excluded from this charmed circle. His relations with Bourke were correct and cordial but he was not on the same terms of easy friendship with the Governor as were his brother judges.[8]

While there is a foundation of truth in that assessment, especially in its discerning a sense of isolation felt by Dowling, the concept of a "charmed circle" cannot be adopted here. Forbes' relationship with Bourke, officially and personally, was cordial and amicable – the exact opposite of the relationship between Forbes and Darling.[9] But it was entirely transcended by the friendship established between Bourke and Burton at the Cape and continued in New South Wales. That was a friendship built on the *esprit de corps* natural to members of the armed forces. Burton had begun in life as a naval man and seen active service. His demeanour, temperament and experience would all have appealed to Bourke. Only in political attitudes would they diverge. Burton, to adopt Chief Justice Forbes' analogy, would have been one of those "high Tory counsellors" advising the Whig-inclined Governor.[10] Burton also bore through life a naval sense of command and superiority that Forbes would have found so uncomfortably reminiscent of the style of Admiral Hamilton in Newfoundland[11] that none but ordinary terms of professional concord between them, falling well short of genuine friendship, could have subsisted. Burton's appointment to New South Wales, at Bourke's instigation, was a curious one in the sense that one of Burton's brothers, in England, had been consulted about the matter and acquiesced in it, committing the judge, as if by proxy, to go to Sydney.[12] As Dr King records:

> Goderich had forthwith appointed him and directed him to proceed immediately to New South Wales from the Cape. Burton had been obliged to leave at short notice, to sell his house at a loss, and to travel to Australia at a dangerous season of the year. He had, then, arrived in New South Wales in a very disgruntled state of mind. The only thing which made the change supportable, he told Hay at the Colonial Office, was the kind attention of Bourke.[13]

But, if Bourke and Forbes were on friendly terms, and Bourke and Burton the more so, that did not create a "charmed circle". The link needed to complete the circle, that of complete amity between Forbes and Burton, did not exist. Their quite radical divergence in legal views, and the lofty and disdainful manner in which Burton often dissented from the other judges in open court, are mentioned elsewhere, as are Burton's criticisms of the court as Forbes conducted it.[14] For present purposes, suffice it to say that no evidence has come to light in support of the suggestion that any triumvirate, social or otherwise, subsisted between Bourke, Forbes and Burton, such that Dowling was excluded, or that Forbes would have been a willing participant in such an alliance even informally. Nevertheless, it was clear that Dowling was not at ease with the gubernatorial and judicial company in which he was placed from 1832. As he confided to Lord Brougham, the Governor had given him very few opportunities of "private communication, though on terms of the greatest intimacy with my brother judges".[15]

Bourke did not actively dislike Dowling, nor yet did he have any particular warmth of feeling that permitted relaxation of the politeness appropriate to official duties. Dowling, although in later years drawn closer to Forbes, was somewhat overawed by the breadth of the Chief Justice's legal knowledge and colonial experience. At the same time, he was suspicious of Forbes' "political" allegiances, and persisted, long after he must have known it to be untrue, with retailing a seriously distorted impression of the first Chief Justice.[16] As late as 1836, Dowling was putting it forward to Brougham that, "Forbes is a most shrewd and liberal man in politics, and from early education his mind is imbued with American sympathies".[17] To Dowling, Forbes never lost that "round head republican look" discerned on first arrival.[18]

Dowling may well have foreseen that Burton might become a threat to his own expectations; but he could not have calculated in what a sinister and awkward way the threat would be manifested. While anxious to affirm publicly that "cordiality and good feeling" had been maintained between himself and Burton as judges,[19] Dowling privately insisted that Burton was "anything but an amiable man".[20] Burton had qualities not unknown within the legal profession. Self-assured to the point of arrogance, he combined a bullying style with an ability to take minute but astute legal points to his own advantage. The air of command he inherited from naval days was augmented by the standing he arrogated to himself as one translated by direct order of the Secretary of State to greater service in New South Wales where his special qualities were needed. That translation, he was convinced, demonstrated an encouragement of his avowed intention to climb as high as he could on the judicial ladder in the colonies. Dowling would discover that anyone blocking Burton's access to a higher rung of the ladder, would be pushed hard to make way. And Dowling would soon find his own relatively modest aspirations for advancement under abrasive challenges by his new "brother" judge.

The selfishness of Burton, in pressing to be appointed Acting Chief Justice when Forbes sought leave in 1834 and 1835, is noticed below.[21] Forbes had to defer taking leave (at a devastating cost to his own health) lest open friction exist on the Bench in his absence.[22] Dowling would find out, abruptly, that the same considerateness he had applied to the feelings of John Stephen, when questions of seniority and precedence arose in 1828, would not in turn be applied to him by W.W. Burton.

Bourke had taken it for granted that, as Dowling, without contest, had occupied the office of Senior Puisne Judge since the resignation of John Stephen, the temporary appointee as *locum* of the Chief Justice while on leave should automatically be Dowling. That appointment, Bourke decided, would be made once Forbes departed. Burton immediately "took huff" and there followed for a time "a considerable coolness" between him and the Governor.[23]

Burton's plans had been laid long before that difference occurred. As early as January 1834 he had written, petulantly, to his brother Edmund in England:

> My request to you now, is that you would take an opportunity of seeing Mr Hay [the Under Secretary at the Colonial Office] and state to him that I am not yet promoted – that I am displeased at being kept here as a puisne judge – that in fact it is not worth my holding – and urge that no opportunity may be lost of appointing me [Chief Justice] . . . I find my income worse here than at the Cape in every way . . . the appointment literally affords only a simple maintenance.[24]

It followed that Burton was in a truculent mood when nothing had flowed from his brother's solicitations, and, by July 1835, Bourke had made known to Burton his intentions. Bourke insisted that he had no alternative but to recognize Dowling's seniority. The very next day, Burton sat down with sophistical pen and argued a specious case for his own advancement.[25] Dowling, he asserted, had been "nominated" as a judge in May 1827, whereas Burton had been "nominated" as a judge (for service at the Cape) in March of that year. Burton was sworn into office at the Cape "at the close of the year 1827": Dowling was not sworn in at Sydney until the February following.[26] While Dowling was Burton's senior at the Bar, that had nothing to say as to seniority as a judge: and, so Burton maintained, as in England, judicial seniority was ambulatory and followed a judge from court to court – a practice that should be recognized as operating between colonial courts. Moreover, the assurance he had been given by R.W. Hay that, in waiving his intended right of precedence at the Cape, Burton would "forfeit no prospect of future advancement",[27] had ripened and was overdue, he thought, for harvesting in New South Wales. His own delicacy, in not having insisted on taking the second place on the Bench since 1833, could not be construed, he insisted, as renouncing any rights he may have had.

The matter was then strung out over months. Colonial Secretary McLeay was deputed by the Governor to advise Dowling of Burton's claim and, in effect, to shift the onus of proof to Dowling to demonstrate why his seniority should be preferred to that claimed by his colleague. Dowling reflected on his position before rejoining, "I do not at all feel disposed to admit this claim . . . but on the contrary . . . strenuously . . . assert my seniority".[28]

In the first place, Dowling relied on Burton's acquiescence. From his New South Wales gazettal as a judge in December 1832 for two years and a half Burton had said nothing about seniority, and had given no "personal or private notice" of his intentions to Dowling, but had "silently acquiesced in the post of juniority".[29] Dowling's trump card was, of course, the despatch by which Goderich had "instructed" Darling that Dowling on his original appointment "will take rank in the Supreme Court next to the Chief Justice".[30] Dowling had never forfeited that entitlement, but had deferred to John Stephen in the interests of judicial harmony – a course commended by the Colonial Office. Nothing, said Dowling, would dissuade him from asserting judicial seniority over Burton "but the express decision of His Most gracious Majesty in Council".[31]

McLeay advised Burton accordingly, indicating that the Governor was determined to refer the matter for decision to Chief Justice Forbes and the Crown Law Officers (Attorney-General Kinchela and Solicitor-General Plunkett).[32] As the Governor explained to Glenelg, he had hoped by taking that route to "obtain some insight into the merits of the case".[33] But his hopes were disappointed. Forbes prudently side-stepped what was largely a political issue, indicating that he could not recall a similar question being raised before and knew of no precedent to settle it. But he volunteered his opinion (which, as so often was the case, would be vindicated) that, "there is no community of jurisdiction between the judges of different colonies – their authority and their rank are confined to the particular colony for which their appointment is made". Nevertheless, the matter, he thought, should be "determined by the authority of His Majesty".[34]

The advice of the colonial Law Officers proceeded so obtusely as to suggest sole authorship by Kinchela. After much prevarication it concluded that "we are unable to give a decided opinion".[35] But their inclination, according to their view of English practice, tended to favour Burton as having "seniority" to Dowling.

Bourke decided to keep his own counsel, though he was probably impressed by Forbes' personal opinion. While not predisposed to advance Dowling, and wishing, if he could, to accommodate the aspirations of Burton, the Governor none the less was a fairminded man. He perceived that, if Dowling did not become temporary Chief Justice, he would seem to the public to have suffered an "actual degradation". Dowling was entitled to preferment, wrote Bourke, "not only by his station and general respectability of character, but on account of the very laborious attention he paid to the duties [of the court] during the protracted illness of the late Mr Justice Stephen".[36]

"I am Desirous of Meeting the Question Fairly"

When advised of the Governor's decision, Burton was furious and told Bourke so. The latter regretted that the judge was "so much aggrieved by this simple and natural course of proceeding".[37] But, for Burton, self-interest was at stake, and considerations of friendship or regard for the circumstances of others (including the Chief Justice's impaired health) must not stand in the way. Burton defended that self-interest so energetically and aggressively that he overreached himself. He prepared another lengthy assertion of his alleged rights, in terms very similar to those of the letter he had sent to Bourke in the preceding July. This time, he addressed the Secretary of State and insisted that the Governor transmit it officially.[38]

Burton wrote according to the precept that attack was the best defence, such that he appeared to be the party wronged and entitled to make complaint, especially as he had been removed from the Cape "not at my own request, but upon His Majesty's most gracious command".[39] His expectation of being considered the senior judge was more than a claim: he perceived it to be his right. With that sophistical skill characteristic of his class of lawyer, he proceeded to pull himself up by his own bootstraps. The "facts" he had put to the Secretary of State were, he insisted, correct as they were not capable of contradiction. He was supported, he said, by s. 24 of the *Australian Courts Act* 1828 (as to the reception of English laws so far as capable of applying in the Colony). The English rules as to seniority of judges were, he contended, applicable under s. 24 (a contention that begged the very question to be proved)[40] and, if his case was the first test of the application of those rules, that had nothing to say by way of objection to the rules.[41] Burton's ego enlarged as the words flowed. "I have further to complain", he wrote, "on the ground that I had reason to expect, in the event of a vacancy occurring in the office of Chief Justice here, and of my being found the best qualified to succeed to it, that I should obtain that elevation".[42] He rested those expectations on the "very great personal inconvenience and sacrifice" he had suffered by his removal, the "zeal and usefulness of [his] public services" in the Colony, and on the testimonial to those services Bourke had promised to furnish to the Secretary of State.[43]

Proceeding then to the highest ground of his outrage, Burton was convinced that it would be obvious to the Colonial Office:

> that I cannot but look upon my prospects in this Colony as entirely changed, and I trust that I shall not be thought unreasonable, when I earnestly make my appeal, as I now do, to be relieved from my present situation, unless some previous arrangement more favourable to me shall have been made by His Majesty's Government, or such should occur before my removal from hence.[44]

He continued, as if to call the Colonial Office's bluff, that because he was "considerably worse in worldly means" than when first appointed a judge, his resignation must be conditional on the making of some better provision for him.[45] He would best like an appointment in England, or otherwise a return to the Cape. It would not be within his power, as he put it, to:

> accept an appointment in a Colony situated in a higher latitude than 50 degrees north, or on the coast of Africa except the Cape of Good Hope, or in any part of the West Indies to the southward of the Island of Jamaica, or in any of the Colonies where the "pleadings and proceedings of the Court" are in any other language than English, or in any of the Australian Colonies but this.[46]

With those exceptions, a colonial Chief Justiceship, at an appropriate level of remuneration, would be an acceptable alternative.

Sir George Grey, then Political Under Secretary, plodded through Burton's 18 manuscript pages with yet further annexures, but disposed of them unsympathetically. He minuted:

> Mr Dowling and Mr Burton held precisely the same position in the respective colonies – that of Second Puisne Judge. But it might have been naturally considered a hardship by Mr Dowling if, on the retirement of Mr Stephen, who was advanced in years, and to whose retirement he might naturally have looked forward, Mr Burton a comparatively young man had been placed above him. Mr Burton . . . if placed below Mr Dowling would have suffered no loss of rank.[47]

On the very same day, 2 September, Burton acquitted himself of seven further pages of private manuscript letter to the Permanent Under Secretary, R.W. Hay. While he conceded that he had little claim upon Hay's attention beyond the latter's unguarded assurances given many years earlier, he wrote because the proposed advancement of Dowling would be "destructive of my prospects in this Colony" and Burton was "by law entitled to be considered the Senior Puisne Judge of this colony".[48] He elaborated upon the regard in which he was held by the Governor, upon the encroachment made into his leisure hours by drafting legislation for the Governor, and upon the zeal he had brought to the judicial office, not least in helping to rescue it from Chief Justice Forbes' supposed reforms:

> when I joined the Bench here, I found much disorder and irregularity to prevail, not only in the departure from fundamental principles of the Law of England . . . but in the conduct of the practitioners of the Court, which was in many instances so disgraceful, that respectable persons against whose veracity there could be no reproach were deterred from giving their evidence in Court, on account of the low and scandalous manner in which they were treated.[49]

The point of all this, Burton hinted, was that his own insistence on the highest standards had attracted the enmity of those (perhaps Dowling was one, or the confederate of others!) "whose unbridled conduct had brought the Court itself into disrepute".[50] Only Burton, according to his account, had attempted to suppress blatant perjury in court: and only he had stood against the negligence of the other judges in allowing court business to become slow, inefficient and costly. All these good works of his were but an earnest of what he would achieve when his just expectations were realized. These remarks in self justification were breathtakingly disingenuous, as they were false, exorbitant or wilfully divorced from their proper context.

Two days after writing that letter, Burton put together ten more pages of manuscript addressed to James Stephen, who, by the time of their receipt, had just been promoted as Permanent Under Secretary to the Colonial Office. This very artful approach was to make sure that no-one in that office could be heard to say that Burton had, as Dowling put it, acquiesced in Dowling's temporary advancement. The thrust of his claim was that Bourke had been reminded by Burton that, "when I first came to this Colony he [Bourke] told me himself, that he had said to Lord Howick that in the event of a vacancy in the Chief Justiceship I ought to succeed to it".[51] As Burton well knew, the preferment was not the Governor's to control, and that expression of opinion could have only persuasive force with those in whose gift an appointment lay.

Nevertheless, Burton was a special pleader. Through such eyes not only was the Governor made to seem to have wronged Burton, but the other judges were made to appear similarly reprobate.

> I feel injured by my brother judges: it was Forbes's duty as C.J. to assign me my proper place in Court, and if he did not know it to enquire. Had he enquired he would have found the right with me – for I have it from authority I do not doubt, that altho' I was ignorant of my right, Judge Dowling was aware of it – but never told me of it – he took advantage of my ignorance and took his place before me.[52]

Then these extraordinary utterances degenerated into gossip. Burton could prove that Dowling's sons had been heard to say on Burton's arrival in Sydney, "Judge Burton is before our father" – though what the probative value of such a remark by mere youths might be was not pursued. Burton was content merely to float the question how Dowling's own family might know even of a rumour to that effect unless through domestic discussion. Burton then recalled that Dowling openly admitted to Burton's seniority, *by nomination*, but only when Burton told him that he would insist upon it – "I am *hurt* to think that he did not tell me so when I arrived – *he knew the date of his nomination, I did not*". He claimed, then, to have been "cheated by one of my brother judges and that other was an accessory to it".[53]

Lest the point have missed its mark, Burton added a postscript that he was not conveying his letter by the normal channel of the Chief Justice – "he will not be the bearer of any communication from me – or in possession of my views, or authorized to act for or pledge me in any respect whatever".[54] Under Secretary Stephen did not react at once to this essay in acerbity, but marked it to be "put by" until Bourke's official representations should arrive.[55] When they did, they placed the matter in perspective. The Colonial Office commended Bourke's reliance on what he called "the rule of conventional seniority" for the purposes of a temporary appointment as *locum tenens*.[56] It also noted that he had applied that rule notwithstanding that, had a permanent appointment been contemplated, Bourke himself "should not have hesitated one moment" in naming Burton, rather than Dowling, as his preferred appointee.[57]

Dowling, meanwhile, was apprised of the enthusiasm which Burton was directing to his claims – though Dowling could not have guessed how harshly he and Forbes had been treated in Burton's aggrandisement of himself. Losing no time, Dowling again committed his future to the hands of Lord Brougham. He may not have realized that his patron had then relinquished the seals of the Lord Chancellorship. But, fortunately for Dowling, Brougham was still a force in politics and well regarded by the government. Dowling had become adept in striking the right balance between obsequiousness and self-promotion, such as would appeal to Brougham. The "exalted station" of the latter, and "the multifarious cares and duties incident thereto", would ordinarily have reduced the humble Dowling to silence, he wrote. But silence in a moment of need was not appropriate, so Dowling had to begin by "indulging a hope . . . that my forbearance from troubling you with many letters, since I have been in this Colony, will not, in your generosity, be attributed to disrespect, or any insensibility to the suggestions of gratitude, for the important benefit I have derived from your friendship".[58]

Dowling then set out his predicament, his arguments in support of his own position, and his supplication to "the great philosopher and philanthropist of the age, to whom he is indebted for every advantage of professional success". Some literary licence was permissible in letters of this kind. When Dowling represented to Brougham that, "I am desirous of meeting the question fairly, candidly, and in good temper. Should the Secretary of State decide the point against me, I shall bow with contentment, because I am thoroughly persuaded it will be the result of fair, just and judicious consideration of the question",[59] he meant to convey a different impression from that borne by the words literally. The "innuendo" was that Burton had been anything but fair, candid or reasonable; and that Dowling would be extremely mortified if such tactics were to prevail over his own faithful discharge of judicial duties and his legitimate expectations of preferment.

Without the intervention of the great philosopher of the age, Dowling's cause might have been swamped by the waves being made by his opponent. There was an added disadvantage in that Dowling was being denied procedural fairness. He knew that Burton had written to the Secretary of State, but was "not apprised of the contents of [the] letter".[60] Accordingly he could not know precisely what case he ought to answer: in particular, as will shortly emerge, the importance being laid upon dates of "nomination" was as yet unclear to him. Dowling had to make his submissions to the Secretary of State as best he could. Unlike Burton's strident tones, Dowling's remarks were measured, temperate and guileless. Dowling's status rested on two propositions. First, that the intention that he be second judge had been explicit at the time of his original appointment: and, second, that the precedency rule among English judges had no application in the colonies.

Enough has been said in earlier pages about the first point.[61] As to the second, it is plain that Forbes was providing Dowling with moral support like that Bourke was giving to Burton. Forbes had obviously given Dowling a copy of the confidential answer he had returned to Colonial Secretary McLeay on the matter of judicial seniority. Dowling copied or paraphrased Forbes' opinion as to there being no community of jurisdiction between judges of different colonies.[62] He added a *reductio ad absurdum* of his own, illustrating how preposterous the Burton thesis could be if carried literally into practice:

> The mere fact of the priority of the appointment of a Judge in point of time, no matter to what Court in any part of His Majesty's dominions, would lead to this consequence (if the rule contended for be irrefragable) that, if His Majesty should be pleased to remove an old Judge from some obscure Colony, and appoint him to the office of a Judge of one of the King's Courts at Westminster, he would be entitled to take precedence of all the Puisne Judges and Barons of those Courts, whose patents happened to be dated subsequently to his own original appointment as a Colonial Judge.[63]

Cast in those terms, Dowling's contention was unanswerable.

While "anxious" that the matter be resolved in his favour, Dowling made it plain that he would not, even were the decision adverse to him, allow personality and private feelings to interfere with the discharge of his judicial duties.

In November 1835, Dowling asked the Governor to transmit another letter to the Secretary of State and simultaneously alerted the Governor to its substance.[64] He had just, felicitously, seen a copy of the Charter of Justice for the Cape of Good Hope, which was the source of Burton's judicial appointment there. It was dated 24 August 1827: Dowling's commission to the New South Wales Bench was dated 6 August 1827. On that basis, Dowling claimed seniority over Burton by 18 days. It followed that if, on the view he had earlier propounded, that dates of commission alone did not determine precedence, the Colonial Office was against Dowling, then it was not a ground on which Burton's claim could succeed. Dowling further argued, correctly, that there could be no substance in Burton's apparent suggestion that dates of swearing in as a colonial judge afforded a test of seniority – still less could dates of nomination (so strongly pressed by Burton behind Dowling's back) have any relevance. The reply by the Secretary of State to the Governor was obviously based on advice. The Colonial Office would not recognize any opinion that succession to a Chief Justiceship, permanently or *ad interim*, was attached as a matter of right to seniority on the Bench.[65] The Government was not only free, but sometimes bound, in the public interest, when filling judicial vacancies, to pass over incumbent judges. It was, however, desirable that appointments by way of *locum tenens* for an absent Chief Justice be of the judge next in seniority, if competent.

> The benefit, which Society might derive from the superior endowments of [a specially elevated] provisional Chief Justice, would not compensate for the evil of subjecting the first Puisne Judge to an apparent degradation, nor is the pain, which must be inflicted on the feelings of that Officer, to be regarded as a matter of trifling concern.[66]

On those grounds alone, Governor Bourke had acted "rightly" in proposing to appoint Dowling *vice* the would-be absent Forbes.

Moreover, Burton's claim was "*not* tenable".[67] The Judges of Westminster Hall were, for all practical purposes, "one Judicial Body or College".[68] But the colonial judges had no such "scene of action common to them all" and there had never, up to that time, been an instance of the judges of any separate colonies sitting together in their judicial character. "The Members of the Superior Court of New South Wales are as completely separate from the Members of the Superior Court of Malta or of Jamaica, as are the members of the Legislatures of those Settlements. The supposed analogy is therefore fallacious".[69] The fallacy could easily be tested in then current circumstances where many colonial Benches, even of superior courts, were occupied "by persons unlearned in the Law". If the Burton claim for reciprocity of precedence were sustained, the absurdity could be imagined of an "unlearned" judge claiming preferment on grounds of long service over a judge of superior legal qualifications.

In short, when Chief Justice Forbes elected to take his leave, Governor Bourke was to call Dowling to the temporary administration of the office of Chief Justice.[70]

"I Have Often Been Obliged to You My Dear Burton"

In between times, Burton had managed to give a strikingly unsolicited testimonial of qualities that should have been foreign to an aspiring Chief Justice. In doing so he incommoded Bourke, turned his fellow judges against him, and came under notice at Downing Street in a manner that could easily have worked to his disadvantage. On 18 November 1835, at the close of Quarter Sessions for the year, Burton felt moved to deliver a "charge" to the assembled, and somewhat palled, petit jurors.[71]

That was not, as Professor Clark represents it to be, the action of a "timid man", but a study in pure egocentricity by a judge anxious to proclaim his self importance to the public.[72] There was ample colonial precedent for ceremonial addresses at the opening of "circuit" sittings of the Supreme Court in country districts.[73] During the brief history of the grand jury in New South Wales, there had been some elaborate charges to that body, in keeping with English practice.[74] But the grand jury had been superseded as to virtually all its legal functions by the appointment of an Attorney-General. Burton's assumption, in 1835, that "he deemed . . . the observations which it would be his duty to make, if he had the opportunity of addressing a Grand Jury in this Colony, might properly be made" to the assembled petit jurors,[75] travelled too far. It might not have mattered had the "charge" been merely formal, but, driven by Burton's religious effusiveness, it ventured, even beyond the ambit of a homily, to commenting on matters that could only be, and were, regarded in Sydney as political and controversial.

Other writers have remarked amply on the consequences of Burton's "charge"[76] and the matter has little further relevance here, save to mention that, in giving it, Burton placed at risk his hopes for advancement in New South Wales. As the newspapers saw it, the "charge" with its emphasis on religious decline leading to unprecedented crime and other excesses, reflected adversely on Bourke's administration, particularly in its alleged return to a Macquarie-like liberality towards the management of the remaining convict community.

Burton was immediately supported by some strident church leaders, among them Marsden and Lang,[77] leaving Bourke, in justifying his own opinion that the judge had indulged in a "gloomy if not morose view of Colonial Affairs",[78] to seek advice from Forbes and Dowling whether the "charge" had been delivered with their concurrence. They disowned any part in it and disputed the conclusions Burton had drawn, as being unsubstantiated by the facts.[79] The latter wrote to Bourke, disclaiming the imputations drawn from his remarks, but the damage was too far gone to be so lightly repaired. As the Governor wrote to him privately:

> I have often been obliged to you my dear Burton and . . . grateful for information freely and most kindly given on public matters and we have more than once both here and at the Cape upon considering such subjects together been led to arrangements of public utility. The information I have derived from the charge brings to my recollection Prior's Epigram:
>
> To Ned I owed great obligation
> But Ned thought fit
> To publish it to all the nation
> Ned and I are more than quit.[80]

Luckily for Burton, he did not literally suffers "Ned's" fate at Bourke's hands,[81] but he had injured his own reputation. To protect himself, Bourke sought, in a despatch to the Secretary of State, to condemn unreservedly the whole of Burton's charge. "I regret much", he concluded, "that Mr Burton should have thought it necessary to put forth an address which dwells upon, and even exaggerates, evils from which none could expect a penal Colony to escape, while it suppresses all mention of the numerous causes for congratulation everywhere apparent".[82]

To almost universal surprise in the Colony, the matter impressed the Colonial Office in exactly the opposite way from that expected. Bourke's assessment was commended for being just, but Burton was entitled to credit for being actuated by "the most humane and upright motives".[83] What had been said in the "charge" was not to be construed as criticizing the Governor or his administration: it was to be seen as reliable evidence that the transportation of convicts was undesirable and in need of reconsideration. Burton's views were received with deference, and described as "the best possible evidence that can be adduced", before the Molesworth Committee which made the formal recommendation, soon implemented, that transportation to Australia cease.[84]

Burton's living to fight another day is of no further concern here. Dowling had been the honourable conqueror in attaining the temporary vacancy caused by Chief Justice Forbes' absence. Yet, in the circumstances that were to happen, what had already occurred was only the first round and the incidents of Burton's "charge" a mere distraction. Burton would soon place himself in even more strenuous combat with Dowling for the prize of becoming the second Chief Justice of New South Wales.

6

"To My Dear Brother Vincent I am Deeply Indebted"

Forbes was, for all practical purposes, farewelled from the Bench in April 1836, shortly before his departure for England. It was generally accepted that he would never resume judicial duties in court, and he never did. The circumstances, a year later, in which he, while in England, sought and was granted leave to retire on a pension, have been noticed in another volume.[1]

When Forbes departed, the Bench, briefly supplemented by the elderly and deaf former Attorney-General Kinchela,[2] was one on which it has been well said that "Dowling and William Burton lived in a temporary but uneasy truce".[3] Behind the scenes, much lobbying occurred. On 7 March 1836, Dowling thought it opportune to "bespeak" the attention of Lord Brougham "to a few lines upon matters of some importance to myself".[4] The pretext was Forbes' imminent departure. Dowling thought it quite possible that Forbes would resign the Chief Justiceship while absent. Forbes' health continued to be poor (he was, wrote Dowling, "truly sick of the Colony"), he was wearied of the political and newspaper attacks upon him and, Dowling suspected, Forbes would find that enemies "who would wish to disserve him in Downing Street" would have done their work before he got there.[5] Forbes' experiences cast something of a cloud over the very office of Chief Justice, but there was no shadow over Dowling's ambitions. As he put it to Brougham, "Envying not his [Forbes'] station, (for it is one necessarily of anxious responsibility) I cannot however suffer myself to be indifferent to any fair and honourable opportunity of seeking to promote my own interests, if such should arise".[6]

Dowling felt entitled to aspire to Forbes' place when it should be vacated. He had endured a life of worrying, ill-paid, labour for eight years. He had applied himself to judicial impartiality and a rigid abstinence from local politics. He added, perceptively, that "the very neutrality I have observed may throw my personal claims, however meritorious, into the shade". The Macarthurs would soon demonstrate that they wanted, not a neutral, but a political ally - especially Burton - as their candidate.[7] Dowling recognized that his recent remarriage - to Harriott Ritchie, a widow, ("the daughter of a most respectable and worthy gentleman . . . and an honest upright man [John Blaxland] . . . who has the misfortune to be a Kentish Whig") - might weigh against him.[8] Blaxland had not been liked by successive Governors, and Dowling feared that, on *noscitur a sociis* principles, he himself would become tainted by the reputation of his new father-in-law. He assured Brougham that, "With this gentleman's politics I have nothing to do,[9] but I suspect that I have not gained golden opinions by this connexion with a certain party, who style themselves *Tories* in this petty community".[10] The "few lines" thus expanded into pages of self-assessment, self justification, and much commentary on colonial affairs.

"To whom could I look in such a juncture, but to you my dear Lord, - my patron and friend!", Dowling exclaimed. "To you I appeal for protection against any indirect influence to my prejudice, and I persuade myself that I shall not appeal in vain". Brougham did not disappoint the author of these apostrophes, although it is remarkable how much depended merely on the invocation of his name rather than on any positive act performed by him. But even more than such an influential name would be needed, for Brougham had ceased to be Lord Chancellor and, while remaining active in public life, commanded a good deal less of the authority he had formerly enjoyed.

Dowling also called in aid the invaluable energies of his brother Vincent, in London, to undertake the essential task of canvassing support among politicians and at the Colonial Office. "I am persuaded", Dowling wrote to his son James, "that had he [Vincent] not been on the spot I should have been thrown over the bridge by my un-friends. He has fought the good fight of brotherly love".[11] A few weeks later he enlarged upon that theme, in circumstances that will be revealed presently:[12] "To my dear brother

Vincent I am deeply indebted for the zealous and able manner in which he pushed my just claims to promotion. I believe that if they could . . . push aside my fair right to advancement, after ten years laborious, zealous and honest service in the post of puisne, they would have done so".[13] Much was due to Vincent's "right bulldog manliness" in "*pinning* them down" so that prevarication within the Colonial Office – not least by Lord Glenelg himself – did not work to James Dowling's disadvantage.

When Brougham agreed again to interpose in support of Dowling, there began an exercise in what Dr Hazel King has described as "pulling strings at the Colonial Office",[14] revealing at its most incongruous the then prevailing system of patronage in appointment to public office. In August 1836, Vincent Dowling who, as a newspaper editor, commanded some political notice, began the task entrusted to him.[15] He wrote to Glenelg, forwarding excerpts Brougham had authorized to be made from James Dowling's long letter to him, and supplicating for James' advancement to the office should Forbes resign as Chief Justice of New South Wales.[16]

James Stephen minuted the file that Vincent Dowling should be advised that he need offer no apology for making representations on his brother's behalf, but there was no official reason to suppose that Forbes contemplated resignation: rather it was expected that he would resume his duties as soon as his health had recovered.[17] In those circumstances it would be "impossible for Lord Glenelg to give any pledge, or even to enter into any discussion with reference to the succession to the Chief Justiceship".[18] Nevertheless, Stephen proposed that a mark of esteem be visited upon the judge:

> His Lordship however gladly avails himself of this opportunity of stating that during the whole course of Mr James Dowling's service in the Colony, no instance has occurred in which his name or his conduct has been referred to by the successive Governors in any other terms than those of respect, *and in the recent promotion of that gentleman to fill the office of Chief Justice provisionally the Governor was avowedly actuated, not only by Mr Dowling's seniority on the Bench, but also by the high estimate he had formed of his public and private character – a testimony the more valuable, because Sir Richard Bourke, at the same time, avows that, in overruling the pretensions of Mr Burton, he was called to a painful sacrifice of the feelings of a long established personal friendship, to the sense of public duty.* [italics added][19]

The passage here italicized – and struck out of the draft – shows that Dowling's reputation stood high in the estimation of James Stephen, whose influence at the Colonial Office was in the ascendancy. Sir George Grey countermanded those observations as being otiose and likely to carry the implication that Burton's public and private character stood less high than did that of Dowling.[20] With that excision made, Stephen, on Glenelg's behalf, so replied to Vincent Dowling.[21]

There the matter rested until Forbes' deteriorating health dictated a new course. On 27 April 1837 the Chief Justice bowed to the inevitable and sought leave to retire.[22] He wrote soon afterwards, telling Bourke so. No doubt in ignorance of Bourke's active championship of Burton, Forbes remarked, "I cannot tell who will succeed me, I take no part – indeed I have no means of doing so, but I think that Dowling's is the stronger claim, and it is, I know, backed by Lord Brougham".[23]

Despite the disavowal of taking any part, it is impossible not to conclude that Forbes had decided to even a score with Burton and to give Dowling a head start. On 28 April, Vincent Dowling, ever so fortuitously, had "an interview with Sir Francis Forbes . . . at which he informed me he had tendered his resignation".[24] On 29 April, Vincent was able to write to Glenelg reminding him of his brother's claim upon any vacancy in the office of Chief Justice, and of the approbation of it by Brougham.[25]

James Dowling was again well served by the good opinion entertained of him by James Stephen. The latter minuted Vincent's letter to be answered to the effect that, "His Lordship has great pleasure in acquainting the writer that he proposes to submit Mr Dowling's name to the King for the office of Chief Justice of N. S. Wales".[26] It was as simple as that – or so it seemed at first. Glenelg approved, and Sir George Grey signed a letter to Vincent in those terms on 5 May.[27] The latter, very wisely, decided to make the news as public as he could, writing immediately to James and disclosing the proposed appointment to many mutual friends. The wisdom of publicity was soon borne out when Burton's supporters realized that they had been outsmarted, and they set about making up lost ground.

"A Public Calamity and the Cause of Most Serious Annoyance"

Burton's supporters included Governor Bourke, Bourke's son also named Richard (then in London), James Macarthur and other connexions of the colonial "tories" or "exclusives". Governor Bourke had given Burton a handsome testimonial when compelled to deny him advancement as Forbes' *locum tenens*. He had then written to Glenelg:

> I consider [Burton] admirably qualified to fill that office [of Chief Justice] in any Colony where English Law is administered. I have reaped great benefit from his Talents and assiduity, both at the Cape and in this Colony. . . Had the vacancy about to be made by Chief Justice Forbes been permanent instead of temporary, I should not have hesitated one moment to name Mr Burton to fill it.[28]

The initiative then passed to Richard Bourke, junior. He approached his father's close friend the Chancellor of the Exchequer, Thomas Spring-Rice, who had previously served a brief term as Secretary of State for the Colonies, seeking to neutralize the groundswell of Whig support for Dowling. Richard wrote that "it is very desirable to get the *junior* puisne judge [Burton] appointed to succeed Forbes",[29] arguing that promotion on colonial Benches was not governed by seniority alone. He believed that his father would not yet have heard of Forbes' resignation or had time to make any consequential representations. Spring-Rice was asked to bring his influence to bear so that the incumbent Secretary of State might know "how desirable in all respects my father thinks Burton's appointment would be".[30]

Such gratuitous interference by Bourke, junior, points to an extraordinary *contretemps*. At the beginning of 1837 Governor Bourke, in a mood of depression after bruising disagreements with some senior public servants, contemplated resignation and sought Dowling's views. With true judicial detachment and none of the personality that might have swayed a lesser man, Dowling coaxed the Governor back from the brink, at least for the time being.[31] "Every honest man must deeply deplore the position into which you have been thrown", Dowling wrote.

> If consistently with your own honour, you could still be induced to retain the command, the interests of the King's government and the welfare of the public, demand the sacrifice. I endeavour to persuade

> myself that your resolution to retire is not irrevocably fixed – for I know that your secession will be regarded and *felt* by the public as a *calamity*![32] . . . When I implore you to pause before the final step is taken, it is for an anxious consideration for the hopeful prospects of the Colony under Your Excellency's enlightened, just, and paternal Government.[33]

One must ponder upon Bourke's thoughts, as the recipient of such a generous and persuasive measure of support and encouragement, had he known that his son was simultaneously straining every nerve to try to block the reasonable aspirations of the writer of that letter.

Meanwhile Burton's supporters had moved up heavier artillery and begun a barrage. James Macarthur fired off one of the lengthy letters he was in the habit of sending to the Colonial Office concerning his family's patrimony of New South Wales. He addressed Glenelg on the pretext that his Lordship had been "pleased to express yourself anxious to avail yourself officially of every means of information with respect to the Chief Justiceship of New South Wales to become vacant".[34] He was moved, he said, by concern for the welfare of the Colony (meaning the Macarthurs and their associates) and by the lack of public confidence (meaning the confidence of the Macarthurs) he detected in the Colony's judicial tribunals as constituted thus far.

Of whatever reforms the Colony's courts and legal system had enjoyed, Macarthur detected only two authors – Burton and Plunkett. He extolled the personal firmness, the excellent decisions, and the professional habits of the former, and the zealous co-operation of the latter. Macarthur could not but "entertain a very strong impression that Mr Justice Burton is the fittest person by becoming Chief Justice to complete the improvements so commenced under his auspices".[35] What those improvements were, Macarthur did not say. Burton's proposed revision of the Insolvency Law was only recently in draft and would take some years and much amendment before being realized.[36] His promotion of the division of the legal profession into the English branches of barrister and solicitor had been more pronounced:[37] yet with that, as with many other plans he cherished to change the court system so that it might run more along English lines than those devised for colonial circumstances by the Chief Justice, he was in necessary collision with Forbes.[38]

But this was no time to be dwelling on mere details:

> Mr Justice Burton is considered in the Colony to unite ability, legal acquirements, and judicial habitude with the most unexceptionable and honourable character, and the knowledge he already possesses of so peculiar a Society, together with his fearlessness in carrying into effect whatever may tend to promote the true interests of the Colony render it very doubtful whether another person could be found so qualified in every respect for the head of that Judicial Bench.[39]

Unless, he might have added, one were to turn to a man of equally great and even longer service in New South Wales, as Dowling was, but who had disqualified himself, for present purposes, by showing no sympathy for the Macarthur interests.

Burton's claim was then shored up with persuasive recommendations, Glenelg being invited to refer to Lord Denman, Baron Vaughan and Serjeant Goulburn as willing supporters of his aspirations.[40] The well known preferences of Governor Bourke were recited again with embellishment. It only remained for Macarthur to reassure Glenelg of his own complete sense of independence and public-spiritedness in the matter such that he had "no personal feeling or motive towards either of the present Judges".[41]

For the moment, James Stephen was unmoved by these submissions and marked Macarthur's letter "put by"[42] – usually his official sentence of death for correspondence. Macarthur persisted in his view that Dowling's preferment would be "a public calamity and the cause of most serious annoyance to the Governor".[43] An English Member of Parliament, P.M. Stewart, was therefore enlisted to advance Burton's cause. He made some representations to Glenelg that obviously worked such an impression that Glenelg wrote to Stewart seeking further information.

Stewart obliged with a few pages directed to revealing the question of the New South Wales Chief Justiceship "in a strong and clear light".[44] The Macarthur view in favour of Burton was, said Stewart, "the view taken by . . . almost every intelligent person concerned with that Colony". Sensing the death blow James Stephen had delivered to James Macarthur's letter, Stewart enclosed a copy of that letter and urged Glenelg's "kind attention" to its contents.[45] The Stewart manifesto then degenerated into hearsay, for the writer could have had no direct knowledge of the subject: "From all I have heard, I doubt, very much, if you can find one lawyer of any standing who can recommend Mr Dowling as, in any degree, qualified for the high and responsible situation of Chief Justice; while some of our very best professional authorities have given the most decided opinions in favour of Mr Justice Burton".[46]

Stephen tried to kill this also by marking it "put by",[47] but the matter was obviously being agitated "in club" where great pressure was being exerted on Glenelg to change his mind, which he soon did. His political weaknesses were duplicity and indecision, as his somersaults on this occasion would testify. Suddenly, it had been recalled to his mind, so the first two drafts of his awkward letter to V.G. Dowling ran, that Bourke had earlier spoken for Burton "in the most decided terms", giving reasons "which, on referring to them, appear to his Lordship conclusive".[48] Glenelg "deeply lamented" having to revoke his planned recommendation of Dowling to the King, and regretted the disappointment caused to the Dowling family, but "a sense of duty to His Majesty and to the Colony" dictated that course.[49]

"I am Not Yet Certain of the Chief Justiceship"

At the eleventh hour, Glenelg having already initialled one of the drafts, a face-saving miracle presented itself *deus ex machina.* John Lewes Pedder, the first Chief Justice of Van Diemen's Land (Tasmania),[50] who had been on the Bench at Hobart for a term equivalent to that of Forbes in Sydney, decided to seek greater glory. An application by him, to be advanced in the room of Forbes, had just come under the Secretary of State's attention.[51]

Pedder's judicial career is examined in a companion volume and needs no elaboration here except to say that, figuratively speaking, Forbes was a judicial giant and Pedder a judicial pygmy. The appointment of the latter – diligent and painstaking though he may have been – to head the rapidly maturing and important court system of New South Wales seems in hindsight barely capable of being imagined. Yet that is exactly the solution the Colonial Office stumbled upon to resolve its own embarrassment. Never mind a sense of duty to Crown or Colony: Pedder would be translated as Chief Justice of New South Wales; Dowling would go, in his place, as Chief Justice of Tasmania; and Burton – the very catalyst of these changes – would have nothing, but would stay exactly where he was. It seemed to the Colonial Office a brilliant result, as practical as it was "honourable".[52] Vincent Dowling thus received a much longer and more contrived letter than had at first been intended. It recited that Glenelg had "caused a search to be made among the records of this office" which indeed showed Bourke's predisposition to recommend Burton to succeed Forbes.[53] That recommendation had arrived a year earlier and, as it rested on contingencies, "it had failed to attract much of his Lordship's attention or to dwell on his memory". But, then, there was the recent application by Pedder whose "pretensions appear to be of the highest nature".[54] It was now a matter of looking beyond the accommodation of personal desires to securing the best interests of the public – or so the official letter would have had Vincent Dowling believe:

> The intimation which you have received of Lord Glenelg's intention to recommend your brother for the vacant office would in his Lordship's judgment be irrevocable if he were acting in any matter affecting himself merely. But in the selection of a name to be submitted to His Majesty for a high judicial office, his Lordship feels that he is discharging a public trust and that his duty to the King and to His Majesty's subjects must control any decision founded in ignorance of facts which if known would have prevented its adoption.[55]

Glenelg was happy, however, to be the bearer of good news that James Dowling "should at once be spared the pain of being superseded on the Bench by a judge who is junior to himself" and at the same time should receive a mark of His Majesty's favour.[56] Chief Justice of Tasmania he was to be.

This miraculous solution, while it offered no comfort to Burton, brought down the wrath of Vincent Dowling upon the Colonial Office. As a newspaper man he was not to be trifled with by politicians. And, as luck would have it, the death of William IV, in June 1837, necessitated a general election during which the public mind would be judgmental and politicians circumspect. It was also a lucky result for James Dowling that the Whigs were returned at the election and that Vincent Dowling continued to deal with Glenelg and Grey.

In his response, written just before the King's death, Vincent Dowling could not dissemble his feelings of pain and mortification at Glenelg's decision.[57] The magic name of Brougham was again paraded. Vincent Dowling had considered Glenelg's original advice to be conclusive and, as noted above, he had wisely proclaimed its purport to his brother and to many of his brother's supporters.[58] Not the least was Brougham who had already conveyed his congratulations to James Dowling, stating that he "had considered it [Dowling's preferment] quite a matter of course, as soon as Sir F. Forbes's resignation should be accepted".[59]

While not questioning Pedder's merits, Vincent Dowling rhetorically inquired how they could, in justice, displace Glenelg's "distinct pledge" to James Dowling.[60] And, in any event, the Colonial Office could have little appreciation of the distance between Sydney and Hobart Town and the intolerable upheaval for a family man (as James Dowling was, but Pedder was not) in making such a move. The disposal of Dowling's landed property in New South Wales would be unacceptable to him and, even if compelled, would inevitably cause financial loss. Stephen was obliged to mark this "put by" because of government preoccupation with the general election.

Vincent Dowling thereupon made a private representation to Glenelg, reminding him that his newspaper habitually supported the Whig cause.[61] Although that did not receive a substantive reply, the message had its effect on Glenelg whose concern for his public trust suddenly became more accommodating of the Dowling claim. It is likely, though, that this transformation owed more to Vincent Dowling's influencing mightier newspaper proprietors to support him than to the representations of Vincent himself. As Professor J.M. Ward has pointed out, James Macarthur "blamed Black of the *Morning Chronicle* for fastening Dowling on to the colony".[62] Vincent Dowling wrote again formally on 19 July 1837 – this time addressing James Stephen, who had always shown sympathy for James Dowling's advancement. It was a simple letter which mentioned that a ship was due to sail to Sydney shortly, and Dowling would be grateful to advise his brother how the matter stood, should Stephen be able to assist its prompt resolution.[63]

At last the issue was settled. Glenelg discarded Burton's claims and reverted to his original position. James Dowling was to have the Chief Justiceship of New South Wales. Stephen so advised Vincent on 8 August 1837.[64] But it took five months for James to receive the news. As late as November 1837 he was seriously reconsidering what he should do, and was inclined to throw himself upon the Colonial Office's mercy for some better remunerated posting elsewhere in the British dominions. Fortunately he did not take that step, given the forcefulness with which his brother had described his reluctance to remove from Sydney. Meanwhile James Dowling suffered much anxiety about his future. As he then wrote to his son, "I am not yet certain of the Chief Justiceship . . . if I am thrown back on my 1500£ I shall look very *blue*, and must shave as close as a new edged razor".[65]

"Mr Burton is Sadly Cut at His Disappointment"

When the news arrived, in January 1838, of his elevation to succeed Forbes, and the Queen's warrant for a commission appointing him Chief Justice followed in the ensuing month, Dowling found it almost an anticlimax. He reported to his son:

> I have heard, with natural satisfaction, I will not say exultation, that I have been Gazetted as Chief Justice. The promotion makes no alteration in me. I am too old to be elated by such events, for like an old soldier, I know the perils of the field, and how that increases responsibility. Mine will be very much enhanced.[66]

He was irritated though at the treatment he had received from the Colonial Office, especially at the glib manner in which his appointment had been agreed upon, and then recanted, and his own prospects in life trifled with. "They certainly do odd things some times in Downing Street", he wrote to James, junior, "but in this instance they dare not do injustice. Doubtless my merits were fully canvassed with inquisitorial criticism, but as I know that my judicial career hitherto is invulnerable, I feel that I have to thank them for nothing but *naked justice*".[67] As for his rival, who lacked the advantage of relatives with newspaper connexions, Dowling had the last word, "Mr Burton is sadly cut at his disappointment. However he sought promotion by unfair means, so I don't pity him".[68]

That was a fair summation. Burton had travelled far beyond the bounds of reasonable contest and had put forward a case based on much deception. His portrayal of himself as the only able and competent judge in the Colony was a fanciful distortion, and was plainly perceived to be so by James Stephen who consistently gave no assistance to Burton's importunings. On the other hand, the

Dowling brothers had fought a good fight. They had been determined: James Dowling had been entirely honourable and fair. Vincent Dowling no doubt made good use of his calling in life as a journalist, but no more so than Burton's unreasonableness deserved. They were entitled to win.

It may be that Burton had to some extent been unlucky. Dr King remarks that Under Secretary Hay had generally supported Burton, but had had to resign early in 1836, a most inopportune moment for Burton.[69] Moreover, had the Whigs fallen at the general election of 1837, there might have been a very different story to tell. Although slow to respond to the news of Forbes' resignation, Burton's supporters had been energetic, numerous and influential. It was a paradox that, at worst from Dowling's point of view, all that the combined efforts of those supporters seemed likely to produce was a windfall promotion for Pedder and a sideways promotion for Dowling – but nothing for Burton himself.

It is not particularly profitable to reflect on what history might have been. But it is at least curious to reflect that Dowling lived to enjoy his Chief Justiceship only until 1844 when he died in office aged 57. Burton stayed in New South Wales until being transferred to the Madras Bench.[70] After retiring as a judge, he returned to New South Wales and continued in public life for many years. He died in 1888 at the age of 94. Had he been more patient and less abrasive, it seems more likely than not that he would have succeeded Dowling as Chief Justice in 1844, at the age of 50, and occupied that office for decades.

7

"Neither of My Colleagues Particularly Love Me"

For all the energies Dowling applied to winning the prize of the Chief Justiceship, it must be wondered how real and substantial were its rewards. There was the gratification of receiving a knighthood,[1] and the immense satisfaction of achieving his life's ambition. Otherwise, Sir James Dowling would find the fruits of that ambition often illusory or rotten. His health collapsed under the burdens of office – burdens aggravated by the grating and eccentric personalities of some of his judicial colleagues. In many ways the summit of his career was blighted.

At first, there was but a minor irritation. A temporary judge was required during the absence overseas of Chief Justice Forbes in 1836. As Acting Chief Justice, Dowling found himself lumbered with the "assistance" of Dr John Kinchela, the former Attorney-General,[2] so afflicted with deafness that he could no longer perform court duties efficiently. The logic of getting rid of him by promotion to the Bench was not plain: deafness must be as great a disadvantage in a judge as in an advocate. Kinchela nevertheless had some strong supporters. The *Australian* considered that making him a judge was "but an act of justice to him by the British Ministry, who shamefully ousted him from his office of Attorney-General, in consequence of . . . misrepresentation".[3] Privately, Kinchela was not a good manager and accumulated many debts. The Colonial Office soon caused him to be retired from the Bench on a small pension and gave him some paid quasi judicial work for a time.[4] While Kinchela was, by one account, "a good lawyer – and in private life an unassuming and an excellent man",[5] the same could not be said of his successor.

John Walpole Willis,[6] who reached Sydney by the *Samuel Winter* on 3 November 1837,[7] was as troublesome a judge as could be imagined. Since school days, he had thrived on being expelled. He came under the cloud of having ostensibly been "amoved" (the expression for expulsion used in the *Colonial Leave of Absence Act* 1782 (22 *Geo.* III *c.* 75 – ("Burke's Act")) from the Bench of Upper Canada. He would leave Australia under the further cloud of attempted "amoval" from the Bench of New South Wales.[8] High-handed, egotistical, "overspeaking", and suffering from a "functional derangement of the liver"[9] which shortened his temper and warped his personal judgment, Willis was a complete misfit as a judge. His reinstatement to judicial service in 1831 came with a severe admonition from Lord Ripon.[10] Willis' self-esteem had also suffered by his being cuckolded in Canada; a double blow, as his first wife, the daughter of an earl, had secured him attention and preferment. That marriage was dissolved by Act of Parliament. He brought to Sydney a new wife, Ann Susanna, daughter of Thomas Henry Bund: Dowling thought the lady "old maidish".[11]

Dowling's greater concern would be with Willis himself; a concern exacerbated because Burton still smarted at being only a puisne judge. The Chief Justice wrote to his son, in 1838, after testing the new triumvirate:

> Neither of my colleagues particularly love me, but of the two Burton is the least disagreeable. Willis is a fidgety restless conceited self-opinionated fellow and it requires a good deal of forbearance and caution on my part to go on smoothly with him. Some people have the opinion that he is cracked. However I hope to get on without quarrelling. Anything for a quiet life.[12]

Relations started well enough when Willis arrived bearing an introduction from "an old and valued friend" of Dowling's.[13] The Willis family became house guests of the Dowlings and cordiality prevailed. But, when Willis removed to his own residence, and his liver reacted to the stresses of court work, an estrangement began. It degenerated into public hostility between him and the other judges. Dowling, being singled out for attention, recorded that, "a very short time had elapsed before I observed a carriage towards me in tone and manner betokening personal dislike".[14] Willis became distant from, and unsociable to, Dowling off the Bench. On the Bench, he directed sarcastic remarks to the Chief Justice in the

Full Court,[15] and, when sitting alone, parodied Dowling's curious sense of humour, with its penchant for the pun, while declaiming on the need for judicial dignity at all times especially by Chief Justices.[16]

Fortunately for Dowling, the public gauged for itself the true character of J.W. Willis. In July 1838 the latter set out to upstage Burton in a contest in religious intolerance. Burton's commitment to the Church of England, and his efforts to have it recognized as the Colony's "established" church, led him to be outspoken in ecclesiastical matters. He was criticized by Roman Catholic clergy for his perceived religious bias as a judge. Willis decided to go further. As guest speaker at a gathering presided over by Bishop Broughton, Willis declared that "the Church of Rome" was guilty of "idolatrous worship".[17] An ensuing meeting of the Catholic community expressed its outrage. Bishop Polding lamented that his letter to Willis, asking whether the judge had been correctly reported in the press, received "a reply by no means satisfactory", and he condemned the judge's strictures as "unjust".[18] As one historian summed up the result, "[Governor] Gipps, who had other reasons to be disquieted at Willis's erratic behaviour, admitted privately to [Attorney-General] Plunkett that the judge had surpassed himself on this occasion".[19] The *Australian* pondered how Willis "thought to confer benefit upon the holy work by a back-handed hit at the Roman Catholic church – are problems utterly beyond our power of solution".[20] Stung by the reaction, the judge became unusually quiet for a year.[21] Lady Dowling wrote to her step-son, "Willis has withdrawn himself quite into the shade and from his quiet manner of late, I would fancy he has been retired as he deserved to be for the unprovoked attack last year upon the Romanists".[22]

Early in 1839, Burton, with an ease denied either to Forbes or to Dowling, took leave in London, being weary of differences on the Bench, and keen to explore the possibilities of promotion elsewhere. Dowling rejoiced. He remarked, "as to my brother Burton it would not break my heart if he never comes back as he is anything but an amiable man".[23] James Sheen Dowling called on the Burtons in London, perhaps to judge them for himself. He recalled being first received with "a cold handshake" by Burton and "an equally cold one" from Mrs Burton:

> However they afterwards received me warmly when they found out who I was, and were very kind and asked me to stay and dine. He honourably mentioned you and your proceedings. I could see that they had not been frequently at Brougham [Place]. He returns to Sydney, having done his best to get another appointment. . . He is much altered for the worse and looks older. Mrs Burton is very cynical in her remarks. I have no great respect for either of them. I did not like his conduct towards you four years ago.[24]

Burton made a strategic blunder in taking leave. A *locum tenens* had to be appointed and, as circumstances were to turn out, that appointee would come to succeed Dowling as Chief Justice. Meanwhile, Burton, aglow at having been presented to the Queen in London, failed to realize that his absence from Sydney at a critical moment would deny him the very office he had so relentlessly sought. The temporary judicial vacancy was offered in turn to Plunkett and to Roger Therry.[25] As Roman Catholics they would have found any close association with Willis uncomfortable. Moreover: "Each of them declined, evidently thinking that such an appointment offered no future security. They alike made a miscalculation".[26] The occupant of the casual vacancy, Alfred Stephen, went on to obtain a permanent commission, and to secure the Chief Justiceship when Dowling died in 1844.[27]

Stephen was Dowling's candidate to take Burton's place.[28] In thus virtually anointing his successor, Dowling played his greatest part as Chief Justice – that of ensuring stability and continuity on the Bench. But, in 1839, the path was not smooth. As Lady Dowling confided to James, junior, "The conflict of opinion of the Bar with regard to the nomination of a successor to Mr Justice Burton involved your father in much difficulty and his triumph involved sullenness as a matter of course".[29] At the same time, Sir James himself reported, "Burton's place I expect will be filled by, as it has been offered to, Alfred Stephen, Attorney General of Van Diemen's Land *at my suggestion*, as we have not one of our own set who would be acceptable to the Public and palatable to the rest of the Bar".[30]

These ingredients, heaped as they were upon already daunting judicial labours, undermined the Chief Justice's health and equanimity. Then, just when all seemed serene, and almost as Lady Dowling was writing that Willis remained in the shade, while her husband was "particularly well",[31] Willis began a new eruption. In two calculated manoeuvres he sought to unseat Dowling as Chief Justice or, failing that, to cause Dowling great public embarrassment.

"A Spirit of Kindness and Friendship"

He first followed tactics he had already tried in Canada. There he sought to paralyse court business by claiming that a particular Bench, being constituted unlawfully, was unable to sit. In New South Wales he similarly attacked the Chief Justice in person. Early in 1839, Willis, "in a spirit of kindness and friendship", invited Dowling to reconsider his position as Chief Justice, which he had allegedly compromised by accepting "any other office or place of profit" contrary to cl. 7 of the Third Charter of Justice (letters patent of 13 October 1823, constituting the Supreme Court).[32] Dowling, like Chief Justice Forbes before him, had acted as Judge Commissary in the Colony's Vice-Admiralty Court, an ancient tribunal, then the oldest continuous court in New South Wales, being separately constituted from the Supreme Court. Presiding as Judge Commissary brought entitlement to share in the court's fees, a benefit Forbes and Dowling deliberately declined to accept.

Nevertheless, so Willis maintained, the entitlement alone rendered the Commissaryship another office or place of profit beyond that of Chief Justice. Dowling had thus disqualified himself. If he did not resign as Chief Justice, Willis would have to complain to the Secretary of State. Dowling, at first, made light of the question, responding to Willis that "I have not the slightest doubt about the matter, and my mind is very easy on the subject".[33] For more abundant caution, Dowling, shocked that Willis had acted without notice in a "very unfriendly and vexatious manner", sent a report to the Governor requesting its disclosure to the Colonial Office.[34]

Willis meanwhile bolstered up his position with the opinion of a friend of his, Serjeant Henry Alworth Merewether of Whitehall Place. Merewether purported to vindicate Willis' every quibble. He considered that the Commissaryship was "clearly" an office of profit and emolument "and such fact does not in any way depend on the acceptance or non-acceptance of the fees which are due".[35] Conversely, he considered that non-receipt of fees did not prevent the office from being one of profit. Therefore, the acceptance of that office would be "an avoidance under the Charter of the office of Chief Justice".[36] Merewether claimed that, in the month following, he had discussed the case with officials at the Colonial Office and they "are of the same opinion as he is".[37]

But the Law Officers of the Crown, in England, advised differently. In a terse report, they considered that the Vice-Admiralty appointment was "incident to" the office of Chief Justice and was not "another office" within the application of cl. 7 of the Charter of Justice.[38] From this, Willis grandly expressed his dissent, making public Merewether's advice, and pressing for a resolution by a Bench of 15 English judges entertaining a test appeal from any conviction previously pronounced by Dowling in the Vice-Admiralty Court.[39] When, by early 1840, it became clear that he would not have his way in this, he capitulated by letter to the Governor in which he claimed only recently to have seen Dowling's Vice-Admiralty commission. As that instrument was, in Willis' view, "of no legal validity whatever",[40] the office of Chief Justice could not be affected and, in this perverse fashion, Willis' doubts were laid to rest.[41] The second manoeuvre may have been the inspiration for the first, though its effects were felt later. It would reveal Willis as an unmitigated hypocrite. In a rambling letter to Governor Gipps, on 30 March 1839,[42] Willis made much of his indispositions and of financial losses he said he had suffered. Astonishingly, given his recent arrival in New South Wales, he foreshadowed his early retirement from the Bench and sought a pension – a matter quickly settled by the Colonial Office as there was no fund to support such a pension based on service in diverse colonies, even were he eligible.[43] The crowning piece of duplicity was Willis' claim that "I have never had the benefit of any Grants of Land *nor of convict labour*, advantages which, independently of any retiring pension or allowance, were sufficient to have enabled any other Judge in this Colony . . . amply to provide for themselves and their families".[44] Before the Colonial Office's refusal was known, Willis decided to expose the imagined discrimination against him, and to do so at the Chief Justice's expense. Dowling, like most of the free colonists, had the services of assigned convict servants: it was a practice encouraged by the imperial government. In June 1839, circumstances arose in which Willis could manipulate court proceedings to provide a forum for his "exposure" of the Chief Justice.

Those circumstances were the hearing before the Full Bench of an action for damages – *Walker v. Hughes*. As Dowling recorded, Willis "of his own motion, stated [a] question, and forced it upon the parties and required it to be argued".[45] The majority of the court (Dowling and Stephen) were foolish to have allowed this diversion to run unchecked, as the point was not in dispute between the parties even had it been material. But the intended mischief could not have been foreseen. The action was for damages arising out of an alleged breach of contract to sell a sheep station.[46] The contract would have permitted the purchaser temporary use of the vendor's convict shepherds. Willis, in dissent, considered that the provision vitiated the contract on public policy grounds, for it purported to recognize a practice akin to slavery. Suddenly the point of his manipulations became arrestingly plain. To the astonishment of all in court, and to a wider public thereafter, he said:

> I believe that His Honour Chief Justice Dowling has been and is the assignee of the services of very many convicts, or transported offenders . . . I have ever considered the provision of His Majesty's Orders in Council[47] . . . to be most wise in prohibiting the judges from being owners of or in any wise interested in slaves, or their labour . . . I will never permit the possibility of insinuation, that my private interest can in any wise interfere with the honest discharge of my judicial duties.[48]

Dowling, astounded by these reflections and by the use of the court room to proclaim them, at first ignored the slight, attributing it to Willis' constantly troublesome health.[49] The Chief Justice feared that, were the matter pressed, Willis might decline to take his place on the Bench, thus disrupting the court's business and inconveniencing litigants.

There was no reciprocation of Dowling's attempts to be conciliatory. As Professor Clark observed, "Willis was one of those men in whom the slightest suspicion of a challenge to his authority or an outrage to his vanity was followed by a rush of blood to the head and a display of hysterical rage".[50] Things smouldered on until again exploding into flames over a most improbable disagreement. On 28 October 1839, the Full Court (Dowling, Willis and Stephen) pronounced judgment in the *mandamus* application of George Robert Nichols[51] – first Australian-born solicitor and, in the late 1830s, a powerful figure because of his proprietorship of the *Australian* – to compel a magistrate to permit Nichols to appear

Mr Justice John Walpole Willis

Edward Smith Hall (1852)

"Judge Dowling's House" and Darlinghurst Windmills (c. 1833)

before him as advocate for an accused person. The significance of *Ex parte Nichols* is considered elsewhere.[52] For present purposes, suffice it to say that the case travelled far beyond its own circumstances and enabled all persons on their trial before magistrates to be represented by counsel or solicitor without leave of the Bench.

Nichols, who had acted as if an advocate at Quarter Sessions, without objection, for many years, thought it prudent to petition the judges to recognize his customary "right" of audience. They recommended him to apply to the Governor, which he did.[53] The Governor, in whom reposed the relevant rule-making power, circuitously sought the judges' advice as to amending the rules. Hearing of this, and fearing that the judges might be unwilling to exempt him specially, Nichols again petitioned the Bench asserting that a pledge had been given to him by Forbes, when Chief Justice, that the separation of the branches of barrister and solicitor in the Supreme Court was not to apply in the Sessions, or, at any rate, not to his detriment.

Dowling, pressed by other things, wrote on the petition that he would accede to Nichols' claim, on the faith that Forbes had given a pledge.[54] Willis wrote "a simple affirmative".[55] Stephen, on the contrary, considered the exemption undesirable in principle, and found that Forbes disclaimed any knowledge of a pledge.[56] When Stephen told Dowling so, the latter changed his mind. Willis, receiving the news as if a personal affront, began a tantrum. He insisted that the memoranda written by himself and by Dowling on Nichols' petition constituted an order of the court.[57] The order had become public knowledge, for Willis had shown the memoranda to Nichols – a course condemned by Dowling as "a breach of judicial confidence and out of the ordinary course of official communication with a petitioner to the judges".[58] There followed "an actual altercation" in the judges' robing room on the morning of 10 February 1840.[59] As Dowling recounted the event:[60]

> immediately on His Honour [Willis] entering, he with great heat and anger depicted in his manner, voice and countenance, began to reproach me with want of fairness towards him, in not shewing him my letters to [the Governor] on the subject of the Vice-Admiralty Judge question, and also about the affair of Mr Nichols. I was almost speechless[61] with astonishment at his demeanour and language.[62]

Willis renewed his attack on Dowling when Stephen entered the room. He claimed that Dowling's treatment of the memorandum on Nichols' petition amounted to a suppression of the truth. From what Governor Gipps was told of the altercation, he was satisfied that "words had passed . . . in the presence of witnesses, which were, to say the least of them, indecorous".[63] There was injury to honour, pride and reputation. Willis did not cool after reflection: he offered no apologies. Instead, he made available to a member of the Bar,[64] obviously for wider dissemination, a selection of the correspondence passing between the judges on all the sensitive issues Willis himself had raised. He turned his attack as well on Stephen, accusing him of discourtesy and want of fairness to a brother judge.[65]

Dowling begged for the Governor's mediation in the interests of restoring public confidence in the judicial Bench. To assist reconciliation, Gipps proposed that the "most neutral" method would be by a memorandum to both parties, after prior discussion with them separately.[66] His memorandum called for such propitiation with "no concession or apology . . . required on either side", and suggested a meeting at Government House. The Chief Justice yielded, as he said, out of respect for the Governor. As the party aggrieved, he was displeased with the unconditional nature of the proposal, offering as it did no atonement for the affronts by Willis upon Dowling's "private honour and personal self respect".[67] Only a sense of public duty decided him to "endeavour to forget what has passed in the hope of a better state of things in future".[68] The two judges dined with the Governor and, although appearing to be reconciled,[69] new troubles quickly emerged.

"Willis Continues the Same Disagreeable Person He Always Has Been"

The *Administration of Justice Act* 1840 was a significant measure having unexpected consequences for Willis, as will gradually emerge.[70] The Bill for the Act was reviewed in correspondence between the Governor and the judges, in which were passages exposing the differences between Dowling and Willis. The Legislative Council ordered the letters to be printed. Despite an assurance from the Governor that all inflammatory passages would be excluded, one was inadvertently published.[71] It related to Willis' preoccupation with convict servants, and his idea that a special Act be passed to prohibit judges from being the assignees of such servants. Dowling's attempts to remonstrate with Willis, on this and related matters,[72] were treated with contempt by the latter who had written, as if the injured party:

> I have now before me the Governor's note of *thanks* for the letter you complain of, and His Excellency, I think, would hardly have thanked me for *personalities uncalled for* [Dowling's phrase] or have forwarded them to Her Majesty's Government. The tone your correspondence has assumed of course prevents all further intercourse in any matter where consistently with public duty it can be avoided.[73]

Dowling had been further isolated when Burton and Willis insisted that they make individual representations to the Governor about the Administration of Justice Bill, and declined to furnish a joint opinion with the Chief Justice.

The substance of Willis' letter published by the Legislative Council, incorporated remarks he had made from the Bench in *Carr v. Stephen,* further criticizing the Chief Justice's allegedly improper engagement of assigned convicts.[74] Dowling again applied to the Governor for redress, urging that the entire exchange of judicial correspondence be transmitted to the Colonial Office for adjudication.[75] Dowling resented Willis' attempt to portray him as "influenced in his decisions by private and personal considerations" and complained that it was the first time in his judicial career that his integrity had been so called into question.[76] A copy was sent to Willis.

Gipps, anxious not to have to report the matter to Downing Street, insisted that the fault, for the inclusion of the troublesome letter in the Legislative Council papers, was his alone.[77] At the same time, other pressures were obviously being placed on Willis. Leaders of the Bar were against him. Stephen remarked to Dowling, with satisfaction, that "Willis is at last evidently in a *fright*".[78] In that state, there came from Willis something close to an apology to Dowling. "I lament", wrote the former, "the seeming disposition to take offence where none was intended".[79] And, even more surprisingly, Willis waited on the Chief Justice, Stephen being present, and "personally expressed to me [Dowling] his sorrow and regret . . . at having wounded my feelings and given offence. Having tendered his hand in the genuine spirit of conciliation, I accepted it with corresponding emotion".[80] Confirmatory letters of good will were exchanged: Gipps was relieved that the differences seemed at last to be settled.[81] Yet they were not.

Willis rejected all overtures by Dowling to re-establish any private friendship "and he has emphatically limited our communications to mere official business".[82]

For a little while, all were diverted by the news that Burton would soon be back in Sydney. In October 1840, Willis sent a very cheerful note to Dowling, well realizing that its contents would be dispiriting to the recipient. "Have you seen the *Colonial Magazine*[83] for May?", Willis inquired. And then, affecting to be a detached observer and critical of Burton's position, he added:

> If not you *ought* to do so for it seems to me you are placed by our Brother Burton's article in a position that *may* require an answer. I do not think our learned Brother ever was up to the first six Books of Euclid or I think he would have argued somewhat more logically. . . A more *washy* production I have seldom read.[84]

Willis had probably received the publication from Burton himself. Dowling had seen nothing of it, so Willis was delighted to pass on a copy.[85] Burton's article "Observations on the Constitution of the Government of New South Wales", reflected adversely on the constitutional position of the Governor, and was very critical of the "official members" of the Legislative Council. He did not name the Chief Justice, but his remarks, when read by those who would fully understand their import, reflected disapproval of the joint holding of judicial and legislative offices.[86]

Dowling strengthened his resolve, as announced to his son the previous February, to seek two years' leave of absence on Burton's return.[87] As things were to turn out, Willis would frustrate those intentions. In November 1840, Dowling summed up his unhappy relations with two of his three judicial colleagues: "I find Burton is really coming back, which I am sorry for, as he is an unfriend of mine . . . Willis continues the same disagreeable person he always has been . . . here, and I believe, everywhere. I am very happy with Mr Stephen whom I fear I shall lose as a colleague, as I think he is going as resident judge to Port Phillip".[88]

"I Am by No Means Anxious for the Office of Equity Judge"

In the last assumption, Dowling was wrong. Events unfolded very strangely in the final stages of the Willis saga. The grand climax would be precipitated by complaints, agitated by Willis himself, about the conduct of equity business in the Supreme Court. It will be convenient to defer that matter for the moment, and examine yet another cause of dispute between Willis and his colleagues arising out of a Bill enacted in October 1840 for the taking of a colonial census in 1841.

On 2 November, Dowling and Stephen protested to the Governor about parts of the Bill. Their complaint went to the authority proposed to be given to census collectors, to demand whether persons had been transported to the Colony.[89] Considerable latitude was to be allowed to collectors to pursue that inquiry, which Dowling and Stephen thought illegal, degrading, and invasive of privacy, especially when coupled with penalties for refusal to answer or to co-operate. In their joint view, invoking the test in s. 24 of the *Australian Courts Act* 1828, the Act would be repugnant to the laws of England.[90]

As Governor Gipps put it, Willis then "turned out of his way in order to express his dissent".[91] Before the Council had met to consider the protest of his colleagues, he decided to emulate Burton's notorious "charge" to a petty jury.[92] Addressing the jurors at the opening of the Criminal Session,[93] he declared that the Census Bill was perfectly legal. He was less concerned with the Bill than with some supposed injury to his pride in having been excluded from the joint representations of the others. He claimed that he had not seen the joint representation when he addressed the jury.[94] Dowling rejoined that Willis could not deny that he knew of the joint intention and had originally agreed with it.[95] There followed a frenzy of correspondence, concerning this and the Equity Judge question to be noticed shortly, all stimulated by injured vanity and wounded honour. The letters were laid before the Governor. Willis wrote a remonstrance of over 40 manuscript pages – Dowling submitted about half as much.[96] It would be tiresome here to examine the details. Dowling rejected Willis' contention that the dispute was inflamed "by the heat of the present season", and insisted that Willis stood condemned by "his temper, and [by] the spirit, and feeling, which are entertained by His Honour against me".[97] Dowling further told the Governor:

> I must express my extreme surprize and regret, at the fact, now, for the first time discovered to me, that Mr Justice Willis has been in the habitual practice of making disparaging communications privately to Your Excellency respecting me; and these, not merely on matters

> relating to official business, but relating also to my personal and private character, habits, manners and feelings.[98]

Into this poisoned atmosphere had intruded the question of the Equity Judgeship. Willis at last would exceed all bounds of propriety and rationality, and cause his own downfall. For years he had made much of having been bred to the Chancery side of the law. His colleagues were experienced in the Common Law. In his early, wheedling style, he had sought an advantage by protesting that his health was unequal to the stresses of criminal business (which preoccupied so much of the court's time). He would better serve the interests of the public and of himself by remaining in the secluded, and little invoked, areas of equity and probate, coupled with greater responsibilities in the insolvency (bankruptcy) jurisdiction. He claimed that he was:

> so feeble and debilitated from frequent pain in my side (proceeding, it is feared from derangement of the liver) pain which is greatly augmented whenever I sit for any length of time in a crowded Court, that I feel myself almost incapable to discharge my Judicial Duties, especially when under the excitement and anxiety of Criminal and Nisi Prius Proceedings.[99]

Why, it might have been asked, was so incapacitated a judge foisted upon New South Wales, with its judicial resources already much over-stretched?

Moreover, Willis was blatantly disingenuous. The letter, in which he made so much of his alleged debility, was the very one in which he supplicated for a pension. His preoccupation, always with self interest at the expense of public duty, was persistent. Months later he repeated his aversion to the "heat and agitation of a crowded Criminal or Nisi Prius Court", while urging that his duties be limited to the "quiet discharge" of equity business.[100] The Colony had never hitherto had much need for a "Chancery" side to the Supreme Court: Chief Justice Forbes discouraged it.[101] Nor was Willis' timing felicitous as the Colony was already drifting into the deep financial depression of the 1840s that would not conduce to the refinements and delays of Chancery litigation.

The other judges, preoccupied with the court's common law civil and criminal business, humoured Willis by acceding to an informal (and, strictly speaking, irregular)[102] arrangement under which he alone disposed of the more specialized matters that appealed to his temperament. Not content with that, he proceeded publicly to deprecate the professional stature of all Judges of the Supreme Court of New South Wales, past and present, excepting, of course, himself. From this pinnacle of Bumbledom, he proclaimed on the Bench, during an admission ceremony in October 1840, that at his very arrival, "I found the practical proceedings [in equity] a perfect chaos of irregularity; of the orders and decrees which had been made, I shall say nothing more".[103] Privately, he assured the Chief Justice that: "I believed also from the state in which I found the proceedings, and I still believe, that my Brethren, (neither of whom had ever practised in a Court of Equity) were incompetent to perform the duty with credit to themselves or benefit to the public – of this I could easily adduce sufficient proof".[104] To Governor Gipps, he expostulated:

> Was it to be wondered then that being brought up, and practising for the most part of a long professional life in Courts of Equity and Civil Law, I should have discovered *flagrant errors* in the proceedings of those who had never been previously accustomed to this branch of judicature, and therefore could not be expected to know the principles and practice of this Science, as Fortescue . . . very justly calls it, by Inspiration?[105]

So all were out of step, save Willis himself.[106] In his own assessment, he was the only competent person to adjudicate upon such intricate matters in the Colony. That should be recognized by creating a separate Court of Equity for the Colony in which Willis would be Chief Baron. Personalities aside, the Chief Justice was appalled by the expense that would flow from such a proposal.[107]

Willis, who was no tactician, decided, in May 1840, to call everyone's bluff, being convinced that they must capitulate to him. If the equity business of the court were to continue merely as a "matter of arrangement", he would for the future take only a share in it by rotation with the others.[108] Those others, being so inadequate in Willis' fields of experience, must, he supposed, quickly yield. To his surprise, they did not.[109] When, half a year later, he wrote to the Chief Justice, complaining that permanent equity arrangements had yet to be made, he again criticized the past conduct of the judicial business in that department. Dismissively, he added words that would be his undoing, "I assure you that I am by no means anxious for the office of Equity Judge nor will I now take it merely as a *locum tenens*[110] if with decency and a regard to the public service I can avoid it".[111]

"Even a Lamb Will Flinch Against the Knife"

Dowling, who, at the time, was "almost worn out with fatigue",[112] showed that letter to Stephen who came up with a bold suggestion.[113] Stephen himself had drafted, from a model prepared by Willis, the Bill for the *Administration of Justice Act* 1840.[114] Section 20 empowered the Governor to appoint "either the Chief Justice or *if he shall decline*[115] such appointment then one of the puisne judges" to determine all causes or matters in equity. The decision of that judge was to take effect as if a decree or order of the Full Court, subject to an appeal permitted by s. 21. Stephen recalled that, at a meeting of the judges concerning the draft Bill, sections 20 and 21 had been discussed. He had recognized Willis' expectation to be the equity judge, and had made some jocular remark that it would probably be so. Stephen was convinced that, at that time, "the idea of your [Dowling's] taking the office never entered my own mind".[116] Willis insisted that it was "perfectly understood" by all that the Chief Justice "would not accept the Equity Judgeship".[117] Stephen did not recall that the Chief Justice had committed himself one way or the other: Dowling denied that he had undertaken not to accept the office.[118]

Stephen said that, afterwards, when reflecting on the curious wording of s. 20, he offered a "suggestion" to Dowling on the matter – indubitably the suggestion that Dowling not decline the equity appointment.[119] Dowling took the hint and so advised Gipps. The Governor, perplexed, thought that Willis would have been the proper appointee, and was quite prepared to have appointed him, until finding that "the clause was so worded that I could not refuse" to appoint Dowling.[120] "It is due to the Chief Justice to say", wrote Gipps, "that I believe he had not originally any intention of claiming the office, and that he has now done so, in consequence of what he considers the injurious statements of his want of ability to discharge the duties of it, which have been made by Mr Justice Willis".[121]

The Governor's fears, that the public might believe that equity business would not be conducted expertly, had already been fulfilled. Willis' friend, the attorney G.R. Nichols, proprietor and editor of the *Australian*, obliged with an attack on the very day of the appointment. According to the *Australian*, "We believe that His Honour the Chief Justice never practised as an Equity Lawyer, and that he understands about as much of the *principles* of *legal* Equity as one of our printer's "devils". We think the selection very unfortunate".[122] Objections of that kind counted for little: the jurisdiction was a backwater. Nevertheless Willis was vexed at being outmanoeuvred, especially on the basis of the very words he had used in trying to call his colleagues' bluff. As Dowling wrote to the *soi-disant* Chief Baron, "I did myself the honour of waiting upon [the Governor] yesterday, and again pressed the matter on his attention, when he was pleased to signify his pleasure, that I should be appointed [Equity Judge], unless I declined it, which I have not done".[123] Then came the reasons, for Willis most bitter, based as they were on his pretended disinclination to continue with the private arrangement among the judges to leave the equity business to him. "I do not exactly recollect", Dowling wrote:

> how it happened that this duty, which you appeared to have undertaken willingly, devolved upon yourself, but so it did – certainly not from any disinclination on the part of Mr Justice Burton, Mr Justice Stephen or myself to take a full share of equity business, although the amount of it pending was very small compared with other branches of jurisdiction.[124]

Dowling had only delayed bringing the matter before the Governor because he was unsure whether Legislative Council and existing judicial duties would permit him to take the equity burden as well. He had decided not to shrink from the position, he said, as soon as he read the letter of November in which Willis declared himself "by no means anxious for the office".[125] If Dowling found that he could not continue the equity work because of other pressures, the Governor would decide which other judge should be assigned. At the very least, Dowling promised to hold the office until the return of Burton "who, as Senior Puisne Judge might be disposed to accept it".[126]

Willis responded in a rage. "I confess that I am of opinion", he wrote to Dowling, "that a Chief Justice duly qualified by previous study and experience, should exercise this jurisdiction – but I did *not* imagine that one who never I believe, save since his arrival in this Colony, was engaged in any equity proceedings, would have accepted an office so vitally essential in its due performance to the public welfare".[127] If Willis were to sit as a judge of appeal in equity matters, he could not henceforth offer the Chief Justice any private assistance should difficulties arise at first instance – and the proposed savaging by Willis, on appeal, of any decrees made by Dowling, could only be imagined. Willis complained that he had not been treated with the candour due to him, and he requested that the exchange of correspondence be forwarded to the Governor.[128] Dowling at once put himself in touch with Stephen, declaring that, unless he were "better advised" (by Stephen) the time had arrived for taking a stand, and "throwing myself upon the Secretary of State". He wrote, "You know that I am a placable person – but even a lamb will flinch against the knife. I shall see you tomorrow morning, and hear what you have to say".[129] The Chief Justice's heavy reliance on his lieutenant is remarkable. But Stephen's great abilities, in proceedings that fell somewhere between politics and warfare, were outstanding throughout his career. With his perceived family connexions in Downing Street,[130] and his political astuteness in Van Diemen's Land, he came as if a seasoned campaigner to deal with Willis. Had it not been for Stephen's intervention and his determination to quell Willis' antics, the Sydney Bench might have been encumbered with the troublemaker for many years.

Meanwhile Gipps feared to dignify the judicial disagreements with too much notice lest they reflect badly on his administration. Burton, out of the way, probably would have sided with Willis unless in competition with him. Dowling was too weary with worries over the court and too frail in health to do more, without Stephen's support, than be over conciliatory to Willis. Dowling must have seen that concession upon concession, which he had made in the name of peace and harmony, had gone for nothing.[131] The only reasoning Willis understood was that based on firmness and authority. As recently as September 1840, Dowling was still deferring to Willis:

> I personally acknowledge the very large and meritorious share you have taken in the Equity Branch of the Court, and beg to assure you that I shall always be ready to take my turn without flinching, notwithstanding your peculiar aptitude from your professional celebrity while at the English Bar which fits you for equity business, and which is I believe universally acknowledged.[132]

To return to the December discussion, Stephen advised Dowling to ask Gipps, not merely to review the disagreement as Willis had proposed, but to transmit to the Secretary of State all relevant public correspondence between the judges. Dowling, being so persuaded, wrote to Willis, on 5 December, advising him that he had made representations to Gipps the previous day,[133] warning the Governor that the character of the court and the administration of justice risked being prejudiced "by the public character and demeanour of one of the judges".[134]

Over the next week Willis so busied himself with a rearguard action that he could have had scarcely any time for court business. He sought support from members of the colonial Bar. To judge from the response of Attorney-General Plunkett, he could have found little. Plunkett said that he would not be "mixed up in the squabbles of judges".[135] He would not decline giving his opinion at a proper time and place to a proper authority, but he suggested to Willis "the expediency of having no such questions put to him [Plunkett]".

Willis then decided to smother the opposition with words. His manuscript address of over 40 pages to the Governor, sought to vindicate himself. It survives as an overblown, self-serving document, that took nice points of detail at the expense of substance.[136] The broad issues of judicial comity, frankness, pre-eminence of public duty over private dispute, and commitment to supporting the court – all of which had been advanced by Dowling – were little regarded in Willis' remonstrance. Much of his material was personal and defamatory criticism of others. For instance, he selected some high sounding phrases Dowling had written about himself in his letter to the Governor, and attempted to turn them back on the Chief Justice:

> It matters not, I think, how long his Honour has been on the Bench – with what ability has he discharged his duties? and in what estimation is he held by the most respectable portion of the community? seems to me to be more material. Of the recent Honours of which Sir Jas. Dowling boasts, I sincerely wish him the utmost joy: but "Virtue is its own Reward". "Labour and anxiety" [which Dowling applied to the discharge of his judicial duties] are not terms synonymous with talent and reputation.[137]

In this partly rhetorical, partly insinuating, manner, Willis tried, without adducing a scintilla of evidence, to charge the Chief Justice with incompetence and want of public esteem or confidence. Willis' remarks served only to confirm how apt were the complaints made against him.

Gipps was aghast at being asked, as Dowling had persuaded him to do only just over a year before, to agitate such matters again with the Colonial Office.[138] He told the Chief Justice that he would prefer not to act, offering the excuse that the correspondence, being unofficial, had not been preserved in Government House files.[139] Dowling remained insistent. Willis, in any event, foreclosed any other resolution by demanding a thorough colonial investigation. "I trust", wrote Gipps to Lord John Russell:

> Your Lordship will think I have acted discreetly in not acceding to such a request; the only investigation, I could institute, would be one before the Executive Council; but such an investigation, in a case where the personal demeanour of one judge towards another is principally concerned, ought not I think to be instituted without more urgent grounds for it than any as yet exist.[140]

Not content with the Governor's management of the conflict, Willis turned to an English patron, Viscount Morpeth,[141] seeking to solicit "one more, in addition to the very many acts of kindness I have received from you".[142] Willis made it appear that, contrary to the Governor's wishes, accusations were being made against Willis about his public speeches (of which he still felt "rather proud") exposing "the incapacity of a very vulgar, uneducated man, who by accident, I believe, became Chief Justice of this Colony".[143] Willis requested Morpeth to solicit the support of the Secretary of State or, at the least, procure the tabling in the House of Commons of the correspondence. "I have no doubt", wrote Willis jubilantly, "that your Lordship's good offices with Lord John Russell will at once produce all I can desire".[144]

Morpeth passed on the letter to the Colonial Office. It chanced to arrive ahead of Gipps' despatch with the whole array of correspondence. Gairdner, (the officer responsible for New South Wales matters), in answer to the question "What do we know of this?" minuted:

> We know nothing of this, but we know a great deal of the writer. He is one of the weakest men I ever knew so far at least as want of sense and a considerable amount of ability are compatible with each other. He has within my knowledge been ruined three or four times over by sheer vanity and an absurd self-importance, and I have no doubt that he is in a fair way to do the same over again.[145]

Willis, who had told the Chief Justice of his grand moves to have the matter agitated in the House of Commons,[146] could scarcely have realized that his fame had preceded him to the Colonial Office in a manner so contrary to his real intentions. His own intervention had cast the first objective light on a controversy he himself had agitated among all the judges continuously since his arrival in Sydney. The Colonial Office at once perceived the man, not the administration of justice, to be the ill. The question became one of finding a remedy.

"Willis is Playing the Very Devil at Port Phillip"

Section 4 of the *Administration of Justice Act* 1840 empowered the Governor to appoint a Resident Judge at Port Phillip. Dowling feared that Stephen would be sent there,[147] the time having arrived when Dowling, whose remaining life span measured less than four years, desperately needed Stephen's support in Sydney. Stephen, no doubt, considered his own prospects best served by staying there. The question of the administration of justice in Melbourne was discussed inconclusively between all the judges in December 1840.[148]

It was due to Gipps that s. 4 of the 1840 Act was invoked to get Willis out of the way. The news Willis proclaimed, of his privately seeking the endorsement of the Secretary of State, became the catalyst. Gipps, at a meeting with Willis, put to him various courses of action so bluntly, and yet so dextrously, that it was made to appear that Willis had volunteered to go to Port Phillip. "It is due to Mr Justice Willis", the Governor reported, "that he has not only acquiesced in this arrangement, but that he himself proposed it".[149] Even before 1840 closed, Gipps was able to advise Superintendent La Trobe in Melbourne that "Judge Willis is to be your resident Judge – and I believe he will leave Sydney in about a fortnight".[150] It could not have been a very happy New Year for Willis as he moved house, and came to realize that the Secretary of State had expressed his "entire approbation" of the Governor's actions.[151]

The southern climate worked little benefit on the judge's deranged liver and, in his judicial isolation, he quickly reverted to his former ways. His shortness of temper, imperious intolerance and penchant for demonstrations in court, persuaded Melbourne citizens, who then had no theatre, to attend the court house for dramatic entertainment. Dowling wrote to his son, in February

1841, that "Willis is going to Port Phillip as a Resident Judge where I pray he may stick and that I may never see his face again".[152] The second part of the prayer was answered: the first was not. Willis did not "stick" in Melbourne because he made his own continuance in office insupportable. He was opposed by almost all of the legal profession, many litigants left court feeling that they had experienced but a parody of justice, and there was a strong popular demand for his dismissal.[153] As the Chief Justice wrote, "My brother Willis is playing the very devil at Port Phillip and has contrived by his outrageous doings to put the province in a flame".[154] Gipps peremptorily – too peremptorily as it was to turn out – invoked "Burke's Act" to "amove" Willis from office yet again. Bundled off the Bench in June 1843, and consumed by indignation, Willis left the Colony. Dowling reported, in advance of the event, that, "Judge Willis is likely to go to England . . . (with the consent of everybody) and may the ----- go with him, for he has been a curse in my path and has been a source of trouble to all who have come in his way".[155]

In England, Willis defiantly sued Gipps and won a hollow victory before the Privy Council, which declared that his "amoval" was void.[156] He had been denied natural justice in not being given any opportunity to consider or respond to the charge made against him. Nevertheless, his judicial career was over and the Colonial Office offered him no new position. As Dr C.H. Currey summed up the result, "Unfortunately for Willis, his tongue was more disturbing to his peace than his liver. Its unbridled and rasping use deprived him of the very work for which he was best fitted and would otherwise have been given".[157]

The place at Port Phillip, involuntarily vacated by Willis, next caused the Chief Justice some anxiety. In contrast to his enforced association with Willis, Dowling had established a working relationship, based politeness not on friendship, with Burton. In August 1841 the Chief Justice observed that "Judge Burton and I agree very well".[158] Gipps proposed that Burton go to Melbourne as successor to Willis. The Chief Justice demurred, realizing that Burton would hate being in a backwater. Gipps wrote:

> The person who is to succeed Mr Willis is Mr Jeffcott[159] who arrived in Sydney only in January last. He is a man of mature age, very quiet, and I hope prudent in his demeanour, *though an Irishman* . . . I was fully prepared to insist on Mr Justice Burton's going to

> Melbourne – but in consequence of the representations of the C. Justice, the Ex. Council decided that it would be better to send Mr Jeffcott – first because he is entirely free from all admixture in the dissentions or party politics of the Colony: and secondly because Actions may be brought against Mr Willis at Melbourne which Mr Justice Burton would scarcely be a fit person to try.[160]

Urged on by restless ambition, Burton continued to supplicate for preferment commensurate with his own exaggerated impression of his status. In 1844 his efforts achieved his translation to the Bench at Madras[161] – an appointment carrying prestige, high remuneration and a knighthood. Burton, who did not last in India, but eventually returned to New South Wales, miscalculated yet again. Had he gone to Port Phillip, it must have been more likely than not that he would become the first Chief Justice of Victoria. And, as earlier mentioned, had he stayed only a few months longer in New South Wales, he would almost certainly have succeeded to the Chief Justiceship of that Colony on Dowling's death in September 1844. Impatience and misreckoning thus conspired to deny Burton the position, he had so much coveted, as the head of a judicial Bench.

8

"A Victim to Scrupulous Anxiety"

"A Certain Monosyllable Attached to Your Name"

Thomas Callaghan,[1] a young Irish barrister admitted in 1839 to the Sydney Bar, and destined to be a foundation Judge of the District Courts in New South Wales, kept a diary for some years after his arrival in the Colony. On 25 March 1841 he reported in it his doings for the day, including attending at the Supreme Court when Chief Justice Dowling presided at the swearing in, to the acting offices of Attorney-General and Solicitor-General respectively, of Roger Therry and William a'Beckett.[2] Callaghan, soured by the slow progress and mean income he was then making at the Bar, confided very harsh assessments of men and affairs to his diary. He found the swearing in "an amusing scene", criticized irregularities he noticed in the court dress of the participants, and concluded that "the Chief Justice seemed anxious to assume the dignity of a Chief Justice if he could".[3]

While coloured, as much of his diary was, Callaghan's observations on the Chief Justice contain particles of truth. Dowling always felt a need to look equal to his judicial part, for which he feared his background denied him the best credentials. He had no classical education: the humanities were, to him, a sealed book. He had none of the ease in colonial administration that his predecessor as Chief Justice (Forbes) and his successor (Alfred Stephen) brought to their offices through experience in Atlantic colonies. Dowling often felt insecure as a judge. He need not have done so. His practice as a barrister had been at least equal to that of J.L. Pedder who had moved so easily from obscurity at the English Bar to the first Chief Justiceship of Tasmania. Moreover,

Dowling's celebrity as a law reporter quite eclipsed Pedder's reputation.

Still, Dowling reproached himself that he could never bring to the Bench the same qualities of intellectual and juristic dominance the Colony had already seen in Chief Justice Forbes. Dowling had different attributes as a remarkable court administrator and as a meticulous legal mechanic. But, try as he might, he could never make title to outstanding excellence as a lawyer. Hence his need, as witnessed by Callaghan, to reassure himself, shore up his status, and prove himself to the colonial community, by giving great emphasis to show, ceremony and appearance. As the *Sydney Morning Herald* recalled, "He was a Judge of the old school; whose wig was always powdered, and who paid a most rigid attention not only to the duties but also to the punctilios of his office. He did not . . . display any extraordinary acuteness as a lawyer, but he was an able man, nevertheless, and his industry has never been surpassed".[4]

Sir Francis Forbes had needed none of Dowling's preferences for mere ceremony. It mattered not to him that there be the slightest pomp or outward affectation in conducting his court. He could, by his powerful presence, control a court without the need even for the wearing of traditional English judicial costume. He could open court sittings with dignity but without the need for rhetoric or public display. He could, as he did in Newfoundland, deliver to grand juries charges that were direct, practical and concise. His public utterances, whether in his judgments or other pronouncements, had Georgian qualities of austerity, balance and reason.

Dowling, on the other hand, spoke discursively and didactically. His addresses were of the Victorian style, being over-ornate and confusing in their intricacy. He liked to give public addresses though he was but a poor public speaker. The result was a hybrid, partaking partly of a lecture and partly of a homily, and being invariably dull. Those addresses raised barely a spark of public interest, in contrast to the conflagrations that could be provoked by Burton or Willis in their ill-considered "charges" to juries.[5]

There were many instances of Dowling's sense of occasion, going back to a series of sittings of the Supreme Court by adjournment from Sydney to outer centres in 1829.[6] Chief Justice Forbes modestly managed the sittings at Campbelltown, agreeing to be received only by a guard of honour of four troopers bearing drawn swords.[7] Mr Justice John Stephen's comparable sitting at Windsor was even more restrained.[8] But Dowling's attendance at Maitland was made into a truly grand occasion with all the trappings of an English assize.[9] The press roundly criticized such extravagance, particularly at "a juncture when the Colony is not in a condition to pay its own debts".[10] Poor Forbes, whose intentions in proposing the adjourned sittings were to save public expense, was castigated by Governor and Secretary of State alike (the latter on quite unreasonable grounds) because nearly £400 had been expended in those three adjourned sittings.[11]

Maitland, however, seems to have been regarded as a special case and, notwithstanding the expense, Dowling went back there, in April 1830, to clear an accumulation of criminal business. At these "assizes", as the press still called them, Dowling persisted with the attendant ceremony, and delivered another pretentious address. In the latter he lauded the zeal of the magistracy and the ability of the colonial police forces. He believed that, notwithstanding the need for his second visitation, serious crime in the Hunter River region was in decline, and he congratulated the community that, despite torrential rain "and the almost impassible [*sic*] state of the rivers", a "highly respectable" and numerous attendance of citizens had appeared to show their support for the regional administration of the King's justice: "Indicating, as this attendance does, a strong desire not only to cherish those rooted attachments for which the subjects of His Majesty are distinguished in every quarter of the globe, but also an ambition, by example and influence, to strengthen and harmonize those bonds of society".[12] Dowling heaped praise upon the Governor, whose "deep interest" in the country community was exemplified in his anxiety to save public money by "bringing justice to the very doors of the settlers" and at the same time provided a "powerful check" on local crime. Such an instalment of wise gubernatorial influence could well be enhanced by the construction of a more serviceable road to the Hunter district and the building of a secure and suitable gaol. It was not, of course, the Governor's fault that these essential measures were delayed.[13]

In 1842, then elevated as Chief Justice, Dowling presided again at Maitland with "excusable exultation",[14] not least because his taste for formal circuit courts (not merely sittings by adjournment) had won favour with the government.[15] These visitations of the judges to country communities would continue as a significant part of the regional administration of justice for the remainder of the 19th century and beyond.

Only the year before, he had applied himself with similar ceremony to the opening of an "assize" sitting at Bathurst. Although he urged all present to "proceed to the despatch of business in a frame of mind befitting this solemn occasion", he must severely have wearied their attention with a long "charge" that lacked eloquence or substance, and, by his own admission, must have been "thought to have exceeded the bounds properly limited to this occasion". It cannot have been of much consolation to his auditory, after 30 minutes of this, to know that the Chief Justice felt "assured of the devoted attachment of her Majesty's loyal subjects in this district to those principles of action which distinguish the British character all over the world".[16]

While the legal profession and the public generally regarded the Chief Justice's preference for display and verbosity as overdone, it was habitual as it was characteristic of his notions of how justice should be administered. It bolstered his sense of the dignity and importance of his office, of which the community, he thought, needed constant reminder.

Another instance of Dowling's preoccupation with ceremony was the part he played in establishing the wearing of traditional court dress, or modifications of it, in the Supreme Court. Enough has been said about that matter elsewhere.[17] At least in this, his divergence from Forbes' preferences matched the inclination of immigrant barristers from England or Ireland, that the courts in all their aspects be modelled on the superior courts "at home".

In April 1839 Dowling received news of having been appointed Knight Bachelor.[18] Although he affected to make light of the distinction, and to protest that his own modest self was unchanged, the acknowledgement was one he had craved and in which he rejoiced. The title crowned his sense that tokens of public recognition reinforced his official position, and rewarded his life's course of diligence and effort in the public interest. The coveted accolade had been hard won, sharing all the vicissitudes of Dowling's battle to be preferred as Chief Justice. When Vincent Dowling had first written to tell brother James that he had triumphed in the battle (that is, before the Colonial Office changed its mind about the appointment)[19] it had seemed that a knighthood would be only a matter of form. Vincent advised that a letter of request and payment of the necessary fees and duties would suffice to have "a certain monosyllable attached to your name".[20]

But James Dowling was obliged to be patient before he could become Sir James and, even when the Chief Justiceship was securely his, the accolade was not a matter of course. In those days, supplication for the dignity had to be made. Pleading his "utter ignorance in these matters", Dowling wrote to Glenelg in July 1838, trusting that:

> I will not be deemed presumptuous if I indulge the ambition of being raised to the honour of Knighthood, as a suitable distinction to the office, however slight the pretensions may be of its present possessor . . . [and] however personally and privately, I might, from the unpretending habits of my life, deem such a favour not desirable.[21]

It would, nevertheless, be appropriate that his office be recognized, he submitted, when knighthoods had been conferred upon all the East India judges, the Chief Justice at the Cape, and those of many other colonies – including, latterly, Sir Francis Forbes. Dowling's efforts in self-effacing humility were transparently insincere.

Glenelg saw no obstacle to the appointment, save a reassurance that someone would pay the fees and duties (£225) on the letters patent.[22] Loyal Vincent Dowling instantly put up that significant sum on his brother's behalf. The gazettal of the ensuing knighthood was all but ignored by Sydney's newspapers.[23] Perversely, the short-lived *Sydney Standard* offered editorial panegyrics on Burton (departing for England) in several issues at the material time, but published not one word about Sir James Dowling.[24]

In reporting his new distinction to his son, Sir James wrote that outward trappings did not alter his affected modesty – "no one shall reproach me with forgetfulness of myself" – yet he was demonstrably elated at being:

> now raised, from my humble beginnings, to the highest grade in my profession. . . The news created a great sensation here, and I have been most cordially congratulated on the event in all quarters. Even the newspapers, which are not wont to say many *civil* things of me, have been warm in their expressions of satisfaction that the honour had been, as they say, meritoriously conferred.[25]

His imaginings must surely have possessed him, given the studious silence of the press on the subject. It was, however, of greater importance to him that no obstruction to the knighthood had been offered at Downing Street. After all that had gone before, he felt that at least he was not ill thought of there. He was contemptuous of those who previously declined to recognize James Dowling, but who suddenly found in Sir James a person whose society was to be cultivated. He wrote:

> It is astonishing how *greatness* brings a man into notice. Many "how do you do?" acquaintances have . . . addressed me in the most endearing terms of regard – people who would scarcely touch me with the tongs when I was a drudging barrister, and a newspaper man. Plain James Dowling was not acknowledged, but when the same humble individual becomes "the Honourable Sir James Dowling, Knt" . . . his friends become wondrous retentive of the most ordinary recollection. So much for the *world*! God knows, promotion has not in the least altered my nature.[26]

Dowling may have convinced himself that he had not changed. But the reality was quite the opposite. It fitted exactly with his pretensions and his need, as he saw it, to reinforce the Chief Justiceship with distinctions that made the then incumbent seem to be a greater figure than he really was.

"Old Blowhard"

While Dowling's predilections for the ways of the Inns of Court and Westminster Hall made him suspicious of the fused legal profession he found on arriving in Sydney, initiatives for change did not come from him. Too preoccupied with his duties, he left it to his brother judge Burton, and to Wentworth and Wardell of the Bar, to press for the profession's separation.[27] Retaining an English barrister's disdain for those calling themselves attorneys or solicitors, he was horrified to receive a letter from his son, James Sheen, then reading for the law in London, written on the note-paper of an East End attorney's office – at which establishment he was seeking experience in practice. "You must understand", remonstrated the father, "that I am not very anxious that you should apply much of your time to the *mere practice* of an attorney's office".[28] Such a course would tend to fetter the mind and make young James unfit for the profession's higher grade.

More distressing was the discovery that James Sheen had struck up a companionship with a common law clerk in that attorney's office. Sir James thought such a thing an abdication of decorum: "the association with such a gentleman cannot tend to elevate the tone of your own feelings or give you that sort of *stamp*, which I deem necessary to your successful *currency* in the profession of a Barrister, which imports freedom from the sordid sympathies of an Attorney's office in the East End".[29]

Despite asserting that he had "not a particle of ostentation or vain glory",[30] Sir James could be snobbish, superior and overbearing when dealing with subordinates – not least solicitors. There was a double edge to his private remark, made late in 1836, when George John Rogers,[31] Second Clerk of the Supreme Court, relinquished that office to enter practice as a solicitor, "Little Rogers has resigned his berth in the Supreme Court . . . I believe I must appoint little Bradley in his place".[32] Writing directly to Rogers, the Chief Justice cloaked his condescension, regretting that the court would lose the services of one "who has done so much credit to his appointment". Nevertheless, the testimonial was to be understood to be uninfluenced by the "private and personal regard I have had for you from your earliest infancy".[33]

Henry Burton Bradley[34] was noticed diminutively, for he was a nephew of Mr Justice Burton who had supported his original appointment as Third Clerk and now urged his advancement to succeed Rogers. For such reasons, the Chief Justice reminded Bradley, "mere seniority gives no right of succession in the Supreme Court".[35] The holders of ministerial office had to demonstrate competence and efficiency in order to progress. But Dowling accepted that Bradley deserved advancement "on the higher ground of merit". Burton, while recognizing that the promotion was not a personal compliment to himself, offered Dowling his "cordial thanks" for his "unhesitating adherence to the only correct principles upon which such an appointment could be made".[36] By October 1840, when, relying on his position as Second Clerk, Bradley sought and was granted admission as a solicitor, Dowling, at least in public, was expansive. He declared from the Bench that he had "never known a more diligent, active, and zealous young gentleman connected with any of the departments of the court".[37]

Behind the scenes, the Chief Justice's loftiness stood fast. In 1841 yet another shuffle in the ministerial offices was made on the retirement of the Chief Clerk, John Gurner.[38] He had held the office, more or less continuously since the Supreme Court opened in 1824. Being passed over, in 1840, for the office of Master to which he aspired, Gurner secured his admission as a solicitor and, in 1841, went into partnership with the Sydney practitioner William Minithorpe. While Dowling publicly praised Gurner,[39] he wrote less flatteringly to James Sheen Dowling, "Old Gurner has resigned the office of Chief Clerk in the Supreme Court and I have been obliged to promote little Bradley to his berth".[40] If he were so sparing of private praise for those who did well, his public condemnation of those found to have polluted the stream of justice was the more pronounced. Even so, despite his low estimation of solicitors, very few disciplinary cases came before the court at that time.[41] Almost to the end of his days, Dowling remained convinced that attorneys and solicitors in the Colony were not merely the lower branch of the profession, but also that they were "with very few exceptions, . . . very ignorant men".[42]

In public, though, he gave little hint of those depreciatory opinions. Rather, in his final year as an *ex officio* Member of the Legislative Council, he spoke up for the solicitors' branch in the Colony. That was remarkable because Dowling rarely addressed the Council on controversial matters, and more rarely still in opposition to the Governor. On this occasion, Gipps, in an address to the House on a Court of Requests Bill,[43] criticized solicitors and their methods of practice in New South Wales. Although he had "no wish whatever to set the attorneys up in array against himself", Gipps spoke his mind: "If attorneys were admitted [as advocates in the Courts of Requests], much more time would be occupied and the expenses of the courts thereby greatly increased; for where the court would dispose of ten cases with the assistance of attorneys, he had no doubt they would be able to dispose of fifty cases without attorneys".[44] He particularly censured their practices as to fees, concluding that "it must be a fine thing to be an attorney". He singled out what he regarded as a blatant instance of avarice, perhaps not appreciating that the subject of his criticism was the highly respected solicitor, George Allen.[45] Dowling was immediately on his feet to defend "a name which could never be mentioned without honour". The Governor, he maintained, had fallen into an error stimulated by, "the disposition which appeared to be growing on the community to run down lawyers, to cry them down as pests to society, heaping charges upon them which were not fair or capable of being sustained, – which were not founded in truth".[46] Having said which, he perversely showed little enthusiasm for the Courts of Requests or for the appearance in them of the Colony's solicitors. He deprecated the courts' summary procedure as precluding trial by jury and appeals.[47] The new courts, which did not long survive, were virtually absorbed by the District Courts. Meanwhile the Courts of Requests attracted much public support because of their cheapness and expedition in disposing of minor litigation.

Although Dowling himself did nothing to promote the ultimate outcome, this difference of opinion between the Governor and himself had a seminal and lasting effect on the Colony's solicitors as a body. For the first time a sense of corporate concern for the profession was aroused, leading to meetings from which emerged the Sydney Law Library Society.[48] From its hesitant beginnings, societies representing solicitors would come to be formed and emulated throughout Australia.

Another remarkable instance, in which Dowling's public stance conflicted with his private estimation of solicitors, is his judgment in *Ex parte Nichols*,[49] delivered in October 1839. George Robert Nichols,[50] first native-born Australian to be admitted as a solicitor in New South Wales, had been well pleased with the "fused" profession originally operating under the Third Charter of Justice. He practised very successfully as a solicitor-advocate at Quarter Sessions and in the magistrates' courts. His claim, to a personal dispensation from the separation of the profession, provoked the rift between Dowling and Willis noticed earlier.[51]

In 1839 Nichols moved the Full Supreme Court for relief by *mandamus* to compel magistrates to permit him to represent clients charged with criminal offences. In England, such representation had been settled by the *Prisoners' Counsel Act* 1836 (6 & 7 *Will.* IV *c.* 114), the effect of which was to give any person brought before justices on a summary charge the right to be represented by barrister or solicitor. In the Colony, the common law, as recently enunciated in *Collier v. Hicks*[52] (a decision displaced in England by the 1836 Act), was that, without the permission of the Bench, no person could appear as an advocate in criminal trials before justices. The colonial Supreme Court had to decide whether to adapt the law to the English statutory reform or abide by the common law precedent.

Mr Justice Alfred Stephen, still a relative newcomer to the Bench, dissented from his colleagues. In his view, the common law prevailed, because the 1836 Act did not extend to the Colony by express terms: and if it were to extend constructively, there would be no reason to exclude other domestic Acts of the United Kingdom.[53] "The Court", he protested, "will thus have opened a flood-gate, through which, I fear, there will . . . be let in upon us, without preparation or the time for preparation, a host of enactments". Nevertheless he was pleased to see the law changed, agreed that *mandamus* should go to the magistrates, and was gratified "as an individual" that the English statutory reform would be adopted, "because he was sure that it would be in every way favourable to the ends of justice".[54] Equally remarkable was the concurrence of opinion by Dowling and Willis in favour of the reform. Dowling rarely strayed from literal and narrow interpretations of the law. On those canons of construction, Stephen, J., must have been right: though his fears were not in fact realized. Dowling's reading of the troublesome s. 24 of the *Australian Courts Act* 1828,[55] as to the reception of English law in Australia, was surprisingly liberal on this occasion and formed an exception to the general rule that the cut-off date for the reception of purely English enactments in the Colony (if they met the tests for reception) was the date of the passing of the Act (in this case 28 July 1828).[56] The result, extraordinarily lucky for G.R. Nichols, is doubly odd, given that one would have expected Dowling, acting consistently, to have preferred caution to radical law reform and to have been unwilling to add to the stature of the attorneys.

In Dowling's view, an exception could be justified because the Secretary of State had expressly instructed Governor Bourke to cause the *Prisoners' Counsel Act* to be adopted in the Colony.[57] The problem was, that the intention behind those instructions had not been fulfilled. The instructions were that Bourke "take measures for extending to the Colony under your Government" the provisions of the 1836 Act.[58] A colonial Bill had been prepared, but shelved, in New South Wales: an identical Bill had been passed in Tasmania. Dowling decided that the way was open for judge-made law in New South Wales: "Although the Repealing Act has not been adopted in this Colony, it appears to me that we are not now fettered by a decision which is no longer law, and that we are at liberty to decide this question upon principle, and as if no such decision had ever been made".[59] It followed that the colonial judges were not to "shut their eyes" to an Act of the Parliament at Westminster, passed since 1828, which had a direct bearing on the principles in issue.[60] The principles, he said, were these:

> The right of being heard by counsel, it is not disputed, is inherent in every party amenable to the jurisdiction of superior Courts of Justice, and was only limited until lately in Criminal Courts, to the extent of restraining the advocate from addressing the jury on the evidence. The temperate and orderly proceedings of every tribunal obviously require the concession of this privilege, independently of the higher considerations of impartial justice. I am unable to discover any sound reason for making any distinction in principle between a superior and an inferior court, in the all important duty of administering justice.[61]

There was, in his view, so much the less reason for the distinction in the magistrates' courts of New South Wales where, in outlying districts, the advantages of professional assistance would facilitate their functions.

Dowling probably thought that the adoption of the *Prisoners' Counsel Act* would expand the role of the colonial Bar, rather than cater specifically to the ambitions of Nichols. At any rate, he persisted with his private disesteem of local attorneys until being shamed into almost a death-bed repentance. Forced to stand down from the Bench in a state of mortal exhaustion in August 1844, it was plain to all that he would never return to his judicial duties. Sixty-four of the Colony's attorneys, the name of James Norton at their head, caused a touching address to be delivered to "Brougham Place". The address said the expected things about the recipient's "uniform courtesy and impartiality" but did not dwell on platitude. "We desire especially to bear our testimony on more general and public grounds", they wrote. And they acknowledged:

> the unflinching exertions and anxious solicitude for the accomplishment of the ends of justice which have characterised the whole of your Honor's career in this colony; a degree of exertion and solicitude which no ordinary vigour of constitution could have so long sustained without exhaustion and to which alone we cannot for a moment doubt is to be attributed the illness which now unfortunately demands a suspension of those labours.[62]

Mollified, Dowling responded that the document "has not failed of the effect so obviously intended, and I accept with deep emotion this affectionate address".[63] It was timely that he had come to have a better regard for the attorneys – just over a month later he died.

With the colonial Bar, Dowling aspired, not always successfully, to make common cause. He accepted only their number – aside from the judges – as his professional peers. To him, the humblest barrister by call in England or Ireland towered in status over even the most seasoned of colonial solicitors. Hence he persisted in his view, with which Attorney-General Plunkett and some other lawyers agreed, that colonially educated youths were too poorly qualified to be granted admission to the colonial Bar.[64] For battling, briefless barristers from "home", Dowling had abundant regard and sympathy.[65] Ample evidence of his adopting a role like that of a paternal schoolmaster appears in the diary of Thomas Callaghan, the young Irish barrister already mentioned.[66]

While acknowledging that Dowling "was very kind to me", Callaghan showed a contrary gratitude by often referring to the Chief Justice, in his diary, as "Blowhard", "Old Blowhard", or even, quite undeservedly, "the old dotard".[67] The "Blowhard" *sobriquet* recognized Dowling's tetchy temper on the Bench and the effects of his declining health. As he did with most young newcomers to the Bar, Dowling occasionally called on Callaghan at his lodgings to offer encouragement[68] – "He advised me", wrote Callaghan, "if I were idle not to seem idle and if I were poor not to seem poor: I have hopes still". Dowling stimulated those hopes by seeing that briefs in criminal cases were assigned to young barristers to give them a start.[69]

For those established at the Bar, Dowling was a regular convener of dinners, many of them held at "Brougham Place"; and he religiously attended return functions at the homes of leaders of the Bar. Burton and Stephen went along with this show of *camaraderie.* But not Willis. As Dowling wrote to that gentleman in May 1840:

> I propose giving a dinner to the Bar next week and have foreborne sending you any invitation, not from want of respect, but really in consequence of an intimation given me in conversation last week, that you decline all invitations of the kind, except to Government House. I recollect also that you declined a similar invitation to meet Mr Justice Stephen and the Bar last year.[70]

Dowling dropped in at meetings of the Bar that were occasionally convened on matters of common interest, but won little friendship there. Callaghan recorded Dowling's attendance at a Bar gathering on New Year's day in 1841, and "when he [Dowling] retired they were all laughing and sneering at him: he in some degree deserves it: for in many respects he is a nasty old man".[71] At that time there continued a rift, between the Chief Justice and seniors of the Bar, over his part in sponsoring the promotion of Alfred Stephen to the Bench over local heads.[72] Those displaced by Stephen knew that their Chief Justice had, in effect, expressed his lack of confidence in their prospective abilities as judges. Felicitous though Dowling's championship of Stephen may have been for the Colony, it did less than justice to some Bar leaders who were abundantly competent to serve on the Bench. That was the reason for the Bar's "sullenness" expressed to his face,[73] and the belittling of him behind his back that Callaghan so frankly described. Questions of protocol were, no doubt, debated vigorously out of court concerning the propriety of a Chief Justice's not merely involving himself in the nomination of a likely successor but becoming an active partisan in his nominee's cause.

In a profession where things said by lawyers in private about other lawyers tend to diverge considerably from things similarly said or done in public, the Colony's lawyers affected a touching *rapprochement* later in 1841. "Blowhard", constantly handicapped by illness brought on by driving himself too hard in his judicial labours, had surrendered to such "severe indisposition" by April that he could not be in court for some weeks.[74] On his return, there was a spontaneous gesture of good will:

> On the instant of Sir James Dowling entering the Court, the bar and attorneys simultaneously rose from their seats, and by this mark of special attention endeavoured to testify their congratulation on His Honour's recovery from ill health and return to that seat of which he is so great an ornament.[75]

Those public pleasantries aside, the Bar had come to find the Chief Justice difficult when presiding in court. Long years of conflict with Burton and with Willis, and the ever growing burdens of the court lists and judicial administration, conspired with his frail health to make the Chief Justice temperamental. There was regular newspaper comment on the "warmth" or "hotness" of his judicial style, though some of the comment was self-serving.[76] Thus Hall's

Monitor, in March 1829, taunted, "What has often astonished us in His Honour Judge Dowling is, that even when sitting with his coadjutors *in Banco* he declares his oral opinion with warmth, as if he were in a state of perpetual irritation".[77] The repetition by journalists of their impressions of such "warmth" suggests that they were founded in truth.[78] Evidence to the contrary is less convincing. James Sheen Dowling considered that his father, as a judge, "was of a very happy and jovial disposition",[79] but had no qualification to say so.[80] J.S. Dowling left Sydney when aged about 17 and never saw his father again. He could scarcely form any independent view. On the other hand, his elder brother, Vincent,[81] who briefly served his father in the Supreme Court, corroborated the latter's prickly disposition on and off the Bench. He wrote, "I am still my Father's Clerk and come in for the usual blowings up which cannot be helped but there is an old saying money pays for a broken head . . . I am like the Cobbler – I grin . . . and remember it cannot last forever".[82]

Sir Roger Therry, in a guarded recollection of Sir James, remarked that Dowling, as Chief Justice, displayed "the most considerate regard for the feelings of others" and "enjoyed without intermission, great popularity, during his whole judicial career".[83] The contemporary Bar would not unreservedly have concurred. Therry wrote probably of Dowling's social popularity and of his usual demeanour towards witnesses in court.[84] Dowling was less considerate when engaged in argument with counsel. Significantly, the members of the Bar who signed what was effectively a valedictory address to Dowling not long before his death, testified to his "untiring zeal and anxious solicitude", his "indefatigable industry", his "pure and unquestioned impartiality" and his "urbanity",[85] but stopped short of acknowledging the sense of fraternity between Bench and Bar that Dowling had striven to promote.[86]

The eulogy delivered from the Bench by Mr Justice Alfred Stephen, shortly after Dowling's death, was precisely that. It is not in the nature of such forms of praise that any faults of the deceased are made prominent. Moreover, Stephen was greatly beholden to Dowling. Even so, there was a veiled remark recognizing that Dowling's court room deportment was not always unruffled. Stephen asserted that, for the good will and respect shown to him, Dowling had been indebted "less to courtesy of manner, though in this not deficient, than to a conciliatoriness of disposition, and genuine goodness of heart".[87] Stephen continued that the late Chief Justice had been, "Accessible at all times, a patient listener, careful to ascertain every fact, and ready to hear every argument, which might be thought to bear on the case before him, he never failed to make himself its master, in every detail".[88] All would readily have concurred in the latter part of that statement. The extent of Dowling's patience in conducting court proceedings is rather the moot point. The better conclusion, on balancing the evidence, is that Chief Justice Dowling did not have an equable temper on the Bench: nor were his celebrated attempts at humour always well intentioned or well received. He could be sardonic in his persistent puns, and some of his witticisms were at the expense of parties who could not respond or who felt demeaned by jokes made against them.

Thus Callaghan recorded indignantly in his diary for 29 June 1841 that he had attended a Government House ball. He wrote: "On the side of the Vice-regal pair 'Old Blowhard' somewhat good-naturedly held out his hand and jocously welcomed me as 'one of his Children in Law'".[89] Willis had latched on to the Chief Justice's penchant for the pun and other jests to declaim against the injury it allegedly caused to decorum and propriety in court.[90] There were times when Dowling went so far as to display insensitivity. The *Australian* early took him to task on such an occasion, objecting to his retort to counsel's submission that a plaintiff had been hanged before he could commence his action:

> Mr Justice Dowling – "I *cannot take judicial* KNOWLEDGE" that the plaintiff was hanged. (Laughter)
>
> Counsel – Then, your Honour, I must call witnesses to that fact.
>
> "I cannot take JUDICIAL *knowledge*!! "[91]

The *Australian* concluded that this added "another strong proof to the many on record, that an intemperate expression may betray hotness of temper even in a Judge".[92]

If the interpretation here offered has correctly weighed the evidence, it must be said in fairness to Sir James Dowling, that a long course of judicial precedent was in sympathy. Very vigorous, sometimes venomous, exchanges have been the stock in trade of forensic argument in some courts since time immemorial. If Dowling followed that pattern, there was abundant provocation offered to him to have warranted it. But in no case, excepting perhaps the wild allegations of the recalcitrant Hall, was it seriously suggested that even strenuous jousts between Dowling, as a judge, and counsel in court ever led to an ill-considered judgment or any other related miscarriage of justice.

"A Subject of Disagreeable Excitement"

The attainment of trial by jury, in its most complete form, in the Supreme Court of New South Wales, was strung out over a generation, albeit the generation in which the foundation class distinctions of the Colony – between emancipist and exclusive – were worn down by attrition. There are published studies, by the present writer and others, on the history of trial by jury in New South Wales.[93] They displace any need to travel the same path here. The circumstances in which Chief Justice Forbes construed the *New South Wales Act* to permit of juries at Quarter Sessions have also been discussed amply.[94] Forbes' commitment to conventional juries, in place of the seven officers of the armed forces in criminal cases and two civilian assessors in civil matters, set him at odds with the exclusives who did not want the administration of justice entrusted to those who had been, or were the children of, convicts.

In that climate of antipathy, Dowling's views on the jury were at first ambivalent. "Coming fresh from England, with all my prejudices in favour of the jury system", he revealed to Lord Brougham,[95] "I was sufficiently impressed with the novelty of a jury composed of seven military officers in the Crown Court, and of two magistrates called assessors and the judge himself (also a juror) on the *nisi prius* or civil side". "As far as my observation has extended", he continued, "this apparently anomalous system works well in practice, and in candour I cannot but say that if the colony were expected not to make any progression in the scale of improvement, the system would not be ill-adapted to this infant country".[96] If, however, greater plans were held for the Colony's future, he conceded that democratic institutions must guarantee the settlement's rising prosperity, coupled with education, especially of the convict-derived portion of the community, in the workings of the English legal system.

Experience attracted him to Forbes' perceptions of the unfair and inadequate methods of trial imposed on the Supreme Court since its opening in 1824. Particularly objectionable was the lack of enthusiasm by military men and civilian assessors, alike, for court duties. For the officers it was such a tiresome distraction from their proper military functions, that some behaved like mischievous schoolboys while in the jury box. An aggravated incident came to light in 1830 when a criminal trial before Stephen was followed next day by a civil action before Dowling.[97] The assessors, occupying the same jury box as that used by the officers in the criminal proceedings, found scratched on the desk tops in front of them messages intended to insult the assessors, the court and the administration of justice itself. The assessors, by medium of counsel in court, revealed these inscriptions to Dowling. One read:

> Of all the humbugs in this humbugging world, the most detestable is to sit for hours in a blackguard Botany Bay jury-box, on the same seats that have been polluted by the canaille (Anglice, 'mancipists), listening to the prosing blunders of a superannuated old wig.[98]

Dowling ordered that the desks be removed and that Crown Law Officers seek out and deal with the culprits. He delivered a severe criticism of "so scandalous an infraction of public decency". In this he had been encouraged by the Chief Justice who wrote to him, "We must carry our hands with exact equipoise – and if the gentlemen of the military profession, who are by law to adjudge libellers, are to become themselves libellers, and to select the Court as the arena of their performances, why then we had better shut up the Court".[99] The early historian Roderick Flanagan concluded that the incident attracted so much publicity as to hasten, rather than defer, reform of jury trial.[100]

Dowling had also experienced assessors in civil cases treating the proceedings with contempt. In 1828, for example, he was obliged to adjourn the court when the assessors, nominated to sit that day, failed to appear. He condemned their misconduct and the "careless and slovenly attendance of many upon Court business".

> The Court is fully aware that the duty of an assessor is very onerous; but at the same time, when the vast importance of the office is considered, and how deeply the civil justice of the Country is concerned in the gratuitous and independent assistance of gentlemen of mercantile experience and substance, in the department of the

> Supreme Court, the Court regrets deeply that any backwardness should be manifested in serving the office.[101]

All this, however, was forgotten two years later when Dowling gave his heroic address to the first special jury empanelled under then recent legislation superseding assessors in some cases. The judge then declared that "the anxiety of our duties on this side of the Court has been greatly mitigated and considered by the intelligence, experience, and upright integrity of those gentlemen upon whom the duties of assessors have been devolved".[102]

That was one of the few cases in which Dowling gave public form to his private views on jury trial. He developed sweeping generalisations in the ponderous prose he habitually used. In this, his first address to a colonial jury, he proclaimed that form of administering justice to be "coeval with the most ancient institutions of Britain":

> In the progressive advancement of this remote settlement of the British Crown in the scale of Colonial importance, it is not possible to regard with indifference an event so interesting in the annals of the southern hemisphere. Accustomed as I have been from earliest infancy to reverence as holy, all the institutions of my native land, I cannot refrain, as a man, from congratulating you gentlemen upon the inoculation of this great southern continent with an institution – the proudest, the most useful, the most venerated of all that the freest nation on earth can boast.[103]

He proceeded thus for a quarter of an hour, building to an almost religious peroration: "Keeping your hearts and minds in the knowledge and love of truth and justice, I invoke you to enter upon the discharge of your duties, in a frame and temper of disposition, which shall render this mode of trial beneficial to this community, and its determinations respected by all mankind".[104]

The status of jury trial, as an existing or prospective colonial institution, again arose when, in the proceedings by *ex officio* information against the newspaper publishers Hayes and Hall,[105] the defence counsel, W.C. Wentworth, attempted a clever stratagem. He sought to employ an old writ, in the nature of a summons, the *venire facias iuartores*,[106] to require the sheriff to summon a jury to try the issues. The military jury that had been empanelled, so Wentworth's argument ran, was open to a challenge of the array (that is, of the jury as a whole) on the ground of a virtual conflict of interest attaching to the Governor, as prosecutor on the one hand, and nominator of the jury on the other; and also on the ground of the relationship between the officers and the Governor, he being their Commander-in-Chief. Those arguments, said Dowling, might work irresistibly upon those having authority to legislate, but it was not an area ripe for judge-made law, especially as Parliament's intentions were all too plain.

> Sitting in a court of justice, a Judge has no course to pursue but to administer the law as he finds it enacted by the wisdom of Parliament. I consider the sense of the Legislature to have been too clearly and imperatively expressed on this point, to admit of doubt, and therefore I must confine myself to declaring what I understand to be the law.[107]

Dowling rejected Wentworth's submission that, because s. 5 of 9 *Geo.* IV *c.* 83 omitted the word "jury", used in s. 4 of 4 *Geo.* IV *c.* 96 to describe the panel of officers, the latter body was not, legally, a jury. The omission of the word, Dowling ruled, was "intentional and of purpose" in order to mark the legislature's proposal to extend trial by jury at some future time to criminal cases in the Colony. If Wentworth's motion were allowed, and a civilian jury were empanelled by the sheriff, the court would simply act in defiance of the statute: a course it could not adopt. Dowling was against Wentworth on the other points raised.

But the judge made clear his conviction that absurd consequences could flow from the literal operation of the statute law as it then stood. Wentworth's arguments might with greater profit have been addressed to legislators. As to the judges:

> The wisdom of the Legislature having provided this mode of trial as a substitution for the trial by jury, properly so called, we are bound to presume that it was adopted upon the fullest consideration of the state and condition of the Colony. We are also bound to presume, until the contrary is shewn, that the function of nominating [by the Governor] is fairly, honourably, and justly exercised.[108]

Again in *R. v. Farrell,*[109] in 1831, Dowling, while remaining scrupulously non-committal, revealed his underlying sympathy for full jury trial in criminal cases.[110]

Reforms were accomplished in 1832, but only through the persistence of Governor Bourke in urging them upon an unwilling Legislative Council.[111] The new *Jury Act* (2 *Will.* IV *No.* 3) made little impression on the jury of military officers in criminal cases, but substantial concessions at civil trials were made. Trial by a civilian jury of 12 was authorized, with a wide eligibility conferred on men in the County of Cumberland to serve as jurors. Trial by special jury was also conceded. Later legislation continued the 1832 reforms for several years. The Colonial Office offered neither encouragement nor support, and the Legislative Council was evenly divided on the merits of Bourke's proposals.[112]

By 1836, Dowling privately interposed to agitate the subject with Lord Brougham, seeking his influence to secure, through the Parliament at Westminster, an Act that would settle the jury question definitively – "for if it be left to local legislation, it will as hitherto be a subject of disagreeable excitement, tending to destroy the very character of justice".[113] The piecemeal reforms made thus far to the system had not quieted party feeling, but had produced a very anomalous system that did not work well. Even if Brougham supported it, the matter came under no sympathetic attention in the Colonial Office, for the predisposition of James Stephen was against trial by jury as a system of administering justice.[114] Henceforth, when the Imperial legislature acted on this question, it was only to divest itself of future responsibility and leave the arrangements to be worked out in detail in the Colony.

Never stepping far from the strict limits of judicial duty, Dowling would not openly volunteer his views about juries, but disclosed them to the colonial government only if asked. In 1836, for example, Bourke sought the comments of the judges and Crown Law Officers on the prevailing jury system. In reporting the result to Glenelg, the Governor observed that "Your Lordship will be gratified to find how well the civil juries have fulfilled the objects of their appointment, and how unnecessary it is any longer to continue the use of military juries".[115] His Lordship's supposed gratification, which existed only in Bourke's hopes, would not be translated into appropriate action for some years to come.

Dowling, in his reply to Bourke, had been tentative. His conclusion was that civil juries had "in general answered the ends of Law and Justice";[116] but there were qualifications:

> I am not prepared to say that I was satisfied with every verdict delivered by the juries so constituted, but judging from my own close observation of the working of the trial by jury in the Mother Country, after an experience of nearly twenty-five years, and adverting to the inevitable imperfection of a tribunal composed of so

> many various mental capacities, I am of opinion that the jury system in this country, will not bear a very disadvantageous comparison, with that in the Mother Country.[117]

When nothing had been achieved by 1838 and a new Governor, Sir George Gipps, arrived with a determination even greater than Bourke's to bring the matter to a favourable conclusion, Dowling was much more forthcoming. Gipps also sought the judges' opinions on the state of the administration of justice in the Colony. Dowling's principal recommendation in reply was that there should be the complete introduction of petty juries and the reintroduction of grand juries.[118] The time had arrived, he insisted, for abolishing the distinction between civil and military juries. The latter supplied an "unsatisfactory piece of machinery" which was cumbersome, expensive, no longer necessary to the circumstances of the Colony, and an "Anti-British anomaly". The excitability of the debate on juries that had persisted in New South Wales for decades was no longer warranted. In his view:

> The state of Society in New South Wales, both in point of numbers and moral eligibility is now so auspicious, that there is no necessity for this party-colored system; and, I am persuaded, that, with proper care, in the formation of jury panels, justice may be as purely and satisfactorily administered in New South Wales, as in any other part of Her Majesty's Dominions.[119]

His interest in the revival of the grand jury lay, not so much in its functions of general inquisition into public administration as had occurred occasionally between 1824 and 1828, but to oust the "enormous discretion" vested in the Attorney-General to initiate prosecutions. Dowling undoubtedly drew upon his unhappy experiences from the days of Attorneys-General Bannister, Baxter and Kinchela. He might, in fairness, have observed that the Attorney-Generalship, in the competent hands of J.H. Plunkett, was a very different institution. None the less he deprecated the Attorney's discretion as being so repugnant to British constitutional principle as to be referable only to "the state of a society of outcasts".[120] The Colony was no longer in that state, and it would be better, he thought, to commit to the community the largest possible share in the administration of the criminal law. The judge was also persuaded that the time had come for the abolition of the option of trial of civil issues of fact by assessors.[121] Again, he thought it an anomalous procedure which had been overtaken by colonial circumstances.

Dowling returned to his views in another letter, over 12 months later.[122] By that time a colonial enactment, 3 *Vic. No.* 11, had become law, on 20 September 1839, while Sir Francis Forbes was yet alive, its effect being to abolish military juries.[123] When Dowling wrote to Gipps, in March 1840, the Colonial Office was still months away from permitting the royal assent to be given to the enactment.[124] Dowling again called for grand and petty jurors in all criminal trials – their number being drawn from the existing ranks of special jurors. He repeated his view that there was no continuing role for assessors on the civil side of the Supreme Court. He further reiterated his opinion that denial of comprehensive jury trial was seen as a general grievance, when he spoke to the Municipal Bill in the Legislative Council in August 1840.[125]

In all of these endeavours, one is struck by Dowling's earnestness and by the soundness of his opinions so far as they concerned petty juries. Yet one is left with the impression that, though he was Chief Justice, Dowling's observations counted for very little. The recommendations he made were almost categorically ignored. The reason was to be found in his unwillingness to promote his own ideas, or, if asked officially to give them, to do anything at all to pursue them once given. That, no doubt, was an unexceptionable judicial position as to matters of policy. It was also unproductive.

No one in the community had a moment's doubt where Forbes stood on the jury question, once he had decided to support reform. Nor could Burton's entrenched antipathy to allowing emancipists into the jury box have failed to impress the public mind. When Alfred Stephen began, in 1839, his long association with the New South Wales Bench, the real impetus for reform in many areas of the law – including the area of jury trial – passed to him. Dowling had been merely a loyal lieutenant in promoting the preferences of Bourke and Gipps for trial by jury in its most complete form. Inwardly he was convinced of the merits of the change: but, outwardly, he would not travel far from his judicial path to support his own beliefs. He again revealed his lack of those qualities of galvanism that distinguished the careers of his predecessor (Forbes) and of his successor (Stephen) in the office of Chief Justice. Had he been more assertive of his commitment to comprehensive trial by civilian juries, the reform might well have been expedited.

"He Thought He Should Die in Business"

Writing of the Year Books, the "law reports of the Middle Ages" in England, Sir William Holdsworth described them as "the exclusive property of the legal profession. Written by lawyers for lawyers". He further pointed out that, "Because they are contemporary reports they are of the utmost value, not only to the legal historian, but also to the historian of any and every side of English life".[126] Inspired by such considerations, translations of the Year Books out of Latin or Norman French and their publication in English continue to the present day.

In Australia, no such national pride surrounds the remarkable collection of Supreme Court reports personally recorded and written up by Dowling throughout his entire term as a judge in New South Wales.[127] Not unlike the Year Books, they present the law as it stood in an evolving and primitive state of society. And, like the Year Books, they were written by a lawyer for lawyers. Yet, because much of the contents of this extraordinary record of early judicial decisions affords no precedent by which to win a modern case, and because there is no other economic value discerned in them, these monuments to judicial industry, and invaluable records of colonial society, have long rested, usually unseen, on archival shelves. As Dr C.H. Currey succinctly summed up Dowling's achievement:

> Two hundred and [forty]-seven notebooks in the [N.S.W. State Archives] preserve Dowling's judgments... When to these are added his official letters and opinions, in five volumes; his three volumes of reports to the Governor on capital cases tried by him; and his six volumes of special cases, all set out in his almost copperplate handwriting[128] and, in many instances, carefully indexed, we can but marvel at the painstaking industry which has provided such a valuable record of the law applied in the Supreme Court of New South Wales from 1828 to 1844.[129]

These original Australian law reports deserve to be cherished by the Australian legal profession, just as the Year Books are cherished by English lawyers. Paradoxically, a selection of them has latterly been wrested from archival obscurity and published in electronic form.[130]

The present point is that Dowling never lost the habits or the discipline acquired on his apprenticeship in the law as a reporter. To him, it was essential to the operation of the Supreme Court of New South Wales as a superior court of record that there be a proper memorial of its proceedings. Newspaper reporting of colonial court cases, as repeatedly demonstrated earlier,[131] was imperfect and wanting objectivity. Resort was had often to Dowling's manuscript record to correct false impressions created by the public prints. In this, as in all his work in office, Dowling was meticulous, thorough and precise. His death deprived the Colony of the continuity of an effective series of law reports that was not made good (apart from some leading cases collected by Chief Justice Stephen)[132] until the publication – in London – of the *Supreme Court Reports,* under the editorship of W.H. Wilkinson and William Owen, in 1896, taking up reportable annual decisions from April 1862. *Legge's Reports* of a selection of cases (taken from newspaper reports) between 1825 and 1862 were published in Sydney in the same year.

An instance of the store set upon Dowling's judicial notes and reports occurred in 1830. The inept Attorney-General, Baxter, submitted what Dowling described as a "requisition" for the production of his notes of the case of *Cooper v. Wiltshire,* so as to make a case of perjury against one of the witnesses. Dowling, taken aback by this "unprecedented and indecorous" demand, declined.

> It is quite out of course for a Judge of the Supreme Court to comply with such a requisition made in the [*sic*] manner and for such a purpose was never presented to any of the Judges in England, and the Attorney-General must know and feel the impropriety of subjecting a judge of his own court to be cross-examined in open court as to the accuracy of his notes.[133]

Realizing, though, that no other course was open to the Crown than reliance on his own records to sheet home responsibility for possible criminal conduct, Dowling was gracious. If a new application were made to him by Baxter "with more courtesy", the Chief Justice "as a matter of favour" would permit his notes to be perused and a transcription made by the Attorney-General's clerk.[134]

The keeping of a proper record was but an instance of Dowling's commitment to an efficient course of court administration. It was, to him, important that the community perceive the court to be efficient and professional. He wasted his own health in his application to court business and, generally speaking, there were few complaints during his term of office of excessive delays in the administration of justice. When there were complaints, as, for instance, a petition by solicitors in 1841 seeking a greater number of cases to be set down for hearing on each sitting day, the Chief Justice's health invariably suffered through his anxiety about them.[135] His preoccupation with the form in which the court went about its business cloaked some insecurity he felt about the substance of some of his judicial decisions. As already noticed, he was uncomfortable in the equity jurisdiction, and there were times when he gave an appearance of unease in the conduct of criminal trials. Therry, who regarded Dowling as a friend, was frank in assessing the Chief Justice's shortcomings. After commending Dowling's conciliatory disposition and freedom from political taint, Therry concluded that:

> With all these estimable qualities, it can be only predicated of his talents that they were not of a very high standard. His range of reading, beyond the books of his own profession, was limited. There was also sometimes apparent in his judgment and address to the jury in criminal cases, a proneness to impart to circumstances, capable of innocent interpretation, a construction on the side of guilt.[136]

That lapse, in Therry's estimation, was due not to "any moral defect" in Dowling's mind, but to his having a much less discriminating judgment than Forbes had had.

Independent evidence corroborated Therry's opinion. The *Sydney Gazette,* for example, protested that the Chief Justice was "too apt on all occasions to be, from almost the commencement of a case, . . . the advocate of one of the two parties before him". But it also acquitted the Chief Justice of conscious impropriety: it asserted, "This is an infirmity (and we call it only an infirmity because SIR JAMES cannot be aware of it) which His Honour, unfortunately, cannot dispense with".[137] Dowling would probably have conceded the justice of most of Therry's remarks. While Dowling was not of the doubting disposition of Chief Justice Pedder in Tasmania,[138] he was sometimes glad that his decisions in criminal cases came up for executive review. Thus, in 1828, in the case of Matthew Miller, where an application for a stay of a capital execution pronounced by Dowling was to be made to the Executive Council, Dowling made extraneous representations to the Governor. "Personally", he wrote:

> I feel the greater propriety of sending this additional document to Your Excellency in consequence of it having been suggested to me privately that the case was not left to the jury with that strict legal accuracy which it required. . . It will be a satisfaction to me if the whole of the case is submitted to the united wisdom of Your Excellency and the Council Board.[139]

If there were small blemishes of that kind, the balance was happily redressed by Dowling's success in freeing the court from the vicious charges of political partisanship that had so dogged Chief Justice Forbes. In many ways Dowling was lucky. The Macarthur influence was already in retreat:[140] the "Parramatta Party" had collapsed: class distinctions, as already mentioned, were in decline. Provided he comported himself with strict neutrality, he could not be attached to any political cause. In that he succeeded very well. Not long before his death, the *Sydney Morning Herald* adopted an opinion that, "He may be emphatically said to be 'one of the people', owing his present position to no political or party influence. . . If Sir James has any political bias, he has, as a Judge, the discretion to conceal it".[141]

One of the very rare instances in which Dowling's political abstinence was called into question occurred in 1837 (when he was Acting Chief Justice), at the instigation of Richard Jones,[142] a nominated Member of the Legislative Council in the conservative (anti-Bourke) interest. Writing to the *Australian*, Jones inveighed against the Supreme Court for having sided with Therry as a candidate in a fiercely contested election (by the Benches of magistrates) for the office of Chairman of Quarter Sessions.[143] According to Jones, "Mr Justice Dowling stopped the trial of a prisoner . . . and allowed a Military Officer, one of the jury in the case, being a Magistrate, to leave the Court to attend the Police-office, where the Election was held, to vote for the Court candidate".[144] Jones was convinced that Dowling had connived in attempting to secure the election of Therry thus gratifying the wishes of Governor Bourke to accommodate the interest of Therry as a personal friend.

Dowling at once met the allegation. He wrote to Jones that he was not in the habit of noticing merely anonymous newspaper criticisms, but Jones' remarks were openly attributed to him, and Jones' standing in the community required the Chief Justice to "step out of my way on this occasion".[145] Dowling insisted that leave was given "as a matter of course under a supposition of personal convenience" for the juryman to retire briefly. His real intention, of participating in the election, was entirely unknown to the court. Dowling complained that his judicial character had been impugned:

> In repelling the insinuation that I was influenced by partisan motives on the occasion in question, I assert that it is false, as the purpose for which it is made, is unworthy. Since I have had the honour of holding the King's Commission in New South Wales I have carefully eschewed the parties of the colony, and appeal to my judicial career, now of nine years' duration, in verification of the assertion.[146]

Therry made a long and public attack on Jones in the columns of the *Australian*, including the apostrophe: "The statement you make respecting the conduct of the Chief Justice Dowling is another of the gross misrepresentations with which [your] letter abounds. Shame! Shame! Sir."[147]

Jones simultaneously had second thoughts, and returned to the pages of the *Australian* to retract his offensive representations,[148] though no hint of an apology to Dowling was forthcoming. The Acting Chief Justice felt his pride to be injured, his stature to be demeaned, and his future prospects to be threatened. He wrote directly to Lord Glenelg,[149] submitting that on this, the first occasion in the Colony when anyone had imputed to him a departure from his strict detachment from politics, the Secretary of State ought not to think the worse of Dowling's reputation in the light of Jones' public attacks. He wrote, he said, "from a desire of reassuring Your Lordship, that notwithstanding the difficulties in which a Judge in this Colony is often placed, I have kept myself untinged by local dissentions and still retain a just sense of what is due to His Majesty's Service – and the honour and integrity of the Bench of Justice".[150] Glenelg was not allowed to be reassured. James Stephen tartly minuted the letter, "This should have come, if at all, through the Govr. I think it may very properly be put by unanswered".[151] Dowling's sensitivity on the point is the more understandable when it is considered that he was acting in the seat of the Chief Justice and was, as it were, on probation. But his taking a stand had been salutary. When he succeeded Forbes as Chief Justice he was not again to be accused of political partisanship.

Curiously, it was the same Richard Jones who, from his place in the Legislative Council, acknowledged a few years later, the impossibly heavy burdens the Chief Justice discharged so diligently. Supporting a Bill for extending the jurisdiction of the Courts of Requests, Jones saw it as a means of relief for the overtasked Supreme Court judges, "His Honour [the Chief Justice] himself had told them the other day that the duties of his office were becoming so arduous that he thought he should die in business".[152] His prognosis was all too accurate, for Dowling "worked himself to death".[153]

9

"Nolens Volens a Politician"

Mindful of what had become of Forbes, by being "dragged into politics" and thrust into the conflicting roles of judge and parliamentary legislator,[1] Dowling, as Chief Justice, tried to avoid the same fate. He did not succeed. Despite reform, the legislature, by 1839, remained anchored to official control secured by the appointment of Crown nominees and, *ex officio*, of some holders of senior office, including the Chief Justice. Although Dowling assumed much extra-judicial work as a Legislative Councillor, most of it was veiled from public view. He drafted Bills, guided the House through procedural difficulties, and gave general advice behind the scenes. Otherwise, he felt out of place there and followed so detached a course as to seem often insensitive to great legislative issues. As a politician he was the antithesis of his patron Lord Brougham.

In seeking to sever the links between his office and the Council he had history as a guide. With Forbes' health so failing, in 1836, that his resignation seemed imminent, Dowling had written to Brougham, soliciting his renewed patronage should the Chief Justiceship become vacant. He remarked:

> I am satisfied that it is a vice in the government of the colony to allow a judge to take any part in the legislation of the country. It renders the individual unhappy and uncomfortable by making him *nolens volens* a politician, and thereby destroying his character as a judge . . . I earnestly trust that when the new Bill comes under consideration the situation of the judges will be borne in mind.[2]

For the time being, on his own elevation as Chief Justice, the legislative institutions remained static and Dowling had to accept his seat in the Council. But he continued to protest that "the legislative and judicial functions are incompatible and should be kept as distinct as possible, especially in so small a community as ours".[3] It did not take long for that precept to be tested vigorously.

"Mr McArthur was Greatly to Blame"

In November 1839, Dowling presided at the hearing of *R. v. Trougher and Kelly*,[4] a case with sectarian and other overtones that eventually attracted attention at the Colonial Office. The prisoners, convict servants of a settler near Parramatta, had been given a pass to attend church on Sunday, but instead got themselves drunk and molested a woman who was walking alone on a public road. The woman providentially escaped when a horseman came by and, whatever her attackers' design might have been, it was not accomplished. They were charged, in the alternative, on counts of assault with intent to commit rape, assault with intent to rob, and of common assault. As Dowling remonstrated, the prisoners "might have been dealt with by the neighbouring Magistrates in their summary jurisdiction"; but Attorney-General Plunkett ensured that the matter went to trial in the Supreme Court because the case raised greater public issues.[5] Dowling came to the proceedings by chance as the rostered judge in the criminal sittings for the day.

Agnes Catherine Byrne, the victim of the assaults charged, had attracted much publicity by her conversion from Catholicism to Protestantism, the more so because, since her arrival in the Colony, she had prominently supported the Roman Catholic faith. Not only did she convert, but, as the *Colonist* put it, she began to expose "the delusions and impostures of popery".[6] Dr William Ullathorne, for the Catholic Church, denounced Miss Byrne from the pulpit so strongly (including purporting to excommunicate her notwithstanding her defection)[7] that many believed that she had been assaulted, in retribution, by virtual agents for the Church. Dowling thought that the press, which had stirred religious discord in the Colony for months, greatly distorted the facts in this case. The accused men were common labourers: they had no idea who the woman was. "There was not", said Dowling, "a particle of proof, which could be tortured into a suspicion that these ignorant men were at all influenced by religious motives in their conduct".[8]

The jury found the prisoners guilty only of common assault and Dowling sentenced them to be worked in irons for one year – half the punishment they would have received if found guilty on the whole charge. To Dowling's dismay, the issue attracted sensational journalism, with himself as a principal target. The leading attack was by the *Sydney Gazette*, then controlled by Richard Jones, a Sydney merchant and Legislative Councillor hostile to the Chief Justice.[9] The *Gazette* denounced Dowling as "a wrong-headed man" who was too often disposed to abandon judicial impartiality and advocate the cause of one side of a case before him – a practice which had become an "infirmity" with him. It considered the sentence passed in this case as "falling very little short of offering a premium for the commission of crime".[10]

Other newspapers concurred. The *Sydney Herald* assured its readers concerning the case, "That murder and something worse than murder were intended there is little reason to doubt, but no, says His Honour the Chief Justice, after one of his usual displays of forensic balderdash – bad logic – and threadbare casuistry, this is a mere case of common assault".[11] The *Colonist*, under the question-begging headline "The Trial of the Popish Assaulters of Miss Byrne", declared:

> For the summing up of the Judge we cannot account, unless it was founded on some weakness . . . The charge which was addressed to the jury in this case was more like the apologetic harangue of a fee'd counsel in defence of the prisoners . . . than the strict and discriminating analysis and just development of evidence, which might be expected from a sternly-dignified and uncompromising judge.[12]

Dowling condemned this editorial licence as being "the most offensive libel".[13]

Public attacks by the press were one thing. What disconcerted Dowling more was further agitation of the question in the Legislative Council, of which Captain Phillip Parker King, R.N., and his brother-in-law Hannibal Macarthur, were members.[14] Neither supported Dowling. Extraordinarily, at the trial of her alleged attackers, Miss Byrne cut a very ostentatious figure, being attended by "two Dissenting Ministers" and, as Dowling reported, she was

> ushered into Court, with great parade, by Capt. King R.N. . . . and whilst the witness [Miss Byrne] was in the box, and about to give

> evidence, he was seen to speak to her under her bonnet, in the face of a crowded Court. In the discharge of my duty, I admonished [King] of the unseemliness of this proceeding, and told him mildly, I thought he ought to have known better than to speak to a witness in that manner in a Court of Justice.[15]

King regarded the admonition as a slight. When the Council met on 13 November, the Chief Justice was not in the chamber. Hannibal Macarthur used a debate on the Appropriation Bill to attack Dowling, asserting that his remarks to the jury in the Byrne case would disadvantage the community, by tending to encourage, rather than to prevent, crime. He described the Chief Justice's lenient doctrines (particularly Dowling's view that drunkenness might extenuate crime) as "monstrous". Governor Gipps, as chairman, insisted that Macarthur curtail his remarks until the Chief Justice should be present.[16]

Next day Dowling was there and demanded that the attacks made in his absence be repeated to his face. Macarthur obliged in unrepentant terms. Incompatibility between the duties of judge and legislator became plain when Dowling tried to rebut the criticisms. "The Chief Justice . . . protested against the right of the Council, or of any Member of it, to sit in judgment upon the conduct of the Judges of the land". King maintained that the newspaper comments had been fair. Attorney-General Plunkett "in a speech of great warmth"[17] supported the Chief Justice, contending that the charge to the jury had been distorted by a "factious press" – a contribution for which the newspapers did not forgive him.[18] Gipps fairly remarked to the Secretary of State that, while he would feel it necessary to preserve order by interposing were any "intemperate attack" made in the Council on the character of a judge, he did not see that vigorous debate, even of an unpleasant and personal kind, could be limited by him "in a body in which freedom of discussion is allowed".[19] Dowling submitted to the Secretary of State that, by joining in the debate, he had vindicated "the right of being exempted, as a Judge, from the fettering influence which a Legislative Council, composed as ours is, might exercise over the highest Tribunal in the land".[20] If, however, the Chief Justice wished for such exemption, he should have declined taking his place in the legislature.

In this dispute the Colonial Office took Dowling's side. James Stephen caused the Governor to be advised that no representations or complaints about the Chief Justice's conduct in the Byrne case had been received.[21] Lord John Russell, recently appointed as Secretary of State, demonstrated that his sympathies were not with Dowling's critics. "It is my opinion", he wrote to the Governor, "that Mr McArthur [*sic*] was greatly to blame in bringing the subject before the Legislative Council without sufficient information, on which to accuse a judge of partiality in the administration of justice; but that he was still more to blame in doing so without notice to the Chief Justice and during his absence".[22]

"No Place for Him to Express His Opinion of the Law"

In those circumstances of personal disagreements with fellow Councillors, and to some extent because "he did not shine as an orator", and further because he eschewed strong political views even privately, Dowling usually kept his peace when attending parliamentary debates.[23] But he took the responsibility seriously. He wrote, for example, in April 1838, of his alarm at heavy court lists coupled with "the prospect of a laborious session in the Legislative Council".[24] But he intervened in the proceedings usually on only procedural questions, or to lend terse support to the Governor's preferred position. In some ways, his diffidence exposed him to more criticism than if he had done nothing.

Thus, in August and September 1841, Dowling took up the cause of grain growers from the Hawkesbury and elsewhere, who petitioned for protection from flooding of the market by foreign wheat and flour. Dowling moved that the duty on those imports be increased from 5 to 15 per cent. Beyond reading some representations by the petitioners, he declined to do more: "He had performed a naked duty in thus bringing the matter under the notice of the Council . . . He should not, however, give his own opinion on the matter until called upon by his Excellency as his sworn adviser".[25] He declared that he would vote against the very resolution he had sponsored. The Governor, presiding, called for two seconders of the motion. After some cheerless procedural debate, Dowling said he would withdraw the motion, and all were happy that he should. Journalists seized upon the absurdity of a "politician's" moving a *pro forma* resolution, doing nothing to see it through, and promising not to vote for it. The *Australian* jeered that:

> The Chief Justice, as usual, had no opinion at all . . . The platitudes of the learned member are enough to try severely the patience of any mortal man . . . A fig for such an advocate, say we. It is very clear that the Hawkesbury settlers committed a capital error in entrusting their Petition to the hands of the Chief Justice.[26]

In such ways, the friction between making and interpreting the law, which Dowling hoped to avoid, was exacerbated and made public.

Nevertheless, there were times when, unobtrusively, he assisted popular causes. In August 1840, the Macarthur interests energetically – and, for a time, successfully – tried to defeat or defer debate on a Municipal Bill for central Sydney.[27] In their view, incorporating Sydney under a form of local government, would encourage democracy and demands for even wider popular concessions. Vested interests, like those enjoyed by the Macarthurs and their colleagues, would be at risk. Therefore, the Bill must be stopped: and the cry was got up that the Legislative Council lacked power to pass it.

While reserving his own position ("the Council was no place for him to express his opinion of the law"), Dowling could see no impediment to the Council's legislative powers. Creating a form of local government by statute contemplated a law "for the peace, welfare and good government" of the Colony, and s. 21 of the *Australian Courts Act* 1828 confirmed such a head of power.[28] The Governor had undertaken to reserve the ensuing Act for the Royal Assent in England. Nothing else stood in the way. Dowling insisted that, "The Council was as well prepared now as ever it would be to pass the Bill . . . If the people . . . were prepared to receive Municipal Corporations, why should they [the Council] for a moment delay them?"[29] Those remarks helped briefly to sway the Council against adopting the Macarthurs' delaying tactics. James Macarthur, and his cousin, Hannibal, proved to be more than equal to the Chief Justice's urgings. Moreover, they still had a score to settle with him. They discerned in the Bill elements of taxation, possibly without representation, that had almost American overtones. That suggestion, pursued with great zeal along with other fabian tactics, stalled the legislation for two years.

In June 1842, Governor Gipps, strengthened by instructions from Lord John Russell (which affirmed precisely what Dowling had said – that the Council enjoyed all relevant legislative power),[30] introduced the Sydney Corporation Bill and appealed to the Council, after so long a delay, now to yield. Attorney-General Plunkett supported the Bill in a "long and eloquent speech". There was nothing, he submitted, in the taxation argument, given the circumstances of the Colony and its residents, "nor was there anything to tax in the Country but kangaroos and opossums". There would have been a truly representative legislature in New South Wales, he asserted, had Huskisson lived to see through his promises which accompanied the *Australian Courts Act* 1828. But those benefits had not been realized and "it was the balanced state of parties at home which had been the cause of their [the colonists'] being so long kept out of them".[31]

Dowling's contribution was equally long, and, by his standards, almost eloquent. He was irritated that legislative power was still being agitated, as it was very forcefully by the Macarthurs who had got up a petition.[32] The opinion of the Secretary of State had disposed of any doubt that might have lingered; Dowling "did not think that this Council had any right to question the authority on which they acted" and, if they did dispute their own powers, they did so at the cost of stultifying themselves.[33] He contended that the Legislative Council had the same legislative powers for local purposes as the Parliament at Westminster had for its purposes.

Creating a municipal government was, he insisted, an exercise in legislating for the peace, welfare and good government of the Colony, as the Council was specifically empowered to do. The taxation argument was equally specious and "a mere perversion of the terms of the English law". What was contemplated was, not legislative taxation, but the imposition of rates levied for the supply of public services and utilities: and levied, moreover, by persons elected democratically. To call this a delegation of legislative powers of taxation was "ridiculous in the extreme". Dowling regretted that opportunities for civic improvement should be obstructed by "merely formal" quibbles,[34] and he "lamented to see a hostile spirit in any quarter arising to oppose this first and preparatory step towards higher and more important privileges".[35] Nevertheless, the Macarthurs continued to try to manipulate the Council, in the teeth of the wishes of the Secretary of State and of the Governor, and to press for the question to be deferred.[36] At length the *Sydney City Incorporation Act* (6 *Vic. No.* 3)[37] was assented to on 20 July 1842 – an achievement that owed much to Dowling's determination and persuasiveness.

The Chief Justice won praise from some journalists when he supported a Press Regulation Bill in 1841[38] – a measure introduced by Gipps to consolidate the law and to repeal repressive measures introduced by Darling. The Chief Justice applauded "the uniformly creditable and respectable manner" in which the colonial press latterly had been conducted, and considered that new privileges were well deserved. He commended the "carrot" offered by Gipps, while implicitly condemning the "stick" so severely applied by Darling.[39]

For the moment, the newspapers were placated. The *Australian* singled out the speeches of the Chief Justice and of James Macarthur as being "the expression of sentiments which are alike creditable to them as legislators, and honourable to them as men".[40] The *Sydney Monitor* thought the measure "a good one" and "a satisfactory enactment".[41] The *Sydney Gazette* published a precis of the Bill without comment.[42]

"The Judges had Been Called Upon Somewhat Out of Their Way"

As one of the few legal men in the Council, Dowling rarely joined in debates unless about "lawyers' law" and then in fields of little continuing interest. Of greater moment was his approach to the tensions that always at times exist between the judiciary and the executive government or the legislature. Governor Darling's aggressive determination to have his own way in government has been amply noticed on earlier pages. By the time of Governor Gipps, the collisions were less frequent and were managed with greater civility. But they had not ceased.

In 1842 the Council entertained a Registration Bill which proposed, as an interim measure, the establishment in Sydney and Melbourne of registries of deeds and other instruments, separated from the Supreme Court registries. That was to be only a "temporary measure to [a] more comprehensive one". Gipps protested to the judges that he could not authorize creation of a new registry office. There were not funds enough to employ extra staff. If a Registrar of Deeds were required, the Supreme Court should dispense with its office of Registrar.[43] Dowling, in the legislature, remonstrated that:

> The objections came upon him by surprise. He did not think that his Excellency had followed the most fair and proper course, in referring to what had passed between the Judges and himself. It could only lead them into detail, and then the Judges had not the opportunity of explanation which they might be considered entitled to.[44]

Moreover, the judges could not concur in lessening the court's establishment authorized by the Charter of Justice. Although Chief Justice Forbes had attenuated the offices specified in the Charter, that was an expedient. "With the growth of population, and consequently of business in the colony", said Dowling, "the wisdom of the old regulations [devised by the Colonial Office] became gradually developed, and the respective offices were now found to have a quite sufficiently onerous share of duties". He was not prepared to dispense with a Registrar in the Supreme Court.

Plunkett interposed, at what might otherwise have been an awkward point, to explain that the Bill was an enabling, not an imperative, measure. The authority for creating a separate Registry of Deeds could be given in principle and acted upon when convenient, without discommoding either of the public interests advanced by Governor and Chief Justice respectively.[45] After that calming suggestion, cordiality was restored and it was agreed that a new office of Registrar-General be established separately from the Supreme Court. Accordingly, a *Registration of Deeds Act* (7 *Vic. No.* 16) was assented to on 20 December 1843.[46]

Dowling's most conspicuous contribution in the Legislative Council related to bankruptcy law measures debated in 1840 and 1841. He was left with their carriage in the House: a paradox, as their original sponsor and draftsman had been Dowling's brother judge and "unfriend of mine", Mr Justice Burton.[47] Finding a balanced regime in bankruptcy (or "insolvency" as, for jurisdictional reasons, it was then called in the Colony) for New South Wales had been a problem since commercial enterprises began to flourish from the 1820s. The matter was examined by the legislature periodically, but *ad hoc* – remedies alternating between the impossible harshness of debtors' prisons and a relaxation that allowed insolvent debtors to laugh their creditors to scorn.[48]

In 1839, in *Ex parte Lyons*, the Supreme Court declared the English *Bankruptcy Act* 1825 (6 *Geo.* IV *c.* 16) not to have effect in the Colony. Dowling thought it "absolutely necessary" that New South Wales have some bankruptcy law of its own, devised by the colonial legislature in the light of local circumstances. A mere copying of English laws and procedures could not work in the Colony. He praised Burton's efforts to achieve reform, and concluded that: "Nothing but the grave importance of the measure (which is, as yet, ill understood, though simple and admirable in principle) has delayed its adoption, but I think we may indulge a sanguine persuasion that early in the next session [of the Legislative Council] the urgent want of some Bankrupt or Insolvent Law in the Colony will be satisfied".[49]

The Governor, perhaps taking his cue from *Ex parte Lyons*, and perhaps sensing that New South Wales was slipping into one of its cyclical disasters of drought-induced depression, decided to press harder for bankruptcy law reform. Although the Council resolved in 1840 to continue the existing colonial law for two years, Gipps sought the Chief Justice's advice. The latter replied that it would be "inexpedient" to persevere with the current enactment because it was "defective in almost all its provisions, and radically erroneous, as respects those principles which should characterise every insolvent law". Dowling told the Governor that he would be willing to move, in the legislature, for the introduction of a new Bill. But he hedged his offer about with so many doubts that Gipps was deterred.[50]

By 1841 colonial economic conditions had so deteriorated as to compel bolder intervention. A group of merchants caused a revision of Burton's Bill to be prepared and submitted to the judges for comment. At the Governor's behest, the Bench agreed informally to appraise the measure.[51] They deliberated over it for five days, before settling a form of words that they considered fit for enactment. Gipps was determined that the Bill go before the Council and, this time, Dowling agreed unequivocally to introduce it. Nevertheless, in doing so, in December 1841, the Chief Justice was almost apologetic for participating in making any law:

> The Judges had no interest to serve which should induce them to crave the management of the Bill. They had been called upon somewhat out of their way to revise and superintend the drawing up of the present Bill, and in the management of the Bill they would incur another addition to their already laborious and responsible duties.[52]

His observations, supporting the measure, were technical. His strongest commendation was merely that "he believed, and was told, that the earlier the Bill came into operation the better, as it would be some protection against the gross frauds now practised".[53]

Dowling was embarrassed that the Governor, without reference to the judges, had added clauses to the Bill, the effect of which would throw the cost of administering the proposed bankruptcy law on the funds of the Supreme Court. Torn between loyalties, the Chief Justice had to side with the court and assert that the judges would not be coerced by the Governor's threat to withdraw the Bill if the Government were put to further expense by its enactment. Dowling protested that "the expenses attendant upon the Insolvent Court, were, in England, defrayed by the Crown".[54] The same rule should apply in the Colony. The judges and ministerial officers already had "as much business to transact as they were competent to perform" and, without extra staff remunerated from the colonial treasury, extra duties could not be performed. "He would now", he said, "candidly state that without government aid it would be impossible to carry the Bill into effect". He threw down a gauntlet to the Governor: would his Excellency adhere to his declaration and withdraw the Bill, leaving "this Colony [to] stand alone, as being without an Insolvent Law?". The Governor, being obdurate, Plunkett interposed, again using diplomacy to avert a rift and to allow the parties to reflect before debate resumed.

Over the following two days, the judges considered the Governor's new clauses. Dowling probably had a private discussion with Gipps. On 17 December 1841 the Council met in a better humour and honour was seen to be done. The Chief Justice declared that:

> The clauses proposed by His Excellency required some slight modification, and whatever the opinions of the Judges might be with respect to [funding arrangements], yet they were desirous to make the Bill work as cheaply and as much for the benefit of the public as lay in their power.[55]

There was none of the animus that had clouded the vision of Darling when obstructed by opinions of Chief Justice Forbes he found unwelcome. With Gipps, Dowling was deferential yet firm. The Governor yielded to the proposed modifications and thanked the judges for their help. The 5 *Vic. No.* 17[56] repealed all previous insolvency measures and established a legislative system based on the English laws of bankruptcy. For all practical purposes – so far as concerned New South Wales – the breaking down of the barriers between insolvency and bankruptcy statutes meant that the new Act applied equally to traders and to non-traders.[57] While it represented a new start, it was not an unqualified success.

The Colonial Office caused the Queen's assent to the Bill to be "suspended":[58] a gesture amounting, not to disallowance, but to reserving the future of the Act to see how it worked during a trial period. A Select Committee of the Legislative Council, appointed to review the Act, suggested that the measure was sound in principle but needed amendments as to details.[59] The legislation, essentially derived from the authorship of Burton, perpetuated his name for over 40 years. But much of the credit for the translation of the Bill to the statute book was due to the parliamentary skill of Plunkett and to the perseverance of Sir James Dowling.

"A Competent and Independent Director of the Debates"

Dowling's involuntary association with the legislature had an eccentric sequel in which he canvassed his own appointment as Speaker on the reconstitution of the Council in 1842. He made the suggestion for at least three reasons, though he at once disclaimed the first, and most obvious, of them – that of self-gratification. "So far as I personally am concerned, the question is one of indifference", he assured Gipps.[60] "A seat in the Legislature or even the post of President of that Body could add nothing to the dignity of my Office, and nothing to my personal ease". Nevertheless, he was convinced that the only way, in "this still young and excitable community [of] securing a competent and Independent Director of the Debates in the House, will be to place the Chief Justice in the Chair".[61]

The second reason was found in a curious attitude of approbation and reprobation, in which Dowling deprecated the role of a judge as a "debating Member" of the Council, but saw great merit in the concept of the Chief Justice as Speaker of the House:

> In a body constituted as this will be, some person should be at its head, accustomed to preserve order in debate; and to whom, from his station and the weight attached to the judicial character, the Members, on both sides of the House would be likely to look, not less for direction on points of form, than for independence and impartiality in his decisions.[62]

Qualities of that kind, he was convinced, would commend themselves by facilitating debate and committee business, especially if the "Speaker" or "President" were made chairman of committees. His chief reservation was that the government was committed to having an elected Speaker, and he could never allow himself to be a candidate for such an election.

A third, and more subtle, reason, lay in the perception that, if the time of the Chief Justice became entangled in even more pressing legislative duties than in the past, the government would be the more readily disposed to appoint an additional judge.[63]

As it turned out, Gipps was not persuaded by any of the grounds advanced by Dowling. The Governor well knew that the Chief Justice's health was in such decline that Dowling would be an insecure appointee. Above all, Gipps was convinced that judges should remain in their courts. He wrote very tersely to Dowling that "it does not seem to me that the occupation of a seat in the Council by the Chief Justice would conduce to the public good". He also reported to the Secretary of State that he doubted the propriety of the union of the offices of Chief Justice and Speaker. His opinion was correct.[64] He was probably surprised at Dowling's persistence, given the diplomatic but blunt terms in which he had made plain to the Chief Justice that the time had come for Dowling's severance from the new legislature and that, "I can indeed scarcely doubt that to be relieved from the duty of sitting in the future Council of this Colony must be agreeable to yourself; and therefore I feel confident that you will not take any thing amiss, which I have herein written".[65]

Lord Stanley approved of the course taken by the Governor.[66] Dowling's contribution, industrious but unspectacular and awkward, in the Legislative Council, was at an end.

Conclusion

Sir James Dowling died in harness on 27 September 1844.[1] His death could not have been unexpected. Illness and chronic fatigue, in attempting to discharge his official duties, had been the principal subject of family correspondence for years.[2] But fate dealt him a doubly cruel blow. A month before his death Dowling's medical advisers certified that a change of climate was imperative to restore his health.[3] The Executive Council granted him leave to visit England, and he booked his passage.[4] In the Legislative Council, speaking to a motion to pay the Chief Justice's full salary during his absence, Plunkett affirmed "the patient attention which the learned Judge had devoted to the duties of his office, to the injury of his own constitution".[5] Wentworth, in support, thought the proposal well-merited. The wider community farewelled Dowling as if for a temporary journey: "Addresses . . . of the most flattering description, had been presented to him by the Corporation and almost every public institution in Sydney".[6] The Bar prepared a generous address which, with "a piece of plate of colonial manufacture", was to have been handed to the Chief Justice.[7] But his final illness, and death, interposed.

In a supplement to the *Government Gazette*, the Governor declared his confidence "that the public in general will join him in deeply regretting the loss which the colony has sustained".[8] He personally attended the funeral. Newspaper notices, however, were ambivalent. They ranged from affected overstatement, to understatement, or even disregard, of Dowling's character. One journal asserted that the Chief Justice had been "universally beloved by all classes in the Colony, not only for his high legal knowledge, humanity and integrity, but for his private worth and extensive benevolence".[9] The *Australian*, long hostile to Dowling, published so exaggerated an appraisal of him as to cast doubt on that journal's credibility and motives. At least it plausibly recognized him as one of the "ornaments of our Colonial history" who had been "a warm friend of that genuine social liberty, which is but another name for the highest and most comprehensive justice".[10] Probably the most balanced assessment came from the short-lived *Morning Chronicle* (Sydney) which commended the late judge's "enduring name for unbending uprightness, clear perception, luminous argument, [and] singular felicity of expression. . . In court he knew no man by his country, his creed, or his complexion".[11]

The *Sydney Morning Herald*, while thoroughly reporting Dowling's death and funeral as news items in mourning borders, abstained from any editorial notice of his worth.[12] The ephemeral *Sydney Dispatch* did not interest itself in the comings and goings of Chief Justices. The *Sydney Gazette* and, more significantly, that gadfly, the *Sydney Monitor*, had predeceased Dowling by two years. But Edward Smith Hall, though a spent force, survived them all!

Sir Alfred Stephen, who succeeded in the office, supposed that "the name of Chief Justice Sir James Dowling will doubtless be remembered and honoured so long as the Supreme Court of New South Wales shall exist".[13] That was not to be. Already, by the end of the 19th century, Dowling, whose judgments were even then rarely referred to as precedent authorities, had been all but forgotten. Neglect of his memory was so much the greater among lawyers of the 20th century. It may be, however, that, due to the initiative of Professor Kercher in making Dowling's reports of cases readily accessible to modern readers,[14] the name of Sir James Dowling will be better recognized, and his work better understood, in the 21st century and beyond.

History will acknowledge Chief Justice Dowling for two principal qualities – the extraordinary industry evidenced in his law reports (a work far transcending contemporary needs), and the relative stability he brought to the court. Disregarding the unique circumstances of the appointment of (Sir) Julian Salomons as Chief Justice in 1886, and his resignation before being sworn in,[15] Dowling's was the shortest term of any Chief Justice in 19th century New South Wales. He was, among the same company, the least distinguished judicial lawyer. But he compensated for those shortcomings by unremitting dedication to his work and to the public interest. That dedication consumed him. He allowed himself no leisure. He even reproached himself, as a religious man, for having to apply Sundays to keeping up with his public commitments.[16]

As a sheet-anchor to the Supreme Court in tempestuous times, he was firm when challenged by abrasive and selfish judicial colleagues. He stood in the way of the court's attachment to the Macarthur interests and of its submission to any other form of politics. Given that the Colonial Office had first appointed him – a man of no relevant experience – as a matter of expediency, Dowling had risen to the challenge and discharged, admirably and honourably, the trust committed to him.

To adapt the words of the Psalmist, James Dowling had taken the wings of the morning to dwell in the uttermost parts of the sea.[17] In New South Wales he founded a dynasty that included some generations of lawyers, and endures still. He achieved public distinctions he could never have won "at home", and he served his adopted country with the most conscientious ability in furtherance of the institutions of its laws and constitution.

Abbreviations

(Used in the following notes)
(Conventional abbreviations are given to Law Reports)

A.D.B.	*Australian Dictionary of Biography* (Melbourne fro 1966).
Callaghan's Diary	"The Diary of Judge Thomas Callaghan, B.A." (M MSS 2112/1).
C.O.	Colonial Office, with particular reference to pape of that office in the Public Record Office, Kew, Richmond, U.K., citing class, piece and folio numbers.
D.N.B.	*Dictionary of National Biography* (Oxford 1917).
Dowling Correspondence	Letters to and from Sir James Dowling, identified Ch. 1, n. 1.
H.R.A.	*Historical Records of Australia* (Commonwealth Parliament, Library Committee, 1914-1923), citin series, volume and page.
J.R.A.H.S.	*Journal of the Royal Australian Historical Society.*
Letters and Opinions	Sir James Dowling, "Copies of Semi-Official Lette and Opinions" (see Ch. 8, n. 127).
M.L.	Mitchell Library of the State Library of New Sout Wales.
N.L.	National Library of Australia, Canberra, A.C.T.
N.S.W.A.	New South Wales State Archives, held at various locations by the authority unhelpfully named "St Records".
S.M.H.	*Sydney Morning Herald.*
V. & P. (L.C., N.S.W.)	*Votes and Proceedings* of the Legislative Council o New South Wales.

Notes

Introduction

1. On 25 November 1787, P.C. Mowle, *A Genealogical History of Pioneer Families of Australia* (Fifth ed., Adelaide 1978), 145. Anthony Dowling, *Fortis et Egregius or Dowling of Ballyroan* (Sydney 1996), 6, 63.
2. Dowling, *op. cit.*, early manuscript facing p. 1 and 1-4 ; H.T.E. Holt, *A Court Rises* (Sydney 1976), 27.
3. Dowling, *op. cit.* n. 1; Mowle, *op. cit.* n. 1, 144.
4. Reminiscences of James Sheen Dowling, typescript, Chapter 1 (M.L. C194; Dowling Papers, N.L. MS 3485/2), 1; *Old Times*, May 1903, 115.
5. Mowle, *op. cit.* n. 1, 144.
6. Entry in Dowling family Bible dated 1830.
7. Mowle, *op. cit.* n. 1, 145.
8. Dowling, *op. cit.* n. 1, 7-8; V *D.N.B.* 1295 (*s.v.* Sir James Dowling).
9. Dowling, *ibid.*, 31-32.
10. Anthony Dowling (ed.), *Reminiscences of a Colonial Judge* (James Sheen Dowling) (Sydney 1996), 46.
11. *See,* for example, below Ch. 8, text to n. 80 and following. Note also the extravagant and inaccurate obituary in *Australian*, 28 September 1844, 727.
12. Of which there are many instances below, *e.g.*, Ch. 2, text to n. 61; Ch. 3, text to n. 18; Ch. 8, text to n. 16.
13. C.H. Currey, "The First Three Chief Justices of the Supreme Court of New South Wales" (1933) 19 *J.R.A.H.S.* 73 at 90.

Chapter 1

1. The letters survive in the Dowling Correspondence 1831-1839 (M.L. A486) and extracts from them are in the Dowling Family Papers (N.L. MS 3485). Letters by Sir James Dowling to his son James Sheen Dowling are here identified by date only.
2. To J.S. Dowling, 16 February 1839 and 15 October 1842 – "From that time [aged 15] I was a *slave,* and have worked my way up by hard drudgery and self-teaching".
3. To J.S. Dowling, 3 February 1838, and 24 February 1843 – "with little intermission my life has been one of drudgery and anxiety".
4. Anthony Dowling, *Fortis et Egregius or Dowling of Ballyroan* (Sydney 1996), 38-39; Sir Roger Therry, *Reminiscences of Thirty Years' Residence in New South Wales and Victoria* (2nd ed., London 1863), 338.
5. Dowling, *op. cit.* n. 4, 63.
6. The date given in *Register of Admissions to the Middle Temple*, Vol. II, 429; J. Hutchinson, *Notable Middle Templars* (London 1902), 76, gives the date as 21 April 1810.

7. Dowling to Lord Goderich, 6 June 1827 [*sic* but 7 June was intended – *see* n. 13], in "Narrative of Proceedings Prior and Subsequent to the Appointment of James Dowling, Esq., to the Office of Judge of the Supreme Court at New South Wales", identified as "Dowling's Journal" (M.L. A485).
8. Republished in 171 *English Reports.*
9. 1 Dowl. and Ryl. (1822), iv.
10 His first wife, Maria (*née* Sheen) whom he had married at St Pancras Church, Middlesex, on 3 September 1814, P.C. Mowle, *A Genealogical History of Pioneer Families of Australia* (Fifth ed., Adelaide 1978), 145.
11. Anthony Dowling (ed.), *Reminiscences of a Colonial Judge* (James Sheen Dowling) (Sydney 1996), 1; *Old Times*, May 1903, 115.
12. "Narrative", cited n. 7. When Chief Justice, and knighted, Dowling was incensed to receive a letter from Lord Lyndhurst requesting his good offices on behalf of a Lyndhurst *protégé*, addressed "My *dear* Sir James": "Now this noble Lord would never *know* me before . . . and I remember well when in 1827 I wrote to him . . . he never even condescended to answer my letter. It is astonishing how greatness brings a man into notice" – to J.S. Dowling, 1 September 1839.
13. C.O. 323/127, f. 81, copied with a discrepancy as to date and with textual variations in the "Narrative", cited n. 7.
14. *Ibid.*
15. *Id.*, f. 82.
16. J.B. Atlay, *The Victorian Chancellors,* Vol. 1 (London 1906), 280-281, 284-285.
17. B.T. Balfour to Dowling, 11 June 1827, "Narrative", cited n. 7 and Letters to Sir James Dowling (M.L. A489).
18. C.O. 323/17, f. 21 at f. 22-22a.
19. *Ibid.*
20. *Id.*, f. 23a.
21. Bayley to Dowling, 8 June 1827, C.O. 323/127, f. 25.
22. Tindal to Dowling, 9 June 1827, C.O. 323/127, f. 27.
23. "Narrative", cited n. 7. For Serjeant Stephen, *see* XVIII *D.N.B.* 1047.
24. Henry Stephen to Dowling, 25 June 1827, Letters to Sir James Dowling (M.L. A489).
25. "Narrative", cited n. 7.
26. *Ibid.*
27. Dowling to Goderich, 5 July 1827, C.O. 323/127, f. 83-84.
28. Burton to Bourke, 28 July 1835, *H.R.A.* I/XVIII, 122 at 125.
29. (1966) 1 *A.D.B.* 184.
30. K.G. Allars, "Sir William Westbrooke Burton" (1951) 37 *J.R.A.H.S.* 257 at 259; Hazel King, "Pulling Strings at the Colonial Office" (1975) 61 *J.R.A.H.S.* 146 at 147-150.
31. Burton to Hay, 15 June 1827, *H.R.A.* I/XVIII, 125.
32. Balfour to Dowling, 6 July 1827, Letters to Sir James Dowling (M.L. A489)
33. Stephen to Dowling, 30 August 1827, *ibid.*
34. Dowling to Goderich, 9 July 1827, C.O. 323/127, f. 87 at 87a.
35. Burton to Hay, 15 June 1827, *H.R.A.* I/XIII, 470 at 472.
36. Below Ch. 5, text to n. 27; Burton to Hay (Private), 2 September 1835, C.O. 201/250, f. 294.
37. Goderich to Darling, 30 July 1827, *H.R.A.* I/XIII, 470 at 472.
38. In which Mr Justice Field (formerly of the Colony's Civil "Supreme Court") encouraged him – "Depend upon it [your] children will be happier and wealthier in the Colony. The girls will marry better than in England, and the

boys will like a farming and wild country life", Field to Dowling, 30 July 1827, Letters to Sir James Dowling M.L. A489).

39. Dowling to Goderich, 9 July 1827, C.O. 323/127, f. 87 at 87a.
40. Dowling to Hay, 9 July 1827, C.O. 201/187, f. 397.
41. C.O. minutes, *ibid.*, f. 399; Hay to Dowling, 13 July 1827, C.O. 202/19, f. 115; Dowling to Hay, 11 August 1827, C.O. 201/187, f. 409 at 409a. The Colonial Office eventually "compromised" with an advance of one-quarter, £375 ("Narrative", cited n. 7 at 47); Goderich to Darling, 4 August 1827, *H.R.A.* I/XIII, 490; Dowling to Hay, 6 August 1827, C.O. 201/187, f. 407; Hay to Dowling, 13 July 1827, Letters to Sir James Dowling (M.L. A489); Hay to Dowling, 9 August 1827, C.O. 202/19, f. 138a; Dowling to Hay, 1 October 1827, C.O. 201/187, f. 421; Horton to Dowling, 2 October 1827, C.O. 202/19, f. 172; Hay to Darling, 14 November 1827, *H.R.A.* I/XIII, 621.
42. The celebrated law reporter John Adolphus not only extended congratulations, but invited Dowling and Rylands to a private dinner to mark the event. Adolphus to Dowling, 28 August 1827, Letters to Sir James Dowling (M.L. A489).
43. S.B. Bosanquet to Dowling, 17 August 1827, *ibid.*
44. Horton to Dowling, 29 September 1827, C.O. 202/19, f. 170a. Dowling, *op. cit.* n. 4, 76-77.
45. Dowling to Brougham, 29 August 1827, Brougham MSS (30,097), University College, London: an excerpt dated "28 August" is in the "Narrative", cited n. 7.
46. Hay took a liking to the new judge and invited him and his wife to dinner, Hay to Dowling, 11 October 1827, Letters to Sir James Dowling (M.L. A489); "Narrative", cited n. 7.
47. "Narrative", *ibid.*
48. Below, text to n. 74 and following.
49. "Narrative", cited n. 7.
50. *Ibid.*; C.H. Currey, *Sir Francis Forbes* (Sydney 1968), 306.
51. "Narrative", cited n. 7.
52. Dowling (ed.), *op. cit.* n. 11, 2; *Old Times*, May 1903, 116.
53. "Narrative", cited n. 7.
54. *Loc. cit.* n. 52.
55. *Australian*, 28 November 1827, 3. Barron Field (n. 38 above) wrote to Dowling, "I congratulate the colony, in which I still have a stake in land and beeves, and shall always take an interest, upon its acquisition of a judge of your law, temper and integrity", Field to Dowling, 30 July 1827, Letters to Sir James Dowling (M.L. A489).
56. "Narrative", cited n. 7. Dowling to Brougham, 1 April 1828, Brougham MSS (30,098), University College, London.
57. 25 February 1828, 2.
58. Dowling to Darling, 24 February 1828, Letters and Opinions Vol. 1 (N.S.W.A. 2/3470), 1.
59. Darling to Dowling, 25 February 1828, *ibid.*, 2; Forbes to Dowling, 25 February 1828 – J.M. Bennett (ed.), *Some Papers of Sir Francis Forbes* (Sydney 1998), 183. Forbes' attempts to invite Dowling to dine were frustrated by competing invitations deliberately issued by the Governor, Forbes to Wilmot-Horton, Bennett (ed.), *ibid.*, 184 at 187.
60. Lady Forbes, "Sydney Society in Crown Colony Days" (M.L. MSS943), 110-112; Currey, *op. cit.* n. 50, 306-307; *Australian*, 27 February 1828, 3.

61. "Narrative", cited n. 7, and quoted, Dowling (ed.), *Reminiscences of a Colonial Judge*, 3; and Currey, *op. cit.* n. 50, 307.
62. "Narrative", *ibid.* The warrant for his appointment is in *H.R.A.* IV/I, 729.
63. "Narrative", *ibid.* Forbes was so unwell that, only two days after Dowling's taking his seat, he could not attend court, *Sydney Gazette*, 5 March 1828, 3.
64. "Narrative", *ibid.*, quoted, Dowling (ed.), *op. cit.* n. 11, 4.
65. *Australian* and *Sydney Gazette*, 5 March 1828, 3.
66. Dowling to Brougham, 1 April 1828, Brougham MSS (30,098), University College, London. The *Sydney Gazette* called it an "elegant cottage belonging to Mr Harper", 5 March 1828, 2.
67. Dowling to Brougham, *ibid.;* Dowling (ed.), *op. cit.* n. 11, 4.
68. Hall to Murray, 2 January 1829, *H.R.A.* I/XIV, 596 at 598; Return of Grants (1828), *id.*, 671; Dowling, *op. cit.* n. 4, 96-101.
69. Dowling (ed.), *op. cit.* n. 11, 7.
70. Reminiscences of James Sheen Dowling, typescript (M.L. C194), 164.
71. (1966) 1 *A.D.B.* 504. As Colonial Architect he was "out of his depth and not very competent", Morton Herman, *The Early Australian Architects and Their Work* (Sydney 1954), 117. The residence was called "Brougham Place", but habitually described as "Brougham Lodge" by others – Dowling, *op. cit.* n. 4, 101, note.
72. Dowling (ed.), *op. cit.* n. 11, 7; *Old Times*, May 1903, 117.
73. To J.S. Dowling, 1 August 1837.
74. Hay to Darling, 17 July 1827, *H.R.A.* I/XIII, 447.
75. *Ibid.*, 490; and Letters and Opinions Vol. 1 (N.S.W.A. 2/3470), 13.
76. Supreme Court Letter Book, quoted, Currey, *op. cit.* n. 50, 309.
77. Darling to Dowling, 24 March 1828, *H.R.A.* I/XIV, 91.
78. *Sydney Gazette*, 5 March 1828, 3. The court then customarily sat on Saturday mornings.
79. Darling to Huskisson, 31 March 1828, *H.R.A.* I/XIV, 86.
80. Stephen to Dowling, 17 March 1828, Letters and Opinions Vol. 1, (N.S.W.A. 2/3470), 6 at 7; and Letters to Sir James Dowling (M.L. A489).
81. *Ibid.*
82. Dowling to Stephen, 17 March 1828, Letters and Opinions Vol. 1 (N.S.W.A. 2/3470), 7-9; copy in Letters to Sir James Dowling (M.L. A489).
83. *Ibid.*, and Dowling to Darling, 22 March 1828, *H.R.A.* I/XIV, 87 at 88.
84. Dowling to Darling, *ibid.*
85. *Id.*, at 90.
86. Dowling to Stephen, 24 March 1828, Letters and Opinions Vol. 1 (N.S.W.A. 2/3470), 38 at 41.
87. Darling to Dowling, 24 March 1828, *H.R.A.* I/XIV, 91.
88. Dowling to Forbes, 26 March 1828, Letters and Opinions Vol. 1 (N.S.W.A. 2/3470), 34.
89. "F.F." to Dowling, 26 March 1828, *ibid.*
90. Dowling to Forbes, 26 March 1828, *op. cit.* n. 88, 35-36. And *see* Dowling to Darling, 27 March 1828, *H.R.A.* I/XIV, 92.
91. Forbes to Dowling, "Thursday evening" [26 March 1828], Letters and Opinions Vol. 1 (N.S.W.A. 2/3470), 46.
92. *Id.*, at 47.
93. Forbes to Dowling, 26 March 1828, *H.R.A.* I/XIV, 93.
94 *Id.*, at 94. For the development of the question, as to the claims of Mr Justice Burton to seniority, *see* below, Ch. 5, text to n. 64.
95 *Op. cit.* n. 76.

96. Darling to Huskisson, 31 March 1828, *H.R.A.* I/XIV, 86 at 87.
97. Forbes had made no such suggestion: he had raised a legitimate doubt about the procedure adopted.
98. Darling to Hay, 3 April 1828, *H.R.A.* I/XIV, 115 at 116.
99. Murray to Darling, 14 November 1828, *H.R.A.* I/XIV, 460 at 461.
100. Dr Currey added the droll remark that "nephew James had obviously miscalculated Uncle John's wishes in the matter", Currey, *op. cit.* n. 50, 310.
101. Dowling to Darling, 22 March 1828, *H.R.A.* I/XIV, 87 at 88.
102. Murray to Darling, 14 November 1828, *op. cit.* n. 99, 460.
103. Darling to Murray, 16 May 1829, *H.R.A.* I/XIV, 743 at 744.
104. Murray to Darling, 14 November 1828, *H.R.A.* I/XIV, 461.
105. The principal sources of Dowling's personal impressions are his record of Letters and Opinions (N.S.W.A. 2/3470 and following), his letters to Brougham (Brougham MSS, University College, London), and, in due course, his letters to his son James Sheen Dowling (n. 1 above). Impressions others had of Dowling appear throughout this work. They include, but are not limited to, many inflammatory remarks by his fellow judges Burton and Willis, highly commendatory statements by Mr Justice Alfred Stephen, and candid comments by Sir Roger Therry and the then youthful barrister Thomas Callaghan.
106. Dowling to Brougham, 1 April 1828, *op. cit.* n. 56; Letters and Opinions, Vol. 1 N.S.W.A. (2/3470), 75.
107. *Cf.* Dowling to James Stephen, 16 August 1828, copy in Letters to Sir James Dowling (M.L. A489) and Letters and Opinions, Vol. 1 N.S.W.A. (2/3470), 109. By that time Dowling asserted that "two thirds of the judicial labours have necessarily fallen to my lot" because of his colleagues' illnesses.
108. *Loc. cit.* n. 106.
109. J.M. Bennett, *A History of the Supreme Court of New South Wales* (Sydney 1974), 81-82.
110. Dowling to Brougham, *op. cit.* n. 106.
111. Dowling to Brougham, 1 April 1828, *loc. cit.* n. 106.
112. *Ibid.*
113. Dowling to James Stephen, 16 August 1828, copy in Letters to Sir James Dowling (M.L. A489).
114. Dowling to Hay, "private", 3 April 1828, *H.R.A.* I/XIV, 115.
115. Charter of Justice, cl. 9 (*H.R.A.* IV/I, at 511).
116. Mowle, *op. cit.* n. 10, 150; Dowling, *op. cit.* n. 4, 106.
117. *See* generally, R.W. Bentham and J.M. Bennett, "The Development of the Office of Master in Equity in New South Wales" (1961) 3 *Sydney Law Review*, 504 at 510-511.
118. Darling to Hay, 3 April 1828, *op. cit.* n. 114, at 115-116.
119. *Cf.* Darling to Hay, 1 September 1828, *H.R.A.* I/XIV, 379; Murray to Darling, 12 November 1828, *ibid.*, 454.
120. Dowling to Stephen, 16 August 1828, *loc. cit.* n. 113.
121. Marginal note to "Paper" of 7 February 1829, Letters and Opinions Vol. 1 (N.S.W.A. 2/3470), 207.
122. *Id.*, at 208.
123. *Ibid.*
124. As against this, Dr C.H. Currey thought Dowling's relevant representations "dictated by fine feelings and great good sense", "The First Three Chief Justices of the Supreme Court of New South Wales" (1933) 19 *J.R.A.H.S.* 73 at 99.

125. Currey, *op. cit.* n. 50, 335-336.
126. Dowling to Brougham, 1 April 1828, Brougham MSS (30,098), University College, London.
127. M.H. Ellis, *John Macarthur* (Sydney 1955), 510; Currey, *op. cit.* n. 50, 323-326; *Sydney Gazette*, 15 February 1828, 2; 18 February 1828, 2; 7 March 1828, 3; 28 March 1828, 3.
128. *Sydney Gazette*, 25 and 28 March 1828, 2; 30 January 1828, 3; 1 February 1828, 2; 6 February 1828, 2.
129. Quoted, Currey, *op. cit.* n. 50, 326.
130. Darling to Stanley, 5 April 1828, "private", *H.R.A.* I/XIV, 119 at 120.
131. Currey, *op. cit.* n. 50, 326.
132. Forbes to the Judges, 16 May 1828, Letters and Opinions Vol. 1 (N.S.W.A. 2/3470), 92.
133. Dowling to Forbes, 17 May 1828, *id.*, 93 at 94.
134. *Ibid.*, 95.
135. Dowling to Stephen, 16 August 1828, *loc. cit.* n. 113.
136. *Australian*, 11 March 1831, 2.
137. *See* further, below, for example, Ch. 7, text to n. 63; Ch. 8, text to n. 131 and following, and n. 153; Conclusion.

Chapter 2

1. Murray to Darling, 31 July 1828, *H.R.A.* I/XIV, 260.
2. At 261.
3. C.H. Currey, *Sir Francis Forbes* (Sydney 1968), Ch. XXIV.
4. *Op. cit.* n. 1, at 270.
5. 5 *Geo.* IV *c.* 84.
6. Darling to Murray, 20 May 1829, *H.R.A.* I/XIV, 762.
7. For a *resume* of the case, particularly through the eyes of Forbes, *see* Currey, *op. cit.*, n. 3, Ch. XXXI.
8. *See* generally, *H.R.A.* I/XIV, note 218 at p. 943.
9. Forbes to Darling, 7 February 1829, *H.R.A.* I/XIV, 763.
10. *Id.*, at 764.
11. Darling to Murray, 20 May 1829, *H.R.A.* I/XIV, 762.
12. The proceedings are in *H.R.A.* I/XV, 670.
13. At 671.
14. *Ex parte Jane New*, *H.R.A.* I/XIV, 765 at 771.
15. *Ibid.*
16. *Id.*, at 772.
17. *Id.*, at 767.
18. *Ibid.*
19. *See* below, text to n. 63 and following.
20. *Op. cit.* n. 14, at 768.
21. *Id.*, at 770.
22. *Id.*, at 773-774.
23. *Id.*, at 775.
24. *Id.*, at 776.
25. *Ibid.*
26. Darling to the Judges, 4 April 1829, *H.R.A.* I/XIV, 764.
27. The Judges to Darling, 25 April 1829, *ibid.*
28. *Id.*, at 765.
29. *Ibid.*

30. Darling to Murray, 20 May 1829, *H.R.A.* I/XIV, 762.
31. They substantially concerned the conduct of John Stephen in relation to the case – Darling to Murray, 29 June 1829, *H.R.A.* I/XV, 28, and Murray to Darling, 12 August 1830 and enclosures, *id.*, 678.
32. *H.R.A.* I/XV, 346.
33. Twiss to Darling, 30 January 1830, "private", *H.R.A.* I/XV, 354.
34. Below, text to notes 58, 59, 87.
35. Murray to Darling, 30 January 1820, "separate", *H.R.A.* I/XV, 346 at 348. For Forbes' private opinion of the criticism, *see* Forbes to Goulburn, 25 July 1820, J.M. Bennett (ed.), *Some Papers of Sir Francis Forbes* (Sydney 1998), 200 at 201.
36. *H.R.A.*, id., at 346.
37. Quoted, *ibid.*
38. "Mr Twiss's Paper", *id.*, 348-353.
39. At 349.
40. *Ibid.*
41. *Ibid.*
42. Currey, *op. cit.* n. 7, 347; David Neal, *The Rule of Law in a Penal Colony* (Cambridge 1991), 111.
43. Currey, *ibid.*, 345-346.
44. *Op. cit.* n. 38, 349.
45. *Id.*, 353.
46. *Ibid.*
47. *Op. et loc. cit.* n. 36.
48. *Ibid.* at 347.
49. *Ibid.*
50. *Ibid.*
51. *Ibid.*, italics added.
52. Dowling to Brougham, 7 March 1836, Brougham MSS (16,882), University College, London.
53. *Op. cit.* n. 7, 346; and Neal, *op. cit.* n. 42, 112 (as to misinterpretation of the issues by social historians).
54. *Op. cit.* n. 7, 347.
55. Dowling to Murray, 10 July 1830, *H.R.A.* I/XV, 709. The letter would have been even more fawning, its first draft (Letters and Opinions Vol. 2 – N.S.W.A. 2/3471, 123) included a sentence, "I candidly hope, Sir, you will forgive me", struck out on revision.
56. *H.R.A.* I/XV, 709.
57. *Id.*, at 710.
58. *Ibid.*
59. *Id.*, at 711.
60. As Forbes insisted (Currey, *op. cit.* n. 7, 347) "in this Colony, where every thing is new and requires to be settled, the Judges are differently situated. The business of the Court must frequently stop, if we adhered to the rigid practice of Westminster".
61. The judges were united in a sequel in *Hall v. Rossi* (below, Ch. 4, text to n. 83) where Governor Darling thought mistakenly that an interpretation of the Act had been offered at variance from Downing Street's "orders". The judges replied (14 July 1830, *H.R.A.* I/XV, 650 at 651) "In none of the cases brought before the Court since that of Jane New, has the construction of the 9th section of the 9th *Geo.* 4, cap. 83 been substantively brought under consideration, . . . and we still hold ourselves ready to reconsider and decide that question, should it ever again be distinctly brought before the Court".

62. Dowling to Brougham, 15 February 1831, Brougham MSS (1260), University College, London.
63. (1966) 1 *A.D.B.* 500.
64. From 1828, the *Sydney Monitor*.
65. *Op. cit.* n. 63, at 501.
66. *The Newspaper Press in New South Wales 1803-1920* (Sydney 1976), 16, and sources there cited.
67. Hall to Murray, 12 March 1829, *H.R.A.* I/XV, 54; 2 May 1829, *id.*, 61.
68. Darling to Murray, 6 July 1829, *H.R.A.* I/XV, 53.
69. 12 March 1829, *H.R.A.* I/XV at 55.
70. *See* also, below, text to n. 76.
71. In legal proceedings, the costs of which were an embarrassment to the government, Darling to Murray, 12 April 1830, *H.R.A.* I/XV, 418. *See* also, Currey, *op. cit.* n. 7, 364.
72. Darling to Murray, *ibid.*
73. Murray to Darling, 8 November 1830, *H.R.A.* I/XV, 811-812.
74. *Ibid.* For Darling's uncontrite reply of 27 June 1831 – *H.R.A.* I/XVI, 289 at 291.
75. Murray to Darling, 8 November 1830, *H.R.A.* I/XV, 812.
76. Murray to Darling, 3 May 1830, *H.R.A.* I/XV, 463.
77. At 464.
78. *Ibid.*
79. Darling to Murray, 12 April 1830, *H.R.A.* I/XV, 418.
80. Darling to Murray, 2 December 1830, *H.R.A.* I/XV, 822.
81. At 823.
82 *Op. cit.* n. 7, 348; *cf.* A.G.L. Shaw, *Convicts and the Colonies* (Melbourne 1978), 232-233.
83. Dowling to Brougham, 15 February 1831, *op. cit.* n. 62.
84. *Ibid.*
85. *Ibid.*
86. *Ibid.*
87. *Ibid.*

Chapter 3

1. J.B. Atlay, *The Victorian Chancellors* Vol. 1 (London 1906), 283.
2. *Id.*, 284. Indeed, Dowling was remembered, long after his death, for alleged severity, In 1829, according to the *Armidale Express*, 24 January 1896, 5, Dowling "sentenced a man to be flogged at the cart's tail from George Street Post Office to Market Street Wharf, Sydney, for stealing a pair of oars".
3. (1831) 1 Legge 5.
4. *R. v. Gully* (1773) 1 Leach 98 [168 E.R. 151].
5. 1 Legge at 9.
6. At 20.
7. At 21.
8. J.M. Bennett, *A History of the Supreme Court of New South Wales* (Sydney 1974), 32, 96, 171, and particularly 173.
9. 1 Legge at 12.
10. At 11.
11. At 16. It scarcely differed, in objects, from some of the British colonies in tropical Africa and in the Caribbean.
12. As summarized in Sir Charles James Tarring, *Chapters on the Law Relating to the Colonies* (London 1913), 3, and by many later writers.

13. 1 Legge at 13.
14. At 10.
15. At 15. *See* also Alex C. Castles, *An Australian Legal History* (Sydney 1982), 503.
16. 1 Legge at 18.
17. At 18.
18. At 19.
19. At 22.
20. Some reliance was placed on the case of *R. v. Yems, Hilton, Gardner and Snell* (1829) where the objection, that the witnesses were convicts attaint, was considered by Forbes as too important to be determined *ex tempore,* and was supposedly reserved – *Sydney Gazette,* 9 April 1829, 2.
21. 1 Legge at 24-25.
22. At 25, italics added.
23. At 12.
24. *Ibid.*
25. At 29.
26. At 34.
27. Particularly the *Civil Rights of Convicts Act* 1828.
28. *See* generally, Castles, *op. cit.* n. 15, 500, 502-503.
29. For example, Gibbs, J., in *Dugan v. Mirror Newspapers Ltd* (1978) 142 C.L.R. 583 at 589; and Castles, *loc. cit.* n. 15.
30. 1 Legge at 37.
31. *Ibid.*
32. Bennett, *op. cit.* n. 8, 169-170.
33. C.H. Currey, *Sir Francis Forbes* (Sydney 1968), 464.
34. Extract from Executive Council proceedings, 22 December 1832, C.O. 201/231, f. 418 at f. 418a.
35. *Ibid.*
36. 18 March 1833, *H.R.A.* I/XVII, 50 at 51.
37. *Ibid.*
38. Stanley to Bourke, 22 October 1833, *H.R.A.* I/XVII, 243.
39. For later statutory developments, *see* Castles, *op. cit.* n. 15, 346.
40. *S.M.H.,* 27 June 1844, 2; Gipps to Stanley, 9 July 1844, *H.R.A.* I/XXIII, 659.
41. This differed textually from the Bill submitted to the Legislative Council, for which *see S.M.H.,* 18 June 1844, 2.
42. *Cross on Evidence* (2nd Australian ed., Sydney 1979), 160. Or, as the sponsor of the Bill for the new colonial Act observed: "the principle was, that a party should not be excluded from giving evidence by the circumstance of his being convicted; or his being interested in the event of the trial in which he gave such evidence, but that the act . . . should go to his credibility only. It had been found that the course of justice had been frequently impeded by the disabilities affecting such parties under the old law", *S.M.H.,* 14 June 1844, 2.
43. *Australian,* 6 June 1828, 3.
44. But *see* generally the references below, Ch. 8, n. 130. For Dowling's part, as judge, in the infamous case of the "Myall Creek Massacre" (1838), *see* the index to the author's companion volume on Sir William a'Beckett.
45. Dowling's report, 3 June 1829, *H.R.A.* I/XV, 84.
46. At 85.
47. *Ibid.*
48. *See* text to n. 51.
49. Dowling's report, 3 June 1829, *H.R.A.* I/XV, 88.
50. Baxter to Darling, 1 July 1829, *H.R.A.* I/XV, 84.

51. Dowling's report, 3 June 1829, *H.R.A.* I/XV, 87.
52. *Ibid.*
53. Darling to Murray, 28 July 1828, *H.R.A.* I/XV, 83. There was soon another ground for complaint when Baxter tried to compel Dowling to produce his judicial notes in evidence – below, Ch. 8, text to n. 133.
54. Above, text to n. 3 and following; *Sydney Gazette*, 22 February 1822, 2; memorandum of F.A. Hely, *H.R.A.* I/XV, 848 at 849.
55. Record of sentence, *H.R.A.* I/XV, 840.
56. Minute of proceedings, 3 January 1829, *H.R.A.* I/XV, 841 at 842.
57. *Ibid.*
58. Order of 3 January 1829, *H.R.A.* I/XV, 842.
59. McLeay to Baxter, 26 February 1829, *H.R.A.* I/XV, 843. *Cf.* the opinion of Hely, *ibid.* at 849.
60. Hely to McLeay, 21 December 1830, *H.R.A.* I/XV, 844 at 845; and McLeay to Hely, 9 January 1829, *id.* at 847; McLeay to Logan, 9 January 1829, *id.* at 848.
61. Below, Ch. 4.
62. 9 March 1829, 1516.
63. Affidavit by J. Weston, 1 September 1829, *H.R.A.* I/XV, 845 at 846.
64. *Times* (London), 10 July 1830, 1. For Darling's response to these and related criticisms, *see* Darling to Murray, 22 December 1830, C.O. 201/213, f. 538.
65. Murray to Darling, 20 July 1830, C.O. 202/25, f. 239.
66. Baxter to McLeay, 6 January 1829, *H.R.A.* I/XV, 850.
67. Manning to McLeay, 21 December 1830, *id.*, 841.
68. Order of Baxter, 3 January 1829, *id.*, 842.
69. McLeay to Darling, 22 December 1830, *id.*, 837 at 839.
70. Chapter 1, text to n. 63.
71. "Proceedings of the Supreme Court of New South Wales" (Dowling's Notebooks) Vol. 14 (N.S.W.A. 2/3197), 20.
72. At 22.
73. The papers were sent to Downing Street – Darling to Murray, 22 December 1830, *H.R.A.* I/XV, 837. The matter thereafter simmered, along with others being agitated against Darling, and eventually petered out. For a summary, *see* Brian H. Fletcher, *Ralph Darling* (Oxford 1984), 306-307.
74. (1966) 1 *A.D.B.* 74 at 75.
75. 8 May 1832, 2.
76. *Ibid.* The *Gazette* further expressed the hope that such admonitions would "have the effect of putting an end to those unseemly altercations which have so frequently taken place at inquests".
77. 12 May 1832, 2.
78. At 3.
79. Trial of Mahony and Bridges, 8 August 1833, *H.R.A.* I/XVII, 360.
80. His visit to Norfolk Island is not otherwise noticed in this book; but *see* Dowling's Journal (M.L. B804) published in (1905) *1 J.R.A.H.S.* 217; and Anthony Dowling, *Fortis et Egregius or Dowling of Ballyroan* (Sydney 1996), 122-124.
81. The Judges to Bourke, 4 January 1834, *H.R.A.* I/XVII, 360 at 360-361.
82. 10 August 1833, 2.
83. Bourke to Stanley, 24 January 1834, and enclosure, *H.R.A.* I/XVII, 359.
84. The Judges to Bourke, 4 January 1834, *H.R.A.* I/XVII, 360 at 363.
85. *Ibid.*, at 364-365.
86. *Id.*, at 362.
87. *Ibid.*

88. In which he also participated as a Member of the Legislative Council, *see* particularly Ch. 9.
89. Chapter 6, text to n. 2, and Ch. 7, text to n. 2-5.
90. The Judges to Bourke, 4 January 1834, *H.R.A.* I/XVII, 360 at 363.

Chapter 4

1. *See* above, Ch. 2, text to n. 83, and following.
2. (1966) 1 *A.D.B.* 500.
3. R.B. Walker, *The Newspaper Press in New South Wales 1803-1920* (Sydney 1976), 16-17.
4. *See* generally, J.A. Ferguson, "Edward Smith Hall and the 'Monitor'" (1930) 17 *J.R.A.H.S.* 163.
5. Above Ch. 3, text to n. 62 following. Darling considered Hall to be "a man so utterly regardless of truth and so totally unworthy of attention", Darling to Murray, 2 January 1829, *H.R.A.* I/XIV, 578.
6. (1967) 2 *A.D.B.* 431.
7. Note 118 in *H.R.A.* I/XIV, 923; Brian H. Fletcher, *Ralph Darling* (Oxford 1984), 271.
8. According, moreover, to Ransome T. Wyatt, "A Wine Merchant in Gaiters" (1949) 35 *J.R.A.H.S.* 145 at 238, "Scott arbitrarily and illegally directed the pew to be disposed of 'to some person of a more respectable character'".
9. Fletcher, *op. et loc. cit.* n. 7.
10. Hall to McLeay, 3 November 1828, *H.R.A.* I/XIV, 584 at 585-586; Hall to Murray, 26 November 1828, *id.*, 596 at 600.
11. 5 July 1828, 1244.
12. John Macarthur, (1967) 2 *A.D.B.* 153.
13. *Loc. cit.* n. 11.
14. *Sydney Gazette*, 1 October 1828, 2; *Sydney Monitor*, 4 October 1828, 1346-1349, but especially 1349.
15. He "could not afford to employ counsel, but pleaded his own cause, though he felt his inability to do justice to himself on points of law", Hall's petition of 20 January 1831, C.O. 201/223, f. 445.
16. *Sydney Gazette*, 1 October 1828, 3.
17. *See* generally, C.H. Currey, *Sir Francis Forbes* (Sydney 1968), 312. Hall attempted, unsuccessfully, to proceed by way of criminal information against Colonial Secretary McLeay for observations made on the Governor's behalf in response to the verdict, *Sydney Monitor*, 8 November 1828, 1388.
18. Hall's petition of 20 January 1831, C.O. 201/223, f. 445-445a; also published in *Sydney Monitor*, 30 May 1832, 2.
19. Petition, *ibid.*, f. 445a. For Hall's later expression of "surprise" at the severity of the remarks, *see* Hall to Murray, 8 May 1830, *H.R.A.* I/XV, 633 at 634.
20. *Australian*, 9 January 1829, 3; Scott to Attorney-General Baxter, 5 November 1829, quoted Wyatt, *op. cit.* n. 8, 241-242.
21. *Australian, ibid.*
22. *Sydney Gazette*, 13 January 1829, 2.
23. *Ibid.*
24. As, when put to the test, it did, *see* below, text to n. 92-97.
25. *Sydney Gazette, loc. cit.* n. 22.
26. *Ibid.*
27. *Ibid.*
28. *Ibid.*

29. Hall to Murray, 8 May 1830, *H.R.A.* I/XV, 633 at 635.
30. *Sydney Monitor*, 26 January 1829, 1474.
31. *Sydney Gazette*, 15 December 1829, 2.
32. *Id.*, 24 December 1829, 2.
33. Hall to Murray, 8 May 1830, *H.R.A.* I/XV, 633.
34. *Ibid.* at 634.
35. Hall applied for a trial at bar (before the Full Court and assessors), but Stephen, J., was unwell, and the Chief Justice considered proceedings at bar inconvenient at first instance. Dowling volunteered to hear the case with assessors – *Sydney Monitor*, 16 March 1829, 1533.
36. *Australian*, 13 March 1829, 3.
37. As to whom, *see* J.M. Bennett, *A History of Solicitors in New South Wales* (Sydney 1984), 47, 49.
38. *Australian, loc. cit.* n. 36.
39. *Ibid.*
40. 14 March 1829, 3. Dowling certified to the accuracy of that report, Dowling to Condamine, 13 July 1829, Letters and Opinions, Vol. 1 (N.S.W.A. 2/3470), 257.
41. Enclosure *No.* 2 in Darling to Murray, *H.R.A.* I/XV, at 132-140.
42. *See* generally, J.M. Bennett, *A History of the Supreme Court of New South Wales* (Sydney 1974), 63-64.
43. *H.R.A.* I/XV, at 133.
44. *Id.*, at 135.
45. *Id.*, at 135-136.
46. *Id.*, at 139.
47. *Id.*, at 136.
48. *Id.*, at 138. The Secretary of State saw no reason "to disapprove or to regret" Dowling's views, Murray to Darling, 20 May 1830, *H.R.A.* I/XV, 475 at 476.
49. *H.R.A.* I/XV, at 140.
50. *Australian*, 31 March 1829, 3.
51. Hall's petition , *op. cit.* n. 15, at f. 445a. In the *Sydney Monitor* of 16 March 1829, 1533, Hall declared that he could give "no idea" of the extent of the proceedings – "so much warmth and irritation prevailed between the Judge, the Crown officers and Mr Keith. . . They complained and recriminated . . . one of the other. The Judge had insinuated that Mr Keith should not lend himself to introduce into a Court of Justice, political and malicious feelings".
52. *See* generally, Alex C. Castles, *An Australian Legal History* (Sydney 1982), 145, 190.
53. *Sydney Gazette*, 14 April 1829, 2-3.
54. *Australian*, 17 April 1829, 2.
55. Hall's petition, *op. et loc. cit.* n. 15; Hall to Murray, 19 May 1830, *H.R.A.* I/XV, 628 at 629. For the alleged libels, *see Sydney Monitor*, 10 February 1829, 1492, 17 February 1829, 1499.
56. For instance, *Sydney Gazette*, 3 December 1829, 2-3; 24 December 1829, 2.
57. *Sydney Monitor*, 6 June 1829, 1627.
58. *Sydney Gazette*, 26 December 1829, 2.
59. *Sydney Monitor*, 19 July 1829, 2-3.
60. *Sydney Gazette, loc. cit.* n. 58.
61. *Ibid.*
62. (1967) 2 *A.D.B.* 582.
63. *Sydney Gazette*, 26 December 1829, 3.
64. *R. v. Mary Ann Carlile* (1821) 1 St. Tri. N.S.

65. 31 December 1829, 2.
66. *Ibid.*
67. *See* Currey, *op. cit.* n. 17, 361.
68. *Sydney Gazette*, 16 April 1829, 3.
69. *Ibid.*
70. 15 April 1829, 2; 17 April 1829, 2, 3.
71. In the case of Hall, to one year for the "seditious" libel of the Governor, and to three months for the libel on Crotty.
72. *Sydney Gazette*, 25 June 1829, 3.
73. *Australian*, 23 June 1829, 3; *Sydney Gazette*, 23 June 1829, 3. Hall thought Stephen's dissent a vindication – "Mr Justice Stephen, on my being called up for judgment, protested against the legality of my conviction ... on the ground that it was contrary to common sense and natural justice to punish Englishmen, who had been tried by a Jury selected by their Prosecutor", Hall to Murray, 17 October 1829, *H.R.A.* I/XV, 442 at 443.
74. Below, text to n. 85 and following.
75. *Sydney Gazette*, 25 June 1829, 3.
76. 16 June 1829, 2.
77. *Australian*, 3 July 1829, 2; *Sydney Gazette*, 4 July 1829, 2-3.
78. *Ibid.* in each case.
79. Above, Ch. 2, text to n. 7 and following.
80. *Australian*, *loc. cit.* n. 77. The quotation is a summary by that journal of Dowling's more extensive remarks, reported at greater length in *Sydney Gazette*, *loc. cit.* n. 77.
81. *Sydney Gazette*, *ibid.*
82. *Ibid.*
83. For his application for trial by common jury, *see Sydney Gazette*, 3 December 1829, 2.
84. *See* generally, Bennett, *op. cit.* n. 42, 178-179.
85. Under 10 *Geo.* IV *No.* 8 and 11 *Geo.* IV *No.* 2; Bennett, *op. cit.* n. 42, 83 and 273 note 235.
86. *Sydney Gazette*, 16 March 1830, 2.
87. *Id.*, 18 March 1830, 2. The first such case was in January 1825, *id.*, 17 February 1825, 2.
88. *Sydney Gazette*, 18 March 1830, 3.
89. Hall had discovered, and sustained, a capacity to succeed before civilian juries, whereas he "inevitably lost" before military juries, *cf.* Ferguson, *op. cit.* n. 4, 189.
90. C.M.H. Clark, *A History of Australia* II (Melbourne 1968), 92.
91. Wyatt, *op. cit.* n. 8, 259.
92. *Sydney Gazette*, 6 April 1830, 3-4; 10 and 13 April 1830, 3; Currey, *op. cit.* n. 17, 312.
93. Hall's petition of 20 January 1831, C.O. 201/223, f. 445a; Hall to Murray (written in gaol), 3 April 1830, Dowling's Letters and Opinions Vol. 1 (N.S.W.A. 2/3470), 300.
94. *Sydney Gazette*, 13 April 1830, 3.
95. *Ibid.*
96. *Australian*, 7 April 1830, 3; *cf.* Currey, *op. cit.* n. 17, 312.
97. Hall to Murray, 8 May 1830, *H.R.A.* I/XV, 633 at 636.
98. *Sydney Gazette*, 20 March 1830, 3.
99. Walker, *op. et loc. cit.* n. 3.
100. As to the costs, *see* Darling to Murray, 12 April 1830, *H.R.A.* I/XV, 418.

101. (1967) 2 *A.D.B.* 204.
102. For a synopsis, *see* (1967) 2 *A.D.B.* at 585; Currey, *op. cit.* n. 17, 355-356.
103. Text of addresses, *H.R.A.* I/XV, 71, 74.
104. Reply by Darling, 4 July 1829, *id.*, 73.
105. Reply by Darling, 6 July 1829, *id.*, 75.
106. Darling to Twiss, 7 July 1829, *H.R.A.* I/XV, 70.
107. *Sydney Gazette*, 1 July 1830, 3, 8 June 1830, 2-4; extract of report by Forbes, C.J., *H.R.A.* I/XV, 653.
108 *Sydney Gazette*, 1 July 1830, 3.
109. *Ibid.*, at 4. The precedent case was *R. v. Wright* (1799) 8 T.R. 293 [101 E.R. 1396].
110 *Cf. Sydney Monitor*, 3 April 1830, 2.
111. Sometimes rendered "Shelly". *Sydney Gazette*, 31 December 1829, 2; Fletcher, *op. cit.* n. 7, 300-304.
112. Particularly *Sydney Monitor*, 21 November 1829, 2.
113. Darling to Twiss, 13 January 1830, *H.R.A.* I/XV, 331 at 332; and *ibid.* note 74 at pp 888-889.
114. Darling to Twiss, 22 December 1829, *H.R.A.* I/XV, 299 at 300.
115. *Sydney Gazette*, 5 January 1830, 2 (editorial).
116. *Australian*, 7 April 1830, 3.
117. Hall to Murray, 8 May 1830, *H.R.A.* I/XV, 633 at 638.
118. *See* below, text to n. 127.
119. *Sydney Monitor*, 3 April 1830, 2.
120. *Australian*, 7 April 1830, 3.
121. *Sydney Gazette*, 6, 8 April 1830, 2-3 in each case; McLeay's "Statement of Facts", July1830, *H.R.A.* I/XV, 595 at 597.
122. *Sydney Gazette*, 6 July 1830, 3.
123. Below, text to n. 145.
124. Above, text to n. 18, 51, 97.
125. The text of the petition is at C.O. 201/223, f. 445a.
126. There still being no civilian jury in the Colony.
127. *Sydney Gazette*, 10 October 1829, 2; 13 October 1829, 2-3; 15 October 1829, 2; Hall to Murray published in *Sydney Monitor*, 6 June 1829, 1628; Darling to Murray, 21 July 1830, and enclosures, *H.R.A.* I/XV, 594; M. Hazzard, *Punishment Short of Death* (Melbourne 1984), 113-117.
128. *Sydney Monitor*, 7 November 1829, 2. Hall would have been predisposed to dislike Wright who was well regarded by Darling and later appointed by him to the Police Magistracy, *id.*, 30 May 1832, 2.
129. Hall's petition, *loc. cit.* n. 125.
130. *Ibid.*
131. Hall to Howick, 23 September 1831, C.O. 201/223, f. 459 at f. 460.
132. *Sydney Monitor*, 6 June 1829, 1628.
133. Report of McLeay, July 1830, *H.R.A.* I/XV, 595 at 596.
134. *Sydney Gazette*, 13 October 1829, 3.
135. *Ibid.* Report of McLeay, July 1830, *H.R.A.* I/XV, 595 at 597.
136. *Ibid.* Darling resented the judicial support for Wentworth, Darling to Somerset, 27 November 1830, *H.R.A.* I/XV, 598 at 599.
137. *Ibid. see* also Darling to Murray, 21 July 1830, *H.R.A.* I/XV, 594, giving particulars of the "conspiracy" at 595; and Darling's "Replies to Accusations", *id.*, at 643.
138. Darling to Somerset, *loc. cit.* n. 136.
139. Hall to Murray, 19 May 1830, *H.R.A.* I/XV, 628 at 631.

140. The expense of legal fees imposed on the government to secure that result was ill accepted at the Colonial Office – Murray to Darling, 8 November 1830, *H.R.A.* I/XV, 810 at 811.
141. Goderich to Darling, 23 December 1830, *H.R.A.* I/XV, 863.
142. Darling to Murray, 27 July 1830, *H.R.A.* I/XV, 626 at 627.
143. Clark, *op. cit.* n. 90, 343.
144. Hall's petition of 20 January 1831, C.O. 201/223, f. 445a.
145. Dowling to Brougham, 15 February 1831, Brougham MSS (1260), University College, London.
146. *Ibid.*
147. *Ibid. Cf.* Dowling to Bourke, 2 June 1832, *H.R.A.* I/XVI, 656 at 657: "During the last four years I have had a most laborious, anxious and I must say an unequal share of the judicial duties of this colony cast upon my shoulders. . . A Judge cannot pick and chuse the cases he will or will not try".
148. Dowling to Brougham, *loc. cit.* n. 145.
149. *Times* (London), 24 December 1830, 2.
150. C.O. 201/233, f. 459.
151. *Sydney Gazette*, 2 June 1832, 2 (Dowling's own report).
152. *Ibid.*
153. *Ibid.*
154. *Sydney Monitor*, 12 May 1832, 3.
155. *Id.*, 30 May 1832, 2.
156. *Ibid.*
157. *Ibid.*
158. *Loc. cit.* n. 151.
159. Dowling to Bourke, 2 June 1832, *H.R.A.* I/XVI, 656.
160. At 657.
161. Bourke to Goderich, 2 June 1832, *H.R.A.* I/XVI, 656.
162. Goderich to Bourke, 30 November 1832, *id.*, 807.
163. *Ibid.* 808.

Chapter 5

1. (1967) 2 *A.D.B.* 477 (*s.v.* John Stephen), at 478.
2. James Stephen to Hay, 2 March 1832; Hay to J. Stewart, 5 March 1832, *British Parliamentary Papers* (Irish University Press series) "Colonies – Australia", Vol. 4, 261-263.
3. *See* below, Ch. 7, text to n. 28 and following; and to n. 113. Dowling wrote to his son: "My new colleague on the Bench, Mr Alfred Stephen, is an excellent person and we agree remarkably well. . . He is a trump of the first water". Letters to J.S. Dowling, 28 November 1839 and 7 August 1841.
4. *See* references to him in the index. Also, generally, (1966) 1 *A.D.B.* 184.
5. Hazel King, *Richard Bourke* (Melbourne 1971), 90.
6. Bourke to Howick, 21 July 1831, C.O. 201/221, f. 375 at f. 376a.
7. Others thought him "a little too fond of judicial display", *S.M.H.*, 5 October 1869, 5.
8. King, *Richard Bourke*, 174. *Cf.* a differently worded conclusion in Hazel King, "Pulling Strings at the Colonial Office" (1975) 61 *J.R.A.H.S.* 144 at 151.
9. For a summary of which, *see* (1966) 1 *A.D.B.* 392 (*s.v.* Sir Francis Forbes), at 394-397.
10. Chief Justice Forbes to Bourke, 19 August 1834, in J.M. Bennett (ed.) *Some Papers of Sir Francis Forbes* (Sydney 1998), 229 at 230.

11. Bennett (ed.), *ibid.*, Introduction, viii-ix.
12. Referred to in Bourke to Burton, 21 July 1835, C.O. 201/250, f. 304a.
13. King, *Richard Bourke*, 174. As to the "kind and friendly attention of Bourke", *see* W.W. Burton to Hay, 6 September 1833, C.O. 201/235, f. 63 at f. 65a.
14. In the writer's companion study of Forbes, *passim*; and, generally, K.G. Allars, "Sir William Westbrooke Burton" (1951) 37 *J.R.A.H.S.* 257.
15. Dowling to Brougham, 7 March 1836, Brougham MSS (16,882), University College, London.
16. Forbes nurtured a corresponding reserve about Dowling and his politics and, before leaving for England, Forbes demanded an assurance of Dowling that he would "support the King's representative in the policy and measures of his government" (Dowling to Brougham, *op. et loc. cit.* n. 15): that Dowling was true to his assurance was attested in Dowling to Bourke, 26 January 1837, Bourke Family Papers (M.L.MSS 403/6), 103-104.
17. Dowling to Brougham, *op. et loc. cit.* n. 15.
18. *See* above, Ch. 1, text to n. 63.
19. Dowling to Brougham, 20 September 1835, Brougham MSS (16,881), University College, London. Also Dowling to Glenelg, 2 October 1835, *H.R.A.* I/XVIII, 119 at 122.
20. To J.S. Dowling, 10 March 1839.
21. Text to n. 37 and following.
22. Bourke to Glenelg, 1 December 1835, *H.R.A.* I/XVIII, 216.
23. R. Bourke, junior, to Spring Rice (n.d.), Bourke Papers, Vol. 11 (M.L. A1738), 612.
24. Quoted, J.M. Bennett, *A History of the Supreme Court of New South Wales* (Sydney 1974), 35. Edmund dutifully pursued his brother's cause, submitting an importunate testimonial to Under Secretary Hay, 12 June 1833, C.O. 201/235, f. 46.
25. Burton to Bourke, 28 July 1835, C.O. 201/250, f. 278.
26. The matter of seniority would, within the same jurisdiction, have been governed by date of commission: Dowling held the earlier commission – below, text to n. 64.
27. Hay to Burton, 26 June 1827, *H.R.A.* I/VIII, 127. Dowling must have been astonished to receive a letter, dated 13 October 1832, from Chief Justice Wylde of Cape Town (latterly Judge-Advocate in Sydney), stating "You will hear from [Burton] how cruelly he has been treated at home; his fate proves that a charter has no seal of security for appointments under it, and the notion of a Patent Place for life under its provisions is all moonshine", quoted, J. Arthur Dowling, "The Judiciary" (1907) 2 *J.R.A.H.S.* 105 at 106.
28. Dowling to McLeay, 8 August 1835, *H.R.A.* I/XVIII 128.
29. *Id.* at 129.
30. *See* Ch. 1, text to n. 75.
31. Dowling to McLeay, *op. cit.* n 28.
32. McLeay to Burton, 11 August 1835, C.O. 201/250, f. 288.
33. Bourke to Glenelg, 3 October 1835, *H.R.A.* I/XVIII, 101 at 111.
34. Forbes to McLeay, "confidential", 19 August 1835, C.O. 201/250, f. 289a at f. 290-290a. Burton condemned it as "an evasive opinion", Burton to Stephen, 4 September 1835, *id.*, f. 302 at 302a. But, *see* C.H. Currey, *Sir Francis Forbes* (Sydney 1968), 494-495.
35. Kinchela and Plunkett to McLeay, 22 August 1835, *H.R.A.* I/XVIII, 129.
36. Bourke to Glenelg, *loc. cit.* n. 33.
37. *Id.*, at 112.

38. Burton to Glenelg, 2 September 1835, *H.R.A.* I/XVIII, 113.
39. *Id.*, at 114.
40. Forbes disagreed: *see* Currey, *op. et loc. cit.* n. 34.
41. Burton to Glenelg, 3 October 1835, *H.R.A.* I/XVIII, 101 at 115.
42. *Id.*, at 116.
43. *Id.*, at 117.
44. *Id.*, at 117-118.
45. *Id.*, at 118.
46. *Ibid.*
47. Minute at C.O. 201/250, f. 269 at f. 273-273a.
48. Burton to Hay, 2 September 1835, C.O. 201/250, f. 294 at f. 294a.
49. *Id.*, at f. 295a. These assertions, and others like them were so exaggerated as to suggest a complete want of judicial objectivity.
50. *Id.*, at f. 296.
51. Burton to Stephen, 4 September 1835, C.O. 201/250, f. 302 at 302a.
52. *Id.*, at f. 305a.
53. *Ibid.*
54. *Id.*, at f. 306a.
55. *Id.*, at f. 300a.
56. Bourke to Glenelg, 3 October 1835, *H.R.A.* I/XVIII 110 at 111, 112.
57. The entire file is at C.O. 201/247, from f. 270.
58. Dowling to Brougham, *op. et loc. cit.* n. 19.
59. *Ibid.*
60. *Ibid.*, and Dowling to Glenelg, 2 October 1835, *H.R.A.* I/XVIII, 119.
61. *See* Ch. 1, text to n. 75.
62. Dowling to Glenelg, 2 October 1835, *H.R.A.* I/XVIII, 121.
63. *Ibid.*
64. Dowling to Bourke, 26 November 1835, *H.R.A.* I/XVIII, 200; Dowling to Glenelg, 26 November 1835, *id.*, at 199; Bourke to Glenelg, 26 November 1835, *ibid.*
65. Glenelg to Bourke, 29 March 1836, *H.R.A.* I/XVIII, 364 at 365.
66. *Ibid.*
67. *Id.*, at 365.
68. *Id.*, at 366.
69. *Ibid.*
70. *Ibid.* That occurred, so far as Dowling's appointment was concerned, in April 1836 – *Australian*, 22 April 1836, 2. Forbes made his greatest show of friendship to Dowling, whom he addressed as "The Honorable Chief Justice Dowling", in a letter from his departing ship on 21 April 1836. "My Dear Friend", he wrote, "This will be my last letter – it is only to say adieu – to thank you, from the bottom of my heart for your affectionate attentions to me", Autograph Letters of Public Men of Australia (M.L. A68), 294.
71. The "charge" was published in the *Sydney Monitor*, 21 November 1835, 2; and in [Macarthur] *New South Wales its Present State and Future Prospects* (London 1837), Appendix 34.
72. C.M.H. Clark, *A History of Australia* II (Melbourne 1968), 92.
73. J.M. Bennett, "Early Days of the Law in Country Districts" (1972) 46 *Australian Law Journal* 578 at 585-586.
74. *See* , generally, Bennett, *op. cit.* n. 24, 69-70.
75. *Sydney Monitor*, 21 November 1835, 2.
76. Currey, *op. cit.* n. 34, 491, 496-499; King, *op. cit.* n. 5, 175-177; Clark, *op. cit.* n. 72, 229; Allars, *op. cit.* n.14, 266-270.

77. Allars, *ibid.*, 269.
78. Bourke to Glenelg, 10 June 1836, *H.R.A.* I/XVIII, 436 at 437; and Bourke to Glenelg, 25 July 1836, *id.*, 456.
79. Quoted, Currey, *op. cit.* n. 34, 498.
80. 5 December 1835, Bourke Papers (M.L. Set 403, item 8), quoted King, *op. cit.* n. 5, 176.
81. *See* King, *ibid.*, at 177, for their *rapprochement.*
82. Bourke to Glenelg, 18 December 1835, *H.R.A.* I/XVIII, 228 at 232, and Colonial Office minutes at C.O. 201/248, f. 235a.
83. Glenelg to Bourke, 21 October 1836 *H.R.A.* I/XVIII, 576. For a comment on the consequences, *see* King, *op. cit.* n. 8 (1975) 61 *J.R.A.H.S.* at 64, n. 33.
84. *Report from the Select Committee of the House of Commons on Transportation* (London 1838), at 14; *see* also, 10, 30.

Chapter 6

1. J.M. Bennett, *Lives of the Australian Chief Justices – Sir Francis Forbes* – and *see* C.H. Currey, *Sir Francis Forbes* (Sydney 1968), 518-519. Dowling recorded that "Forbes seems sadly cut up at being obliged to resign and calls himself a poor gentleman", Letter to J.S. Dowling, 19 January 1839.
2. Kinchela was not confirmed in office – "a Judge, incapable of distinctly hearing the evidence on criminal trials, must be in danger of committing the most fatal errors", Glenelg to Bourke, 25 July 1837, *H.R.A.* I/XIX, 46: *see* also below, Ch. 7, text to n. 2-5.
3. J.N. Molony, *An Architect of Freedom* (Canberra 1973), 21.
4. Dowling to Brougham, 7 March 1836, Brougham MSS (16,882), University College, London. An extract is in C.O. 201/257, f. 412.
5. *Ibid.*
6. *Ibid.*
7. Below, text to n. 34.
8. Dowling to Brougham, *op. cit.* n. 4. P.C. Mowle, *A Genealogical History of Pioneer Families of Australia* (Fifth ed., Adelaide 1978), 54. Anthony Dowling, *Fortis et Egregius or Dowling of Ballyroan* (Sydney 1996), 103-106.
9. A disavowal intended to suggest Dowling's claimed sense of judicial detachment.
10. Dowling to Brougham, *op. cit.* n. 4.
11. To J.S. Dowling, 16 January 1838.
12. Below, text to n. 61.
13. To J.S. Dowling, 3 February 1838.
14. (1975) 61 *J.R.A.H.S.* 145.
15. V.G. Dowling to Glenelg, 26 August 1836, C.O. 201/257, f. 408.
16. At f. 409.
17. At f. 414a.
18. At f. 415.
19. At f. 415-415a.
20. Minute at f. 411.
21. C.O. 202/35, f. 71a-72a.
22. Forbes to Glenelg, 27 April 1837, J.M. Bennett (ed.), *Some Papers of Sir Francis Forbes* (Sydney 1998), 257.
23. Forbes to Bourke, 1 May 1837, *ibid.*, 258.
24. V.G. Dowling to Glenelg, 29 April 1837, C.O. 201/266, f. 248.
25. *Ibid.*

26. *Id.*, at f. 249a.
27. Grey to V.G. Dowling, 5 May 1837, C.O. 201/266, f. 250 and C.O. 202/36, f. 42a.
28. Bourke to Glenelg, 3 October 1835, *H.R.A.* I/XVIII, 110 at 112.
29. R. Bourke, junior, to Spring Rice, (n.d.), Bourke Papers, Vol. 11 (M.L. A1738), 611.
30. *Id.*, at 613.
31. Dowling to Bourke, 26 January 1837, Bourke Family Papers (M.L. MSS 403/6). Bourke's resignation was delayed for a year.
32. Italics added to "calamity", the very word used by James Macarthur to describe Dowling's prospective promotion.
33. Dowling to Bourke, *op. cit.* n. 31.
34. 27 May 1837, C.O. 201/267, f. 539.
35. *Id.*, at f. 540.
36. J.M. Bennett, *A History of the Supreme Court of New South Wales* (Sydney 1974), 116.
37. J. M. Bennett, *A History of Solicitors in New South Wales* (Sydney 1984), 55.
38. Bennett, *op. cit.* n. 36, 35.
39. Macarthur to Glenelg, *op. cit.* n. 34, at ff. 540a-541.
40. *Id.*, at f. 541a-542.
41. *Id.*, at f. 543a.
42. Minute, C.O. 201/267, f. 544a.
43. 22 May 1837, Bourke Papers, Vol. 11, (M.L. A1738), 616.
44. Stewart to Glenelg, 29 May 1837, C.O. 201/268, f. 157.
45. *Id.*, at f. 157a.
46. *Id.*, at f. 157a-158.
47. Minute, *id.*, at f. 158a.
48. Approved by Sir George Grey, but later cancelled – C.O. 201/266, f. 260 at f. 260a, and f. 264 at f. 264a.
49. *Id.*, at f. 261a, f. 265.
50. (1967) 2 *A.D.B.* 319, where the subject incident is not mentioned. *See* Currey, *op. cit.* n. 1, 184, for an earlier suggestion of Pedder's promotion.
51. Grey to V.G. Dowling, 6 June 1837, C.O. 202/36, f. 71 at f. 71a. Pedder is there referred to as "Peddar".
52. *Id.*, at f. 72a.
53. *Id.*, at f. 71a.
54. *Id.*, at f. 72.
55. *Ibid.*
56. *Id.*, at f. 72-72a.
57. V.G. Dowling to Glenelg, 7 June 1837, C.O. 201/266, f. 270.
58. *Ibid.*
59 *Id.*, at f. 270a.
60. *Id.*, at f. 271.
61. 27 June 1837, Letters to Sir James Dowling (M.L. A489); (1966) 1 *A.D.B.* at 318.
62. John Manning Ward, *James Macarthur* (Sydney 1981), 85.
63. V.G. Dowling to Stephen, 19 July 1837, C.O. 201/266, f. 279.
64. Stephen to V.G. Dowling, 8 August 1837, C.O. 202/36, f. 146.
65. To J.S. Dowling, 25 November 1837.
66. *Id.*, 16 January 1838.
67. *Id.*, 3 February 1838.
68. *Id.*, 16 January 1838.
69. *Op. cit.* n. 14, 156.
70. *See* further, below, Ch. 7, text to n. 160-161.

Chapter 7

1. *See* below, Ch. 8, text to n. 18.
2. (1967) 2 *A.D.B.* 51; *see* also above, Ch. 7, n. 2.
3. *Australian*, 12 September 1837, 2 (which represented the opinion of the solicitor G.R. Nichols), and *cf. id.*, 7 November 1837, 2.
4. Gipps later proposed that Kinchela be appointed "Master in Chancery", as he was - Gipps to Dowling, 27 October 1840 (Letters and Opinions, Vol.5 (N.S.W.A. 2/3474). unpaged.
5. *Australian, loc. cit.*, n. 3.
6. (1967) 2 *A.D.B.* 602; H.F. Behan, *Mr Justice J.W. Willis* (Glen Iris 1979), a work that would have been the richer had it been documented.
7. *Australian*, 7 November 1837, 2; Gipps to Russell, 3 January 1841, *H.R.A.* I/XXI, 160.
8. Useful information about Willis' Canadian career is in Behan, *op. cit.* n. 6; and, as to his service in British Guinana, B.A. Keon-Cohen, "John Walpole Willis: First Resident Judge in Victoria" (1972) 8 *Melbourne University Law Review*, 703 at 704, 707-708.
9. Certificate of Dr J. Mitchell, 10 January 1839, *H.R.A.* I/XX, 124 at 125.
10. Minute of James Stephen, C.O. 201/306, f. 329a. The reappointment was to a court in British Guiana.
11. To J.S. Dowling, 28 November 1839.
12. To J.S. Dowling, 20 April 1838. Willis arrived with great hopes for his own advancement. As Mr Justice Burton wrote to his brother Robert, 25 December 1837 (copy in the possession of the New South Wales Bar Association), "You are aware perhaps that a new Puisne Judge has come out, Mr Willis. He was anxious to be Chief Justice, but he had informed me this very day *tiffin* with him, that it was quite impossible, that Dowling had a claim to the office which could not be got over".
13. Dowling to Gipps, 16 March 1840, C.O. 201/306, f. 352 at f. 353a.
14. *Ibid.*
15. For example in *Ex parte Roxburgh* (1838) 1 Legge 86 at 88; Dowling to Gipps, 17 December 1840, C.O. 201/306, f. 394a; Sir Roger Therry, *Reminiscences of Thirty Years' Residence in New South Wales and Victoria* (2nd ed., London 1863), 340.
16. Gipps to Russell, 3 January 1841, *H.R.A.* I/XXI, 160 at 161; *Sydney Herald*, November 1839, 2.
17. *Australian*, 31 July 1838, 2; J.N. Molony, *An Architect of Freedom* (Canberra 1973), 197-198. For further commentary and references, *see* Frances O'Donoghue, *The Bishop of Botany Bay* (Sydney 1982), 49-50: letters of Bishop Polding show that he regarded Willis "as a tool of the more cunning Judge Burton and other hostile Tories" (at 49).
18. *Australian, ibid.*
19. Molony, *op. cit.* n. 17, 198.
20. *Australian, loc. cit.* n. 17.
21. He had little option, having exacerbated the storm by demanding that the Attorney-General proceed by *ex officio* information against Polding for libelling Willis, and Polding insisting that the matter be submitted to the Colonial Office - Gipps to Glenelg, 17 September 1838, *H.R.A.* I/XIX, 586; Normanby to Gipps, 3 March 1839, *H.R.A.* I/XX, 50.
22. To J.S. Dowling, 30 June 1839.
23. To J.S. Dowling, 16 March 1839.

24. From J.S. Dowling, 2 May 1840.
25. As to Plunkett (whom Dowling described as "my excellent friend", letter to J.S. Dowling, 17 March 1841), *see* Molony, *op. cit.* n. 17. As to Therry, *see* J.M. Bennett, Introduction to Therry, *op. cit.* n. 15 (facsimile ed., Sydney 1974).
26. Bennett, *ibid.* [19-20].
27. (1976) 6 *A.D.B.* 180 at 182.
28. The candidate proposed by Willis was William Montagu Manning ((1974) 5 *A.D.B.* 207), son of the court's Registrar John Edye Manning ((1967) 2 *A.D.B.* 202) a confidant of Willis – Dowling to Gipps, 17 December 1840, C.O. 201/306, f. 38 at f. 396a. Manning, the younger, might have had his immediate future prejudiced by Willis' notice of him. But he became Commissioner of the Courts of Requests in 1841 and, after other appointments, a Supreme Court Judge in 1876.
29. Lady Dowling to J.S. Dowling, 16 March 1839.
30. Sir James Dowling to J.S. Dowling, 16 March 1839.
31. Lady Dowling to J.S. Dowling, 20 June 1839.
32. 15 March 1839, C.O. 201/306, f. 559, and Letters and Opinions Vol. 5 (N.S.W.A. 2/3474), 48 at 49. J.M. Bennett, *A History of the Supreme Court* of *New South Wales* (Sydney 1974), 160.
33. 15 March 1839, C.O. 201/306, f. 559. Dowling conceded to the Governor that he had been "startled" by the suggestion, Dowling to Gipps, 16 March 1840, C.O. 201/306, f. 352 at f. 357a.
34. Dowling to Gipps, 17 December 1840, C.O. 201/306, f. 389 at f. 397; Dowling to Willis, 17 May 1839, *id.*, at f. 561; Gipps to Russell, 3 January 1841, *H.R.A.* I/XXI, 160 at 161.
35. Opinion of 3 August 1839, C.O. 201/306, f. 555 at f. 555a.
36. *Id.*, at f. 556.
37. Willis to Gipps, 7 December 1840, C.O. 201/306, f. 410 at f. 428a. Gipps, meanwhile, was so uncertain of the matter that he proposed to preside personally in Vice-Admiralty, with Dowling attending as assessor, 13 April 1840, Letters and Opinions, Vol. 5 (N.S.W.A. 2/3473), 72.
38. Report of 9 November 1839, *H.R.A.* I/XX, 395.
39. Quoted, C.H. Currey, *Sir Francis Forbes* (Sydney 1968), 457.
40. Because it had not been issued in the reign of Queen Victoria – a spurious argument – Willis to Dowling, 8 February 1840, Letters and Opinions, Vol. 5 (N.S.W.A. 2/3473), 17.
41. Willis to Gipps, 10 February 1840, C.O. 201/306, f. 553 at f. 553a; Dowling to Gipps, 16 March 1840, *id.*, f. 352 at f. 358; Willis to Dowling, 7 February 1840, Letters and Opinions, Vol. 5 (N.S.W.A. 2/3473), 13.
42. Willis to Gipps, 30 March 1839, *H.R.A.* I/XX, 118.
43. Russell to Gipps, 28 October 1839, *H.R.A.* I/XX, 374.
44. *Loc. cit.* n. 42.
45. Report of Dowling, C.O. 201/306, f. 354.
46. *Australian*, 25 June 1839, 2.
47. Of 1831.
48. *Australian*, 25 June 1839, 3; C.O. 201/306, f. 355 at f. 426a. The *Australian* later wrote editorially, 27 June 1839, 2, that Willis' judgment reflected "so much honor on him". For Dowling's contrary view, Dowling to Gipps, 17 December 1840, C.O. 201/306, f. 389 at f. 396a-397. Dowling's judgment was published in the *Australian*, 27 June 1839, 2; Stephen's, *id.*, 29 June 1839, 2.
49. *Op. cit.* n. 45 at f. 355a.
50. C.M.H. Clark, *A History of Australia* III (Melbourne 1973), 130.

51. (1967) 2 *A.D.B.* 235.
52. (1839) 1 Legge 123. J.M. Bennett, *A History of Solicitors in New South Wales* (Sydney 1984), 65.
53. Dowling to Gipps, 16 March 1840, C.O. 201/306, f. 352 at f. 359-359a.
54. *Id.*, at f. 359a.
55. To which he resolutely adhered, Willis to Dowling, 28 November 1839, Letters and Opinions, Vol. 5 (N.S.W.A. 2/3474), 2, 6, 9.
56. C.O. 201/306, f. 361; Dowling to Willis, 23 January 1840, Letters and Opinions, *ibid*, 3.
57. Dowling, on the other hand, insisted that "I did not consider my hasty memorandum, on Mr Nichol's petition, as an actual order of Court by which I was bound *per fas et nefas* until it was formally communicated to that gentleman", Dowling to Willis, 23 January 1840, Letters and Opinions, *ibid.*, at 5.
58. C.O. 201/306, f. 360a.
59. Gipps to Russell, 3 January 1841, *H.R.A.* I/XX, 160.
60. Willis' version was that "Sir James Dowling had made use of language so strong that I do not care to repeat it", Willis to Gipps, 22 March 1840, C.O. 201/306, f. 447 at f. 448a; and he accused Dowling of "very gross rudeness" on that occasion, Willis to Gipps, 7 December 1840, *id.*, f. 411a; for which, he claimed, Dowling had instantly apologized, *id.*, f. 419a.
61. Carried almost to a state of paralysis when Willis produced a newspaper reporting that Dowling's eldest brother had suffered a serious coach accident in England, of which news Dowling was unaware (C.O. 201/306, f. 362).
62. *Id.*, f. 361a.
63. Gipps to Russell, *loc. cit.* n. 59.
64. Roger Therry, who prudently declined to be drawn. A. Stephen to Dowling, February 1840, Letters and Opinions, Vol. 5 (N.S.W.A. 2/3474), 20.
65. C.O. 201/306, f. 364. There was also a well-calculated snipe at Stephen, suggesting that his practice as an attorney in Van Diemen's Land had disqualified him from judicial appointment. *See* also, Gipps to Dowling, 17 May 1840, Dowling to Gipps, 18 May 1840, Letters and Opinions, *ibid.*, at 58, 60.
66. C.O. 201/306, ff. 364a, 366a, 367a. Gipps to Dowling, 16 March 1840, Letters and Opinions, Vol. 5 (N.S.W.A. 2/3474), 20 at 43.
67. Dowling to Gipps, 23 March 1840, C.O. 201/306, f. 368 at f. 368a.
68. Dowling to Gipps, 25 March 1840, *id.*, f. 371a. For the strength of Alfred Stephen's support, *see* Stephen to Dowling, 23 March 1840, Letters and Opinions, Vol. 5 (N.S.W.A. 2/3474), 20 at 44-45.
69. Gipps to Russell, 3 January 1841, *H.R.A.* I/XXI, 160 at 162. Willis, however, kept pressing Dowling to yield to Nichol's petition, Willis to Dowling, 27 March 1840, Letters and Opinions, *ibid.*, at 46.
70. Below, text to n. 149.
71. Gipps to Russell, *loc. cit.* n. 69.
72. For instance, Dowling to Willis, 6, 7, 9 March 1840, Letters and Opinions, *op. cit.* n. 64, at 28, 32-33, 35.
73. Willis to Dowling, *id.*, at 37. For Willis' determination to decline all invitations, saving those to Government House – *id.*, 57. Willis to Gipps, 7 December 1840, C.O. 201/306, f. 410 at f. 411; Sir James Dowling to J.S. Dowling, 23 November 1839.
74. Letter of 12 March 1840, (1840) *V. & P. (L.C., N.S.W.)* "Proposed Judicial and Legal Improvements" (item no. 4), 14.
75. Dowling to Gipps, 4 June 1840, Letters and Opinions, *op. cit.* n. 64, at 110.

76. *Id.*, at 113.
77. Gipps to Dowling, 6 June 1840, *id.*, at 122; Gipps to Russell, 3 January 1841, *H.R.A.* I/XXI, 160 at 162.
78. A. Stephen to Dowling, 15 May 1840, Letters and Opinions, *op. cit.* n. 64, at 90.
79. Willis to Dowling, 5 June 1840, *ibid.*, at 115.
80. Dowling to Gipps, 7 June 1840, *id.*, at 126; Dowling to Willis, 7 June 1840, *id.*, at 126; Dowling to Willis, 7 June 1840, *id.*, at 127; Willis to Dowling, 7 June 1840, *id.*, at 128.
81. Gipps to Russell, *loc. cit.* n 77.
82. Dowling to Gipps, 4 December 1840, C.O. 201/306, f. 339 at f. 341.
83. *The Colonial Magazine and Commercial-Maritime Journal* commenced publication in London, under the editorship of R. Montgomery Martin, only in January 1840.
84. Willis to Dowling, 21 October 1840, Letters and Opinions, Vol. 5 (N.S.W.A. 2/3473), unpaged.
85. Willis to Dowling, 22 October 1840, *ibid.*
86. *Op. cit.* n. 83, from p. 332 and especially at p. 351.
87. Lady Dowling to J.S. Dowling, 14 February 1840.
88. Sir James Dowling to J.S. Dowling, 14 November 1840. A month later he wrote, 19 December 1840, "I have been greatly assisted by Mr Justice Stephen but I fear I shall lose him when Burton arrives . . . I fear Stephen will be sent to Port Phillip".
89. *Sydney Herald*, 4 December 1840, 2.
90. Gipps to Russell, 1 January 1841, *H.R.A.* I/XXI, 154. According to Stephen and Attorney-General Plunkett, Willis at first also unhesitatingly agreed that the clause was contrary to the law of England, Dowling to Gipps, 4 December 1840, C.O. 201/ 306, f. 339 at f. 342.
91. Gipps to Russell, 3 January 1841, *H.R.A.* I/XXI, 160 at 163. One record of Willis' grounds of dissent is a memorandum of 29 October 1840, C.O. 201/306, f. 496.
92. According to Dowling, Willis had made a practice of so addressing juries – Dowling to Gipps, 17 December 1840, C.O. 201/306, f. 389 at f. 395a; and Willis conceded the fact, with pride, Willis to Gipps, 7 December 1840, *id.*, f. 410 at f. 414.
93. Willis to Gipps, 21 November 1840, C.O. 201/306, f. 494; *Sydney Herald*, November 1840, 2.
94. Notwithstanding which, he insisted that "a weaker or less convincing paper . . . I never remember to have read", Willis to Gipps, 7 December 1840, C.O. 201/306, f. 410 at f. 414a.
95. Dowling to Gipps, 17 December 1840, C.O. 201/306, f. 389 at f. 396; and Dowling to Gipps, 4 December 1840, *id.*, f. 339 at f. 343.
96. Willis to Gipps, 7 December 1840, C.O. 201/306, f. 410; Dowling to Gipps, December 1840, *id.*, f. 339.
97. Dowling to Gipps, *id.*, f. 390a.
98. *Id.*, ff. 391-391a. Gipps thereafter required that all communications to and from himself and the judges be conducted through the Chief Justice.
99. Willis to Gipps, 30 March 1839, *H.R.A.* I/XX, 118 at 124.
100. Willis to Gipps, 30 April 1840, *id.*, 629-630.
101. Bennett, *op. cit.* n. 32, 94.
102. *Ibid.*, 279, note 11.
103. *Sydney Herald*, 2 November 1840, 2. Dowling's reaction is found in Dowling to Gipps, 4 December 1840, C.O. 201/306, f. 339 at f. 344a-345.

104. Willis to Dowling, 1 December 1840, C.O. 201/306, f. 378 at f. 378a. Willis was not the only one to make public criticisms. In overturning an order of Willis, in *Fisher v. Wilson* (1840) 1 Legge 155 at 157, Dowling deprecated the "loose notes of the evidence taken by His Honor".
105. Willis to Gipps, 7 December 1840, C.O. 201/306, f. 410 at f. 417. Willis further complained (Dowling to Gipps, 17 December 1840, C.O. 201/306, f. 389 at f. 397) that Dowling had written a letter, signed "A Bushman", published in the *Sydney Herald*, 2 December 1840, 2, critical of Willis. Dowling denied the allegation.
106. Dowling to Gipps, *op. cit.* n. 105, at f. 397a.
107. Dowling to Gipps, 4 December 1840, C.O. 201/306, f. 339 at f. 347; Willis to Gipps, 28 February 1840, (1840) *V. & P. (L.C., N.S.W.)*, 169.
108. Willis to Dowling, 29 May 1840, Cases and Opinions, Vol. 5 (N.S.W.A. 2/3473), 105.
109. Dowling to Willis, 2 November 1840, C.O. 201/306, f. 517.
110. This was written to forestall postponement of the matter until Burton's return – Dowling to Gipps, 3 November 1840, Cases and Opinions, *loc. cit.* n. 108, unpaged.
111. Willis to Dowling, 2 November 1840, *ibid.*, unpaged.
112. Dowling to Willis, 1 December 1840, C.O. 201/306, f. 374 at f. 375a.
113. Stephen to Dowling, 5 December 1840, *id.*, f. 384a: for the response of Willis, *id.*, f. 385, and Willis to Dowling, 1 December 1840, *id.*, f. 379.
114. 4 *Vic. No.* 22.
115. Italics added.
116. C.O. 201/306, f. 384.
117. Willis to Gipps, 7 December 1840, *id.*, f. 423; Willis to Dowling, 1 December 1840, *id.*, f. 379.
118. On the contrary, he maintained that "I could not give such a pledge without stultifying myself", Dowling to Gipps, 4 December 1840, *id.*, f. 339 at f. 346a.
119. Stephen to Dowling, 5 December 1840, *id.*, f. 383a at f. 384a.
120. Gipps to Russell, 1 January 1841, *H.R.A.* I/XXI, 155 at 156.
121. *Ibid.*
122. 1 December 1840, 2. Dowling considered its authorship due more to Willis than to Nichols – Dowling to Gipps, 4 December 1840, C.O. 201/306, f. 339 at f. 346.
123. Dowling to Willis, 1 December 1840, C.O. 201/306, f. 374 at f. 374a.
124. *Ibid.*, f. 375. For an *ex post facto* explanation by Dowling, *see* (1842) *V. & P. (L.C., N.S.W.)*, 283 at 284.
125. Dowling to Willis, *op. cit.* n. 123, at f. 376a.
126. *Id.*, f. 377. For Willis' response, that Burton had never wished for the "Chancellorship", *see* Willis to Dowling, 1 December 1840, *id.*, f. 378.
127. *Ibid.*, f. 379a.
128. *Ibid.*, at 380. Dowling urged the Governor to submit the matter to the Colonial Office, *op. cit* n. 122, f. 339a. To his son, Dowling wrote: "A more disagreeable man I never had to do with in my life. If he could truly shelter himself under the plea of *madness* I should look over all; but he is influenced by the most malignant and diabolical dispositions", to J.S. Dowling, 19 December 1840.
129. Dowling to Stephen, 1 December 1840, Letters and Opinions, Vol. 5 (N.S.W.A. 2/3474), unpaged. *Cf.* Dowling to Gipps, 18 May 1840, *ibid.*, 60.
130. James Stephen was his cousin and had brought his influence to bear on the advancement in life of Alfred Stephen's father (Mr Justice John Stephen) and

of Alfred himself - *see* generally (1976) 6 *A.D.B.* 180-181; Paul Knaplund, *James Stephen and the British Colonial System 1813-1847* (Madison 1953), 7-8.

131. As he recognized too late - "I have however been unfortunate in my efforts to establish anything like real cordiality" - Dowling to Gipps, 4 December 1840, C.O. 201/306, f. 339 at f. 341-341a.
132. Dowling to Willis, 2 September 1840, *id.*, f. 517; Dowling to Gipps, *op. cit.* n. 132, at f. 339.
133. Dowling to Willis, 5 December 1840, *id.*, f. 434; Dowling to Gipps, *ibid.*, f. 339.
134. Dowling to Gipps, *ibid.*, f. 340.
135. Memorandum, 16 December 1840, Letters and Opinions, Vol. 5 (N.S.W.A. 2/3474), unpaged.
136. Willis to Gipps, 7 December 1840, C.O. 201/306, f. 410.
137. *Id.*, f. 411.
138. Above, n. 77.
139. Gipps to Dowling, 13 December 1840, Letters and Opinions, Vol. 5 (N.S.W.A. 2/3474), unpaged. Dowling almost immediately tried to force the Governor's hand by making a private approach to James Stephen of the Colonial Office (16 December 1840, C.O. 201/304, f. 184), but engaged no support there.
140. 3 January 1841, *H.R.A.* I/XXI, 160 at 164. The Colonial Office supported the Governor and was sympathetic to Dowling. James Stephen minuted the file that the matter was not material to the general public, C.O. 201/306, f. 329a, 330, 331.
141. George Howard, Sixth Earl of Carlisle (X *D.N.B.* 18), a leading Whig politician.
142. For an earlier instance, *see* H.F. Behan, *op. cit.* n. 6, 39.
143. Willis to Morpeth, 26 December 1840, C.O. 201/306, f. 445.
144. *Ibid.*, f. 446.
145. C.O. 201/306, f. 446a.
146. Dowling to Gipps, 23 December 1840, *id.*, f. 403.
147 *See* n. 88 above.
148. Dowling to Willis, 6 December 1840, C.O. 201/306, f. 438. For particulars, *see* A.G.L. Shaw (ed.), *Gipps - La Trobe Correspondence 1839-1846* (Melbourne 1989), 51; n. 2.
149. Gipps to Russell, 1 January 1841, *H.R.A.* I/XXI, 158 and C.O. 201/306, f. 328.
150. Shaw (ed.), *op. cit.* n. 148, 53 at 54.
151. 29 December 1840, C.O. 201/306, f. 330-331.
152. To J.S. Dowling, 14 February 1841.
153. Dowling's son confirmed that, in England, "all hands speak of Judge Willis' peevishness and crankiness", letter from J.S. Dowling, 20 May 1841.
154. To J.S. Dowling, 20 May 1841.
155. To J.S. Dowling, 2 December 1842.
156. *Willis v. Gipps* (1845) Moo. P.C. 379 [13 E.R. 536], and, generally, Alex C. Castles, *An Australian Legal History* (Sydney 1982), 243.
157. C.H. Currey, "Chapters on the Legal History of New South Wales, 1788-1863" (University of Sydney, LL.D. thesis [1929]), 242.
158. To J.S. Dowling, 7 August 1841.
159. (1967) 2 *A.D.B.* 15.
160. Shaw (ed.), *op. cit.* n. 148, 214-215.
161. Dowling recorded that, "Judge Burton has gotten an appointment to the Bench at Madras at a salary of 4 or 5000£. So much for High Tory friends. His *admirers here* are paying him great worship" - Letter to J.S. Dowling, 22 June 1844.

Chapter 8

1. (1966) 1 *A.D.B.* 195.
2. J.M. Bennett, Introduction to Sir Roger Therry, *Reminiscences of Thirty Years' Residence in New South Wales and Victoria* (facsimile ed., Sydney 1974), [19] [20].
3. Callaghan's Diary, "Thursday" [25 March 1841].
4. 5 October 1869, 5.
5. Above, Ch. 5, text to n. 71 and following; Ch. 7, text to n. 92.
6. J.M. Bennett, *A History of the Supreme Court of New South Wales* (Sydney 1974), 76.
7. Roderick Flanagan, *The History of New South Wales* Vol. 1 (London 1862), 311.
8. *Australian*, 5 August 1829, 2.
9. *Old Times*, May 1903, 119.
10. *Australian, loc. cit.* n. 8.
11. C.H. Currey, *Sir Francis Forbes* (Sydney 1968), 407-408. J.M. Bennett, "Early Days of the Law in Country Districts" (1972) 46 *Australian Law Journal* 578 at 583.
12. *Sydney Gazette*, 27 April 1830, 2.
13. *Ibid.*
14. *S.M.H.*, 9 September 1842, 3; *Australian*, 19 September 1842, 2.
15. Bennett, *op. et loc. cit.* n. 6.
16. *Australian*, 2 October 1841, 3.
17. Above, Ch. 1, text to n. 60. Below, Ch. 9, n. 53. Anthony Dowling, *Fortis et Egregius or Dowling of Ballyroan* (Sydney 1996), 272. For Dowling's introduction of "purple" robes – *Australian*, 11 May 1832, 2.
18. "Thus am I now raised, from my humble beginnings, to the highest grade in my profession", James Dowling to J.S. Dowling, 16 April 1839.
19. Above, Ch. 6, text to n. 61 and following.
20. Vincent Dowling to James Dowling, 6 May 1837, Letters to Sir James Dowling (M.L. A489).
21. Dowling to Glenelg, 5 July 1838, C.O. 201/281, f. 367 (and M.L. Ad 69/2). His further supplication to James Stephen (5 July 1838, *id.*, f. 365) was rebuffed – "I am not the proper channel through which such applications as this should be made", minute, *id.*, f. 365a.
22. Minute of 9 November 1838, *ibid.*
23. There were brief notices in *Sydney Herald*, 11 March 1839, 2, and *Australian*, 12 March 1839, 3.
24. For example, 4 March 1839, 2; 11 March 1839, 2; 25 March 1839, 2.
25. Letter to J.S. Dowling, 16 April 1839. The "warm expressions" of contemporary newspapers have not been found.
26. Letter to J.S. Dowling, 1 September 1839; and *see* above, Ch. 1, text to n. 12.
27. J.M. Bennett (ed.), *A History of the New South Wales Bar* (Sydney 1969), 46-48; J.M. Bennett, *A History of Solicitors in New South Wales* (Sydney 1984), 53, 55.
28. Letter to J.S. Dowling, 25 July 1840.
29. *Ibid.*, and to J.S. Dowling, 18 June 1843.
30. Letter to J.S. Dowling, 1 September 1839.
31. As to whom, *see* J.M. Bennett, *A History of Solicitors in New South Wales* (Sydney 1984), 90.
32. Letter to J.S. Dowling, 30 November 1836.
33. Dowling to Rogers, 30 November 1836, Letters and Opinions, Vol. 4 (N.S.W.A. 2/3473).

34. Bennett, *loc. cit.* n. 31.
35. Dowling to Bradley, 29 November 1836, *loc. cit.* n. 33.
36. Burton to Dowling, 1 December 1836, *ibid.*
37. *Sydney Herald*, 2 November 1840, 2.
38. Bennett, *op. cit.* n. 31, 87-89.
39. *Ibid.*, at 89.
40. Letter to J.S. Dowling, 14 February 1841: contrast lavish praise expressed publicly by Dowling on Gurner's admission as a solicitor – *loc. cit.* n. 37.
41. Bennett, *op. cit.* n. 31, 116-117.
42. Letter to J.S. Dowling, 30 March 1843.
43. Bennett, *op. cit.* n. 31, 141.
44. *S.M.H.*, 25 August 1842, 2.
45. Bennett, *op. cit.* n. 31, 38-41.
46. *S.M.H., loc. cit.* n. 44, 2; *Australian*, 26 August 1842, 2.
47. *Australian*, 19 August 1842, 2.
48. Bennett, *op. cit.* n. 31, 141.
49. (1839) 1 Legge 123.
50. Bennett, *op. cit.* n. 31, 37, 64-67.
51. Above, Ch. 7, text to n. 52, and following.
52. (1831) 2 B. & Ad. 663 [109 E.R. 1290].
53. 1 Legge at 136.
54. *Id.*, at 139.
55. 9 *Geo.* IV *c.* 83.
56. Alex C. Castles, *An Australian Legal History* (Sydney 1982), 430-431.
57. Glenelg to Bourke, 5 September 1836, H.R.A. I/XVIII, 526.
58. *Ibid.*
59. 1 Legge at 125.
60. *Id.*, at 126.
61. *Ibid.*
62. *S.M.H.*, 20 August 1844, 2; *cf.* an address by the Bar, *id.*, 2 November 1844, 2, and Anthony Dowling (ed.), *Reminiscences of a Colonial Judge* (Sydney 1996), 50.
63. Address of 19 August, in *S.M.H.*, 20 August 1844, 2.
64. For example, *Australian*, 13 October 1840, 2; (1840) *V. & P. (L.C., N.S.W.)*, 283 at 284.
65. Nevertheless, he privately admitted, as to the Bar, that "we have some dumb Dollies here . . . especially the Irish men", letter to J.S. Dowling, 30 March 1843; earlier he had written of "two or three *leatherheads*, who do little or nothing" at the Bar, letter to J.S. Dowling, 14 November 1840.
66. Above, text to n.1.
67. For example, Callaghan's Diary, 16 January 1841, 14 October 1841, 1 September 1840.
68. *Id.*, 3 October 1840, 19 March 1840, 13 March 1840.
69. *Id.*, "Tuesday" [23 February 1841].
70. Dowling to Willis, 10 May 1840, Letters and Opinions, Vol. 5 (N.S.W.A. 2/3474).
71. Callaghan's Diary, 1 January 1841. For Plunkett's contrary view – *Australian*, 4 March 1841, 2.
72. Above, Ch. 7, text to n. 27 and following.
73. Above, Ch. 7, text to n. 29.
74. *Australian*, 15 April 1841, 2.
75. *Id.*, 1 June 1841, 2.
76. Above, Ch. 4.

77. *Sydney Monitor*, 16 March 1829, 1533.
78. For instance, *Sydney Gazette*, 8 May 1832, 2, 6 November 1834, 2; *Australian*, 3 July 1829, 2, 16 December 1829, 2; *Sydney Monitor*, 12 May 1832, 3.
79. Dowling (ed.), *op. cit.* n. 62, 48.
80. The likelihood is that J.S. Dowling adopted the exaggerated assessment of his father, published as an obituary in the *Australian*, 28 September 1844, 727.
81. Anthony Dowling, *op. cit.* n. 17, 175-180.
82. Vincent Dowling to his brother J.S. Dowling, 13 February 1837.
83. Sir Roger Therry, *op. cit.* n. 2 (2nd ed., London 1863), 338-339.
84. Although, as to witnesses, he could be severe if they transgressed the court's requirements of punctuality and decorum, *Sydney Gazette*, 8 May 1832, 3; above, Ch. 4, text to n. 129.
85. *S.M.H.*, 2 November 1844, 2.
86. A corresponding address by attorneys referred to Dowling's "uniform courtesy and impartiality", *id.*, 20 August 1844, 2; there was also an address by the court ministerial officers, *ibid.*
87. *S.M.H.*, 22 October 1844, 2.
88. *Ibid.*
89. Callaghan's Diary, 29 June 1841; Dowling had similarly made fun of Alfred Cheeke in public, Therry, *Reminiscences of Thirty Years' Residence in New South Wales and Victoria* (2nd ed., London 1863), 340.
90. The *Sydney Herald* supported the criticism – "Does the Chief Justice imagine that his attempts at punning, when hearing a case, add dignity to his office . . .? Sir James! such conduct is unbecoming a Judge, however characteristic of yourself", 13 November 1839, 2.
91. *Australian*, 16 December 1829, 3.
92. *Ibid.*
93. Bennett, *op. cit.* n. 6, 80-89. J.M. Bennett, "The Establishment of Jury Trial in New South Wales" (1961) 3 *Sydney Law Review*, 463. Castles, *op. cit.* n. 6, 53-54, 186-187, 203-204.
94. Currey, *op. cit.* n. 11, 114-118, 278-279.
95. Dowling to Brougham, 1 April 1828, Brougham MSS (30,098), University College, London.
96. *Ibid.*
97. Roderick Flanagan, *op. cit.* n. 7, 325.
98. *Ibid.*
99. Forbes to Dowling, 7 April 1830, J.M. Bennett (ed.), *Some Papers of Sir Francis Forbes* (Sydney 1998), 200.
100. Flanagan, *op. cit.* n. 7, at 326.
101. *Australian*, 6 June 1828, 3.
102. *Sydney Gazette*, 16 March 1830, 3, address in *Hall v. Rossi*.
103. *Id.*, 2.
104. *Id.*, 3.
105. *Id.*, 25 June 1829, 2.
106. The writ, abolished in England in 1852, was otherwise probably never used in New South Wales.
107. *Australian*, 26 June 1829, 2; and, with textual differences, *Sydney Gazette*, 25 June 1829, 3.
108. *Australian*, 26 June 1829, 3.
109. (1831) 1 Legge 5.
110. At 32.
111. Bennett, *op. cit.* n. 6, 84-85.

112. *Id.*, at 85.
113. Dowling to Brougham, 7 March 1836, Brougham MSS (16,882), University College, London.
114. Bennett, *op. cit.* n. 6, at 86.
115. Bourke to Glenelg, 13 April 1836, *H.R.A.* I/XVIII, 391 at 392.
116. Dowling to the Colonial Secretary, 7 April 1836, C.O. 201/253, f. 64.
117. *Id.*, f. 64a-65. For a criticism, see, *Sydney Herald*, 30 June 1836, 2.
118. Dowling to Gipps, 18 December 1838, (1840) *V. & P. (L.C., N.S.W.)*, 164 at 165. He persisted for some time in this lost cause, *e.g. Australian*, 2 October 1841, 3.
119. *V. & P., loc. cit.* n. 118.
120. *Id.*, at 166.
121. *Ibid.*
122. Dowling to Gipps, 12 March 1840, *ibid.*, at 159.
123. Bennett, *op. cit.* n. 6, 86-87.
124. Russell to Gipps, 11 August 1840, *H.R.A.* I/XX, 754.
125. *Australian*, 8 August 1840, 2; 12 May 1842, 2.
126. *A History of English Law*, Vol. 2 (London 1909), 444, 445.
127. The public archival collection includes his manuscript notebooks "Proceedings of the Supreme Court of New South Wales" (N.S.W.A. 2/3184 to 3396 and 2/3400 to 3433) with indexes (*id.*, 2/3397, 2/3434), and his Letters and Opinions "Copies of Semi-Official Letters and Opinions" (N.S.W.A. 2/3470 to 3474). As well there were his "Select Cases", prepared for publication but never published (N.S.W.A. 2/3461 to 3469); abstracts of "special cases in law" (N.S.W.A. 2/3398 to 3399); and many volumes of equity and vice-admiralty cases (N.S.W.A. 2/3436 to 3460).
128. His Bench books were, however, kept in shorthand which, as Sir Roger Therry (*op. cit.* n. 83, 338) recorded, he accomplished "remarkably well" with complete accuracy.
129. (1966) 1 *A.D.B.* 317 at 320. The original text suggested 237 notebooks, but that was inadvertent.
130. At <www.law.mq.edu.au/scnsw/>. For a commentary, *see* Bruce Kercher, "Publication of Forgotten Case Law of the New South Wales Supreme Court" (1998) 72 *Australian Law Journal* 876.
131. *See*, for example, above, Ch. 3, text to n. 76 and following.
132. And attributed to his son – M. Henry Stephen, *Supplement to the Supreme Court Practice with Acts of Council and Notes of Cases* (Sydney 1851). But, for the particular contribution of a'Beckett's *Reserved Judgments* and *Reserved and Equity Judgments*, *see* the author's companion volume, *Lives of the Australian Chief Justices – Sir William a'Beckett*; and Alex C. Castles, *Annotated Bibliography of Printed Materials On Australian Law 1788-1900* (Sydney 1994), 3-4.
133. Dowling to Baxter, 5 March 1830, Letters and Opinions, Vol. 2 (N.S.W.A. 2/3471), at 11-12.
134. *Ibid.*
135. *Australian*, 23 January 1841, 2.
136. *Op. cit.* n. 83, 339. Contrast *Sydney Herald*, 13 November 1839, 2, which objected that Dowling had "protected" a prisoner on trial.
137. 7 November 1839, 2: and note a critical letter by "*Justitiae Amicus*" in *Sydney Herald*, 6 July 1830, 3.
138. J.M. Bennett, *Sir John Pedder* (Hobart 1977), 8-9.
139. Dowling to Darling, 1 December 1828, Letters and Opinions, Vol. 1 (N.S.W.A. 2/3470), 164 at 166.

140. James Macarthur was convinced that "Dowling was a man of no ideas and deficient in those qualities of political judgment that were then required of the chief justice on the Legislative Council" – John Manning Ward, *James Macarthur* (Sydney 1981), 85.
141. *S.M.H.*, 20 March 1844, 2 (attributed to the *Weekly Register*). Dowling thought well of the piece and sent a copy to his son to "encourage you to aspire to *something*", Letter to J.S. Dowling, 6 April 1844. The suggestion, made provocatively in the *Sydney Monitor*, 10 February 1829, 1492, that "Judge Dowling . . . is begun . . . to be called 'the government Judge'", was without merit.
142. (1967) 2 *A.D.B.* 24.
143. *Id.*, 512 at 513 (*s.v.* "Therry").
144. *Australian*, 17 February 1837, 2.
145. Dowling to Jones, 17 February 1837, Letters and Opinions, Vol. 4 (N.S.W.A. 2/3473), unpaged.
146. *Ibid.*
147. 21 February 1837, 2.
148. *Australian*, 21 February 1837, 2.
149. Dowling to Glenelg, 22 February 1837, C.O. 201/266, f. 218.
150. *Id.*, f. 219.
151. *Id.*, f. 219a.
152. *Australian*, 22 August 1842, 2 at 3.
153. *S.M.H.*, 5 October 1869, 5.

Chapter 9

1. Dowling to Brougham, 15 February 1831, Brougham MSS (1260), University College, London.
2. Dowling to Brougham, 7 March 1836, *ibid.* (16,882). The "new Bill" was not hurried. After temporizing measures, the 2 & 3 *Vict. c.* 70 was passed in 1839 giving the local legislature power to make provision for the better administration of justice. *See* generally, A.C.V. Melbourne, *Early Constitutional Development in Australia* (R.B. Joyce, ed., St Lucia, Qld, 1963), 198.
3. (1840) quoted (1966) 1 *A.D.B.* at 319.
4. *Sydney Gazette*, 7 November 1839, 2; *Australian*, 7 November 1839, 2-3; *Colonist*, 9 November 1839, 2.
5. Dowling to Normanby, 28 November 1839, C.O. 201/288, f. 149 at f. 150. According to J.N. Molony, *An Architect of Freedom* (Canberra 1973), 99, Plunkett, a leader of the Catholic laity, probably so acted "in order to make sure that no accusation could be levelled against him of treating the matter with levity".
6. 9 November 1839, 2.
7. Molony, *op. cit.* n. 5, 198-199.
8. Dowling to Normanby, *op. cit.* n. 5, at f. 151a.
9. 7 November 1839, 2. (1967) 2 A.D.B. 25. Dowling's attempt to complain directly to the Secretary of State was snubbed by James Stephen – "This should have come, if at all, through the Governor. I think it may very properly be put by unanswered", Dowling to Glenelg, 27 February 1837, C.O. 201/266, f. 218-222.
10. *Loc. cit.* n. 9.
11. 13 November 1839, 2.
12. 9 November 1839, 2.

13. Dowling to Normanby, *op. cit.* n. 5, at f. 152.
14. As to whom, *see* respectively (1967) 2 *A.D.B.* 61 and 147.
15. Dowling to Normanby, *op. cit. n.* 5, at f. 150a.
16. *Sydney Gazette*, 16 November 1839, 2. Gipps to Normanby, 26 November 1839, *H.R.A.*, I/XX, 403 at 404.
17. *Sydney Gazette, loc. cit.* n. 16.
18. Molony, *op. cit. n.* 5, 199.
19. Gipps to Normanby, *loc. cit.* n. 16.
20. Dowling to Normanby, 28 November 1839, C.O. 201/288, f. 152a.
21. Minute, *ibid.*, f. 146a.
22. Russell to Gipps, 6 June 1840, *H.R.A.* I/XX, 649.
23. *S.M.H.*, 5 October 1869, 5. Dowling to Glenelg, 22 February 1837, C.O. 201/266, f. 218 at f. 219.
24. Letter to J.S. Dowling, 20 April 1838.
25. *Australian*, 19 August 1841, 2; 2 September 1841, 2; *cf. Sydney Monitor*, 1 September 1841, 2; *Australasian Chronicle*, 2 September 1841, 2.
26. *Australian*, 2 September 1841, 2.
27. For the background, *see* F.A. Larcombe, *The Origin of Local Government in New South Wales 1831-58* (Sydney 1973), Ch. 2.
28. *Australian*, 8 August 1840, 2.
29. *Ibid.*, report of speeches, and editorial.
30. Russell to Gipps, 21 July 1841, *H.R.A.* I/XXI, 440 at 441.
31. *Australian*, 14 June 1842, 2.
32. Larcombe, *op. cit.* n. 27, 87. There were also three vigorous public meetings – *S.M.H.*, 31 May 1842, 2; 7 June 1842, 2; 30 June 1842, 2.
33. *Australian*, 14 June 1842, 2.
34. Macarthur had tried, unsuccessfully, to have the Bill's reading deferred for six months.
35. *Australian*, 14 June 1842, 2; those observations do not appear in the *Sydney Herald*, 15 June 1842, 2.
36. Larcombe, *op. cit.* n. 27, 84-85.
37. "An Act to declare the Town of Sydney to be a City and to Incorporate the Inhabitants thereof" (20 July 1842).
38. Passed on 3 January 1842 as 5 *Vic. No.* 20.
39. *Australian*, 16 December 1841, 2.
40. *Ibid.* (editorial); *cf. Sydney Gazette*, 16 December 1841, 2.
41. 15 December 1841, 2.
42. 18 December 1841, 2.
43. *Australian*, 1 January 1842, 3: *cf. id.*, 16 December 1841, 3.
44. *Id.*, 4 January 1842, 2.
45. *Ibid.*
46. "An Act to consolidate and amend the Laws relating to the Registration of Deeds . . .". It superseded 5 *Vic. No.* 21 of 1842.
47. Letter to J.S. Dowling, 14 November 1840.
48. *See Ex parte Lyons* (1839) 1 Legge 140 at 143, 153-154, and generally, J.M. Bennett, *A History of the Supreme Court of New South Wales* (Sydney 1974), Ch. 6.
49. *Ex parte Lyons* (1839) at 144.
50. Dowling to Gipps, 13 April 1840, Letters and Opinions, Vol. 5 (N.S.W.A. 2/3474), 68-69.
51. *Australian*, 18 December 1841, 2.
52. *Ibid.*

53. *Id.*, 23 December 1841, 2.
54. *Sydney Monitor*, 17 December 1841, 2.
55. *Id.*, 20 December 1841, 2.
56. As Dowling wrote to his son, "After a great fight we have at length passed an Insolvent Debtors Law, of which I fear hundreds will be compelled to take the benefit", Letter to J.S. Dowling, 23 December 1841.
57. Bennett, *op. cit. n.* 48, 116.
58. Stanley to Gipps, 27 February 1843, *H.R.A.* I/XXII, 572 at 573.
59. Such as the abolition of imprisonment for debt, Bennett, *op. cit.* n. 48, 117-118, 121. *See* generally *S.M.H.*, 11 December 1843, 4.
60. Dowling to Gipps, 24 June 1843, *H.R.A.* I/XXII, 812.
61. Dowling to Gipps, 27 June 1843, *id.*, 815.
62. *Op. cit.* n. 60, at 812-813. As Dowling wrote to his son: "It is doubtful whether I am to have a seat [in the Council] which however I decline taking except upon the expectation of being elected the Speaker, for I should not on constitutional principles choose to be there as a debating member. I believe the Governor is scheming to get Therry appointed Speaker", Letter to J.S. Dowling, 18 June 1846.
63. *Op. cit.* n. 60, at 814.
64. Gipps to Dowling, 28 June 1843, *H.R.A.* I/XXII, 816. Gipps to Stanley, 29 June 1843, *id.*, 810 at 811.
65. Gipps to Dowling, 22 June 1843, *id.*, 811 at 812.
66. Stanley to Gipps, 23 December 1843, *H.R.A.* I/XXIII, 268.

Conclusion

1. Supplement to *New South Wales Government Gazette*, 28 September 1844; *S.M.H.*, 30 September 1844,
2. Anthony Dowling, *Fortis et Egregius or Dowling of Ballyroan* (Sydney 1996), 170. Frequent references in the Dowling Correspondence identified above, Ch. 1, n. 1. *Australian*, 5 June 1841, 2; 25 November 1842, 2: *S.M.H.*, 23 November 1842, 2; 19 January 1843, 2.
3. *S.M.H.*, 9 July 1844, 2.
4. *Id.*, 13 July 1844, 2; 14 August 1844, 2.
5. *Id.*, 23 August 1844, 2.
6. *Gentleman's Magazine*, April 1845, 463.
7. *S.M.H.*, 23 August 1844, 2; 2 November 1844, 2.
8. Supplement to *New South Wales Government Gazette*, 28 September 1844.
9. J.A. Dowling, Newspaper Cuttings Vol. 2 (M.L. Q991/N), 59.
10. 28 September 1844, 727.
11. 2 October 1844, 2.
12. 28 September 1844, 2; 1 October 1844, 2.
13. *S.M.H.*, 22 October 1844, 2.
14. Above, Ch. 8, n. 130.
15. (1976) 6 *A.D.B.* 81; J.M. Bennett, "Sir Julian Salomons – Fifth Chief Justice of New South Wales" (1972) 58 *J.R.A.H.S.* 101.
16. *Sydney Monitor*, 17 December 1841, 2; *Australian*, 28 September 1844, 727.
17. Psalm 139, verse 9.

Index